Women, Politics, and Reproduction
The Liberal Legacy

In this book Ingrid Makus examines the position of women and the role of parenting in the thought of three traditional liberal philosophers – Thomas Hobbes, John Locke, and John Stuart Mill. She does so in response to the feminist claim that women are excluded from most models of the political community, including the liberal one, in traditional Western political theory. She finds that in these philosophers' works women indeed fall short of achieving equal political status – but for reasons which feminist interpretations have overlooked.

The relationship between children and both parents is a more fundamental problem for political theory, according to Makus, than addressing adversarial relations between men and women. Traditional liberal thought has difficulty accounting for the care of children without placing women in a role that creates tension between their rights (self-interest) and duties (care for others). She shows how this tension is evident in modern liberal society, where it comes to the forefront in contemporary debates about women's reproductive rights and their underrepresentation in politics.

Finally, Makus explores whether feminist theory, in its various forms, presents alternatives to the liberal tradition or whether it replicates for women the dilemmas of the liberal legacy. She also addresses the potential for feminist theory to encourage a political community inclusive of women, children, and men.

INGRID MAKUS is an assistant professor in the Department of Political Studies at Brock University.

Women, Politics, and Reproduction

The Liberal Legacy

Ingrid Makus

UNIVERSITY OF TORONTO PRESS
Toronto Buffalo London

© University of Toronto Press Incorporated 1996
Toronto Buffalo London
Printed in Canada

ISBN 0-8020-0716-3 (cloth)
ISBN 0-8020-7663-7 (paper)

Printed on acid-free paper

Canadian Cataloguing in Publication Data

Makus, Ingrid
  Women, politics, and reproduction : the liberal legacy

  Includes bibliographical references and index.
  ISBN 0-8020-0716-3 (bound)   ISBN 0-8020-7663-7 (pbk.)

  1. Hobbes, Thomas, 1588–1679 – Views on women.
  2. Locke, John, 1632–1704 – Views on women. 3. Mill,
  John Stuart, 1806–1873 – Views on women.   4. Feminist
  theory.   I. Title.

  HQ1236.M35 1996   305.4   C96-930317-3

This book has been published with the help of a grant from the Humanities and Social Sciences Federation of Canada, using funds provided by the Social Sciences and Humanities Research Council of Canada.

University of Toronto Press acknowledges the financial assistance to its publishing program of the Canada Council and the Ontario Arts Council.

Contents

ACKNOWLEDGMENTS vii

INTRODUCTION 3

1 Thomas Hobbes 10
   Maternal Dominion 15
   Parent-Child Relations 20
   Gratitude 24
   Marriage 26
   Education 34
   Political Participation 42
   Political Power 44
   Political Citizenship: Rights and Duties 47

2 John Locke 54
   Women and Education 57
   Women and Conjugal Relations 62
   Propagation of the Species 67
   Continuation of the Political Community: Education 71
   Accumulation of Property 77
   Women and Conjugal Relations: Rights and Duties 82
   Women and the Political Realm 87

3 John Stuart Mill 93
   Women's 'Nature': Differences 95
   Family Relations 105
   Women and the Political Realm 113

4 Reproduction and Politics 127
   The Liberal Legacy: Parents and Children 127
   The Liberal Legacy: Women and Reproduction 131
   Women and Reproductive Rights: Abortion 134
   Abortion and the New Reproductive Technologies 138
   Women and Politics 150

5 Feminist Alternatives? 157
   Feminism of Sameness 163
   Feminism of Difference: Maternal Feminism 169
   Feminism of Difference: Experiential Feminism 178
   Feminism of Difference: Sexual Feminism 189
   The Feminist Legacy 193

NOTES 199

BIBLIOGRAPHY 247

INDEX 265

Acknowledgments

I am most grateful to Edward Andrew for his generous support, advice, and direction in undertaking this project; to Sylvia Bashevkin, Leah Bradshaw, Ronald Beiner, Lynda Lange, Jennifer Nedelsky, and Melissa Williams for their constructive and encouraging comments on an earlier version of the manuscript; to Don Carmichael and Duff Spafford for their sympathetic response to draft portions of the chapters on Hobbes and J.S. Mill respectively; to David Penner and Anne Ward for their valuable research assistance; and to the readers and editors of this press for their indispensable suggestions and assistance. The Dean of the Faculty of Social Sciences at Brock University provided funds for research assistance.

I am especially grateful to Roger for taking such good care of our children, Kira and Megan.

Women, Politics, and Reproduction

Introduction

Feminist scholars concerned with the position of women in Western political thought have come to an almost unanimous conclusion: women are excluded from most models of the political community the Western tradition has to offer.[1] Even the models of those thinkers who purport to include women in politics or who are silent or ambiguous about the 'woman question' cannot seem to sustain women's full-fledged participation in political life.

To explain this situation, feminist scholars have drawn on a number of partially overlapping propositions. These can be summarized as follows. Women are deemed to be naturally inferior in their biological or bodily make-up and therefore unfit for political life. Their reproductive role, perceived as natural to them and functional for the community, is understood as a further indicator of their unsuitability for political life and embeddedness in private life. Reinforcing this idea is the duality that pervades Western thought in the form of the split or separation between the necessary but subordinate private realm (associated with nature, the body, the emotions, the family, and women) and the superior public realm (associated with culture, the mind, reason, politics, and men).

Furthermore, women's confinement to private life, it is argued, reflects the institutionalization of the male need to ensure sexual access to women and the male desire to dominate them. Since it has been elucidated almost exclusively by male theorists, Western political thought on the whole is marred by a male bias that is unable to take into account women's qualities, values, or experiences. The most blatant manifestation of this bias is that women's subordination and exclusion become requirements rather than mere by-products of traditional formulations of politics.

Kathryn Morgan, for example, maintains that women are considered consistently incapable of exercising an important requirement of political life, moral agency, on the grounds that their bodies destine them to irrational behaviour and thinking.[2] The devaluation of the domain with which women are naturally associated – reproduction and mothering – as 'individualistic, private, and infantile' contributes to the perception of their moral and political incompetence.[3] For Zillah Eisenstein the patriarchal ideology of such thinkers as John Locke and John Stuart Mill defines women as biologically inferior and their role in reproduction as natural.[4] On this basis it assigns women to the private realm: 'Because patriarchal ideology presents motherhood as natural, woman's assignment to the private sphere and dismissal from the public realm is argued as a defense of the natural sphere.'[5] Jean Bethke Elshtain emphasizes the separation between private and public in Western political thought.[6] She concludes that invariably women have been relegated to the private domain, despite changes in the way that it has been defined and distinguished from the public one.

The male desire to ensure sexual access to women, according to Carole Pateman, is evident in the contractual representations of politics found in Western thought.[7] The original political and social contract described by thinkers such as Thomas Hobbes and John Locke is in essence a sexual contract. Its purpose is to give men civil freedom. Since this entails 'the right of sexual access to women, and, more broadly, the enjoyment of mastery as a sex', women's political rights are sacrificed to men's desires.[8] Created *by* men, *for* men, civil society requires that women be subordinate. For Christine Di Stefano, women's subordinate status rests on the 'masculinist orientation' that imbues modern Western political thought.[9] This orientation, evident in Thomas Hobbes and John Stuart Mill, is an expression of male difficulty with the experience of being mothered by a woman.

Do these explanations hit the mark? That is, do they provide a sound and comprehensive picture of why women are excluded from political life in the models of the political community put forth by the Western tradition? This question is important for two reasons. First, if the Western tradition cannot place women, then alternative models capable of fully incorporating women need to be formulated. If the account of why women are excluded in the first place is flawed, however, there is a greater chance of repeating past mistakes or failing to address vital difficulties when sketching alternatives.

Second, the task of uncovering obstacles in Western thought to women's full-fledged inclusion is motivated by, in part, the desire to shed light on their political status in modern liberal regimes. Women's under-representation in politics in contemporary liberal states requires some explanation. So too does the increasing forcefulness of debates over women's reproductive rights in the face of the proliferation of new reproductive technologies. Feminist theorists have looked to the theoretical foundations of liberal polities, as expressed in liberal thinkers, for clues to understanding women's present political predicament.[10] A sound assessment of women's place in those theoretical foundations can lead to a better grasp of the terms of contemporary debates over women's reproductive rights and their under-representation in politics.

This book is informed by both these concerns: to enhance the potential for feminist-inspired alternative formulations of politics that are inclusive of women, children, and men; and to illuminate debates over women's position in modern liberal regimes. To this end, I examine three political thinkers of the Western tradition – Thomas Hobbes, John Locke, and John Stuart Mill – who are also important exponents of liberal thought.[11] I do so in light of feminist accounts of what is wrong with their frameworks in particular and Western thought in general.

The extent to which women participate in politics, wield political power, and exercise the rights and duties of citizenship is a useful indicator of their political status in modern liberal states. 'Political participation' describes one's activity in the political sphere, however that sphere is defined.[12] 'Political power' refers to the impact of that activity. To have political power is to be able to overcome obstacles in order to achieve a desired outcome.[13] To have it is also to be able to determine the political agenda – ultimately, to determine what is considered 'political.' 'Political citizenship' entails having both rights, the exercise of which promotes one's own interest or welfare, and duties, the exercise of which promotes the interest or welfare of others; it provides motivations and benefits for engaging in political activity.[15]

I use these indicators to assess how women fare in Thomas Hobbes, John Locke and John Stuart Mill.[15] The questions I ask of these thinkers include: Do they depict women as capable of participating in politics, wielding political power, and exercising the rights and duties of political citizenship? Are their requirements for these dimensions of political life compatible with or at odds with women's perceived qualities? Do the conditions and ends of political life, as Hobbes, Locke, and J.S. Mill formulate them, preclude women (either implicitly or explicitly) from enjoying or engaging in all facets of political life?[16]

In my investigation I find that feminist interpretations of all three thinkers, drawing on the explanations that I have listed above, are flawed. Women are *not* presented as naturally inferior to men in their capacity for politics in Hobbes and Locke. Hobbes depicts mothering as rooted in rational self-interest rather than nature. The political implications and ends of the 'private realm' of reproduction come to the forefront in Locke and J.S. Mill. And to varying degrees, in all three political life *is* based on qualities associated with women. At the same time, Hobbes, Locke and J.S. Mill either stop short of or point to the difficulties of extending to women equal political status within the framework they set out.

In Hobbes' and Locke's framework (chapters 1 and 2), women's ability to exercise rational self-interest suggests they are capable of political participation at the same time as it makes it difficult to account for their role in reproduction. Women's right to govern their own bodies is latent but unacknowledged. What makes this acknowledgment problematic is not the perception that women are irrational or biologically deficient in reason but the perception that they do have the capacity for rational calculation, which is threatening to the ends of the political community. And in J.S. Mill (chapter 3), equality of opportunity to participate in politics, wield political power, and exercise the rights and duties of political citizenship, resting as it does on the perception of women's differences from men, generates inequality of outcome for women.

In chapter 4 I suggest ways in which paying attention to the status of women in Hobbes, Locke, and J.S. Mill can contribute to our understanding of women's position in modern liberal democratic states such as Canada. In particular I show how it can illuminate our understanding of the terms of contemporary debates over women's reproductive rights and political under-representation.

Current discussions of women's under-representation are frequently under-scored by divisions over whether women have the *same* or *different* political interests and capacities and whether the requirements for politics as a result are compatible with their qualities. Hobbes' and Locke's models, in which women are attributed the *same* capacities as men for politics but fail to achieve equal status, provide a contrast to J.S. Mill's model, in which women are attributed *different* tendencies from men and achieve equality of opportunity (but not equality of outcome). Whether or not women are ascribed the same capacities as men, the outcome may well be some form of inequality.

Furthermore, the framework in which contemporary debates over women's reproductive rights take place is coloured by Hobbesian and Lockean assumptions. The demand to extend reproductive rights to women rests on, in large part, the premise that women are rational and therefore capable of exercising rights, and that they are justified in exercising them as the achievement of their right to govern their own bodies. Paying heed to Hobbes and Locke can alert us to the problems that may ensue in making such demands on these premises. Difficulties arise not because women are perceived as lacking the rational capacity to exercise (reproductive) rights, as some feminist analysts have suggested, but precisely because they are perceived as having such a faculty. Difficulties also arise because the notion of a right to govern one's own body, drawn from liberal thought and framed within liberal terms, poses peculiar complications when applied to women. The complications have less to do with adult male-female relations, which have tended to be the focus of feminist inquiry, than with parent-child relations.

This last point brings me to an important question. Why have feminist interpretations missed the mark? Why have they failed to provide a comprehensive and sound assessment of women's position in Western thought? Perhaps because they have drawn, almost exclusively, on explanations that emphasize the importance of relations (adversarial ones) between adult women and men. The problem of women's exclusion is therefore understood as a problem of adversarial relations between adult men and women. At best, male thinkers, because they are male, have a blind eye when it comes to women. This leads them to believe that women are naturally inferior or that motherhood is the fulfilment of their natures. At worst male thinkers have imbibed or uncritically assumed the need to dominate women. This leads them to construct edifices that are fundamentally grounded in the oppression of women.

I am not suggesting that antagonistic relations between the sexes are inconsequential to explaining women's status in Western political thought. But I am suggesting that they do not tell the whole story. In placing such emphasis on them, feminist scholars have paid too little attention to what may be of more significance – relations between parents and children. They have overlooked a number of related factors, such as the degree to which traditional thought, including liberal thought, is concerned with parent-child relations over and above adult male-female ones, and the extent to which the position of women in traditional and liberal thought is connected to this concern.

Even 'maternal feminists,' who do elaborate on differences between the father-child and mother-child tie, tend to so do so in the context of adversarial adult male-female relations.[17] According to Mary O'Brien, for example, uncertainty over paternity has induced men to attempt to appropriate women's reproductive powers.[18] Men have created an oppressive duality which associates women with nature, the body, and private life and associates men with culture, the mind, and public life. In keeping with this duality, O'Brien then assumes that traditional thought has conceived of women's role in reproduction as overwhelmingly natural. She thereby overlooks the extent to which mothering has been presented as influenced by rational deliberation rather than maternal instinct.

To remedy these oversights I examine Hobbes', Locke's, and J.S. Mill's accounts of the link between parents, mothers and fathers, and offspring. Such an emphasis is vital for improving our understanding of the position of women in their thought. It is also helpful to feminist thought, in so far as it sets itself the task of coming up with alternative conceptions of the political community that fully address the implications of women's reproductive capacities.

Why do women and men have and care for children? Why ought they to do so? How can one ensure that they do so? These questions are addressed implicitly or explicitly in Hobbes, Locke, and J.S. Mill. Feminist theory can benefit from recognizing the importance of such questions and from investigating the way they are posed in liberal theory.

The care of children is necessary for the perpetuation of any political community; accounting for that care is a prerequisite for constructing models of the political community that embody continuity, be they traditional, liberal, or feminist models. To feminist inquiry, the dangers of ignoring parent-child relations are multi-fold. Failing to recognize the importance of parent child relations and their connection to the political status of women in traditional and liberal thought leads to incomplete and distorted interpretations of women's position in liberal thought and practice. Ignoring parent-child relations altogether averts the construction of a feminist-inspired model of the political community that can accommodate its own preservation and perpetuation. And trying to account for mothering and fathering in liberal terms is problematic.

In showing that feminist interpretations are flawed or incomplete, my intention is neither to rescue the Western tradition or liberal thinkers from feminist criticisms, nor to suggest that women's exclusion is defensible. Rather, my aim is to strengthen the feminist potential for coming up with alternatives that are fully capable of integrating women, children, and men. At present, this potential is inhibited by flawed accounts of women's exclusion.

Virginia Held, for example, contends that the main problem with traditional (male) thought, including liberal thought, is that human birth is depicted as a natural event.[19] Not surprisingly, her proposed solution is to present mothering as a rational activity that involves making choices.[20] Counter to Held's assumptions, however, Hobbes *does* present mothering as determined by reason and choice. As a result, moreover, he has trouble accounting for why women or men would choose to care for children. In Hobbes, the difficulties of subjecting reproduction to rational considerations are illuminated. In its eagerness to emphasize the rational element in women's reproductive role, feminist thought might be replicating those difficulties.

There are problems with the status of women in liberal thought (and in liberal states). They have to do with the terms on which liberal thought tries to account for the care of children. And they come to a head when women's reproductive rights are in question.

Has feminist theory, that is the growing body of thought devoted to assessing what is wrong with the place of women in thought and practice, moved beyond these difficulties? In chapter 5 I appraise feminist thought from this perspective. I explore how it responds to the issues of women's reproductive capacities and the care of children. Most varieties of feminist thought, I suggest, even those that purport to reject a liberal standpoint, are beset by liberal assumptions about parent-child relations and women's role in reproduction. This influence is mixed. It has the potential either to facilitate or to hinder feminist thought in directing us to alternative conceptions of the political community capable of fully incorporating women, children, and men.

CHAPTER ONE

Thomas Hobbes

Traditional expositions of the ideas of Thomas Hobbes (1588–1679) have been relatively unconcerned with the position of women in his thought.[1] Feminist interpretations of political thought have tended to ignore Hobbes either by failing to consider him or by grouping him with other contract theorists, most notably John Locke (1632–1704). As a contract theorist, Hobbes is often faulted for barring women from full-fledged participation in civil society. Carole Pateman, for example, has argued that contract theorists simply replaced the old form of patriarchalism, based on the power of fathers over sons, with a modern form of patriarchalism, resting on the power of husbands over wives.[2] The social contract they describe can be read as 'a fraternal pact that constitutes civil society as a patriarchal or masculine order' in which men's power over women is defended as 'natural.'[3]

Pateman's interpretation, however, is less applicable to Hobbes than to Locke.[4] Admitting that Hobbes is somewhat of an exception among contract theorists, she notes that he does attribute a form of natural equality to both men and women.[5] She also concedes that, in the Hobbesian state of nature, women as mothers are endowed with some power.[6] This power, however, according to Pateman, is overridden by the 'sexual contract' which constitutes relations between adult men and women. Ostensibly, the sexual contract in Hobbes is based on consent. But for women, Pateman contends, consent is never voluntary. It is elicited from them by force. Force rather than consent defines sexual relations in Hobbes' account of both civil society and the state of nature.

Pateman confesses, however, that it is difficult to explain why and how, in Hobbes' framework, women lose the maternal power they wield in the state of nature when they enter civil society. She suggests, at one point, that maternal power and the dominion over children that accompanies that power disappear in the formation of the family, when women as wives become subsumed as servants under the ownership of the male head of the household.[7] But this answer is unsatisfactory, given that Hobbes makes allowance for female heads of households.

A different sort of reading of Hobbes is given by Jane Flax.[8] She approaches Hobbes and Locke as thinkers whose representations of the human condition can be understood as expressions of a certain psychological dynamic. At the centre of this dynamic is the attempt to deny or repress the early infant (male) experience of being mothered by a woman. The outcome, as evident in the Hobbesian and Lockean state of nature, is persistent anxiety about separation from the mother, the exclusion of female values of concern for the dependent and helpless, and a failure to address the ramifications of children's dependence on adults.

Although Flax's interpretation is more applicable to Hobbes than to Locke, it leaves a skewed picture of what we uncover in Hobbes. For example, the Hobbesian individual exhibits some traditionally 'female' qualities such as the desire to preserve oneself over and above the desire to act as the warrior-hero. Hobbes excludes maternal values of care and nurture (not maternal powers), but not female values per se. And he does address the implications of an infant's dependence on the care of adults, but he deliberately rejects the infant's dependency as proof that society is natural.

Christine Di Stefano's approach is similar to Flax's.[9] Using object relations theory, which focuses on the role of the pre-Oedipal mother-child relationship in the formation of gender, Di Stefano finds that Hobbes is a thinker whose representations reveal his masculinist orientation. Defining oneself as a masculine subject, according to object relations theory, is a difficult and complex process. It requires that one differentiate oneself from the mother; one may end up trying to deny or repress her. Since the mother is a female she easily becomes an 'other.' Di Stefano uses the term '(m)other' to describe the image with which women may consequently be associated.[10]

The modern masculine formation of self is especially susceptible to what Di Stefano calls 'false differentiation,' whereby the 'the maternal other is strictly and unrealistically objectified in split versions rather than vitally engaged and at least partially accommodated in a more mediated and nuanced manner.'[11] This lends itself to a world-view that is neurotic. Its characteristics include a sense of detachment from the world; a feeling of alienation and estrangement from others; a tendency to see dualism everywhere; a desire to conquer others to compensate for feelings of powerlessness, fear, and hostility; and an obsessive concern with autonomy, to buttress a fragile ego.

These are the qualities that Di Stefano finds in Hobbes' depiction of the state of nature. She cites them as evidence that Hobbes' theory reflects a masculinist orientation. To do so, Di Stefano must convince the reader that Hobbes' theory reflects his own masculine upbringing or his inability to differentiate his identity from that of his mother in a way that does not lead to a severed sense of self, or that Hobbes, because he is a 'masculine subject' working with a certain 'masculine' conception of self, has imbibed certain aspects of modern masculine identity.[12] Although Di Stefano points out that the framework she is using, object relations theory, cannot be used to account 'for the lives of actual men and women whose families do not conform to the white, bourgeois, nuclear model,'[13] and that the conceptions of gender which she is elucidating may never fully be lived by particular men and women, she does attribute Hobbes' thought, in part, to its being part of a canonical literature that has been 'written, interpreted, and formed as a tradition by masculine subjects.'[14]

According to Di Stefano, modern masculinity is an ideology that pervades modern Western thought in general. It lends itself to a predominantly masculine world-view of estrangement and conquest, from which Hobbes is no exception. In making this kind of argument, Di Stefano gets into the uncomfortable position of suggesting that all male thought reflects male upbringing or a 'masculinist' conception of the self which is incorporated by male theorists (and accepted by those female theorists who uncritically appropriate male thought) and which forms their perceptions of what they call 'human nature.' Di Stefano backs away from saying this by pointing out that she is giving a deliberately 'gendered' reading of Hobbes from a particular feminist standpoint.[15] As such, her interpretation is open to being dismissed as just that. However, it is apparent that Di Stefano wants to convince the reader that her explication is not just an alternative to traditional interpretations of Hobbesian human nature, but is both a more accurate and a more fruitful reading in light of current concerns.

Di Stefano is not convincing, however. In order to back up her central assertion regarding Hobbes – 'the most significant finding involves the denial of the maternal contribution'[16] – she must dismiss his explicit discussion of maternal power and dominion. She does so by claiming that Hobbes never fully embraces mother-right; maternal power is cancelled out by the power of fathers as heads of families.[17] Di Stefano dismisses as equally insignificant Hobbes' endorsement of women's ability to inherit sovereign power.[18]

One of the characteristics of modern masculinity evident in Hobbes, according to Di Stefano, is the fantasy that one is self-generating:

> We can discern modern masculinity at work in the fantasy pattern that underlies this account: men magically spring like mushrooms, unmothered and unfathered. While such a fantasy deals a blow to parenthood and to the organic notion of generational continuity, it strikes especially hard at the maternal contribution, whose denial is uniquely remarkable and difficult to implement since it is so biologically and socially apparent (even to Hobbes).[19]

In her interpretation of Hobbes, Di Stefano relies heavily on a passage in which he refers to men springing to maturity like mushrooms.[20] According to Di Stefano, Hobbes is revealing to us and inviting us to engage in his fantasy about springing into the world motherless and fatherless, a fantasy of male independence, derived from the male experience of differentiation from the mother figure. Underlying this fantasy is an attempt to deny the real maternal contribution.

I interpret Hobbes' remark in a different light. Hobbes contends that in the state of nature we must consider men *as if* they had sprung out of the earth and come to full maturity like mushrooms, 'without all kind of engagement to each other' (thereby acknowledging that they do not in fact spring up or come to maturity this way), because in the context of what he tells us about parent-child relations and the absence of a natural maternal instinct, he has no way of accounting for the care of children in that state. In her assessment of Hobbes, Di Stefano seems to conflate the recognition of the maternal contribution to the care of children with the recognition of a maternal instinct to care for children. Hobbes recognizes the former but not the latter.

The mother is present in Hobbes not as the nurturing, benevolent mother assumed by Di Stefano, but as the powerful, fear-inspiring mother who may opt to abandon her child, thereby causing its death. In suggesting that the image of the powerful mother is simply another version of the male fantasy,[21] Di Stefano underplays the extent to which the Hobbesian mother is depicted as having a form of political power, as well as the political implications of her exercising that power.

Moreover, to argue that this image of the fear-inspiring, powerful mother is proof that Hobbes' depiction of her is a masculinist one is to pose an alternative image of the mother, and to present it as being more 'real' and accurate because it has been elucidated by women and consequently reflects women's experience.[22] Di Stefano cautions that she is not undertaking to reveal and criticize masculine conceptions from the standpoint of a more real and accurate 'feminine counter example' or standpoint.[23] I think she does, however, end up interpreting Hobbes from such a reference point, which leads her to suggest that Hobbes' masculinist orientation 'ignores and debases the female contribution to social life.'[24] Di Stefano does not tell us exactly what that female contribution might be. But she hints at it and assumes what it might be when she relies on object relations theory to account for the formation of gender identity.[25] According to object relations theory, the female experience of being mothered by a woman, different from the male experience, lends itself to a greater concern with the (maternal) values of care and nurture. The 'female contribution,' we can surmise, is grounded in maternal values of care and nurture.

By equating the female contribution with maternal qualities of care and nurture, one distorts the position of women in Hobbes. Hobbes may reject maternal qualities of nurture and care as natural characteristics of women, but he does not necessarily reject qualities traditionally associated with female experience (the desire for self-preservation, for example). Moreover, he brings out in stark relief the potential and very modern implications of women's rational control over reproduction.

All three analysts – Pateman, Di Stefano, and Flax – note the significance of Hobbes' portrait of parent-child relations. At the same time, all three either deliberately or unintentionally fail to explore this avenue and the implications it might have for women. Flax suggests that political thinkers, including Hobbes, on the whole have ignored children as irrational.[26] Di Stefano notes that Hobbes 'takes special pains in addressing the particular relationship between parents and their offspring.'[27] Pateman elaborates on this point: Hobbes' theory of consent cannot explain the parent-child bond.[28] But she does not investigate the implications of this failure for the position of women, insisting that what is more important than and what precedes the 'parental contract,' or the relation between parents and children, is the 'sexual contract,' or the relation between adult men and women.[29] Furthermore, Pateman recognizes that Hobbes' description of the self-interested individual makes it difficult to account for the survival of infants in his state of nature.[30] This raises a number of questions which Pateman by her own admission leaves unanswered: 'I am concerned with adult heterosexual relations not parent-child relations, so I shall merely raise and not pursue such questions.'[31] To pursue such questions, however, is to arrive at a fuller understanding of women's peculiar position.

MATERNAL DOMINION

According to Hobbes, there are two ways of establishing civil society – by institution and by acquisition.[32] Both are based on fear and both establish the legitimacy of the subject's obedience to a sovereign authority. Civil societies founded by acquisition, moreover, may be established either by conquest or by generation; if established by generation, they rest on the dominion of parents over children.[33] *Parental* dominion can take the form of either *maternal* dominion or *paternal* dominion. Most striking is Hobbes' suggestion that *paternal* dominion, although more prevalent, is less 'natural' than *maternal* dominion.

Hobbes contends that biological begetting does not confer on fathers the right of dominion over their children, that is the right to obedience from them for having saved their lives in the state of nature. He gives us two reasons for this. The first is that the right of dominion derives from the child's consent, whether express or tacit, to the father's dominion. (I shall return to the problem of the child's consent.) The second reason Hobbes provides for not resting the father's dominion over the child on biological begetting is that this would mean that the father and mother, who have both taken part in the biological act of begetting, would then both have dominion over the child. But two cannot have dominion over the same person. Dominion, or any form of authority, is meaningful, according to Hobbes, only when it is undivided.[34] Only one parent can then have dominion over the children.

If Hobbes were the patriarchalist that Pateman and Di Stefano suggest he is, he might have simply established the father's dominion over the child on the basis of the father's natural dominion over the mother, or the superiority of male over female in the state of nature. But he explicitly rejects the argument that, in the state of nature, the male is always and necessarily superior to the female so that he can always and necessarily acquire dominion over her and her children:

And whereas some have attributed the Dominion to the Man onely, as being of the more excellent Sex; they misreckon in it. For there is not always that difference of strength or prudence between the man and the woman, as that the right can be determined without War.[35]

Hobbes refers directly to the Amazons as an example of women acquiring power over men and dominion over children:

> But what some say, that in this case the father, by reason of the pre-eminence of sex, and not the mother, becomes lord, signifies nothing. For both reason shows the contrary, because the inequality of their natural forces is not so great, that the man could get the dominion over the woman without war, and custom also contradicts not. For women, namely Amazons, have in former times waged war against their adversaries, and disposed of their children at their own wills.[36]

Moreover, Hobbes suggests that, in the state of nature, without any civil authority to artificially establish that dominion over children be given to men, paternal dominion over children is much more unlikely than maternal dominion over children. He cites two important reasons for this. Both have to do with women's peculiar biological relations to reproduction. The first is that the father is uncertain that the children are his. The mother, because she carries and gives birth to the child, knows it is hers. Furthermore, it is up to the mother to testify that the children belong to the father.[37] The mother can establish not only the maternity but the paternity of the child as well, thereby giving her the advantage in acquiring dominion over it:

> For in the condition of meer Nature, where there are no Matrimoniall lawes, it cannot be known who is the Father, unless it be declared by the Mother: and therefore the right of Dominion over the child dependeth on her will, and is consequently hers.[38]

But why should establishing the maternity or paternity of the child be connected to acquiring dominion over it? On the one hand, Hobbes tells us that it does not matter by whom the child was begotten; what matters is who gives it life by nourishing it – and anyone (even a stranger) who does this acquires the right of dominion over the child.[39] He thereby implies that the biological connection between parent and child is of little significance. On the other hand, Hobbes implies that there is some significance to the mother's ability to establish the maternity and the paternity of the child. This can be understood in two ways. First, if dominion entails obedience to an undivided and known authority, a child needs a known master. If it does not know who gave it life, it cannot fulfil its obligation to obey the one who gave it life. The mother then can make it known to the child to whom it owes its obedience. Second, knowing the child is one's own, one may have a greater incentive to nourish it, thereby giving it life and acquiring dominion over it. This is not because there is a natural link between parents and children in the form of a natural instinct to care for one's own children, but because one might derive greater honour, a form of power, from one's own children than from a stranger's children.(I shall elaborate on this point shortly.)

The mother's ability to establish maternity and paternity, therefore, gives her the advantage in the state of nature – it makes maternal dominion more 'natural' than paternal dominion. Another and more important reason that Hobbes cites for the greater 'naturalness' of maternal dominion is that the mother is usually the first to be able to exercise the power of life and death over the infant: 'But it is manifest that he who is newly born, is in the mother's power before any others, insomuch as she may rightly, and at her own will, either breed him up or adventure him to fortune.'[40] Because she bears and gives birth to the infant, the mother usually has the initial access to it. She has the first opportunity either to nourish the infant, thereby giving it life, or to refuse to nourish it, thereby either leaving it to die or leaving it to someone else to nourish and give life to:

> Again, seeing the Infant is first in the power of the Mother, so as she may either nourish, or expose it, if she nourish it, it oweth its life to the Mother; and is therefore obliged to obey her, rather than any other; and by consequence the Dominion over it is hers.[41]

The mother acquires dominion over the child when, having the power of life and death over it, she chooses to give it life. Infanticide, through exposure of the infant, is an option that comes with Hobbes' depiction of maternal power. The infant's dependence at birth means that inaction, the failure to nourish, inevitably leads to death.

Maternal power, as Hobbes depicts it, rests on the exercise of choice. It rests not on the fact that a mother bears the child *per se*, but on the initial access to the child that bearing it gives her and on the option she has to either nourish or expose it, breed it up or adventure it to fortune. But what would induce her to choose one option over the other? That Hobbes implicitly asks this kind of question indicates that the answer is not a given. It also suggests that caring for a child is not an involuntary response to bearing it.

According to Hobbes, all voluntary acts that benefit another have as their object the good of the person perpetrating them,[42] 'because whatsoever is voluntarily done, is done for some good to him that wills it; there can no other token be assigned of the will to give it, except some benefit already received, or to be acquired.'[43] What he must show then is that it is in the interests of the mother to nourish and raise the child. In other words, he must show that saving the child's life, acquiring dominion over it, is in the mother's interest. Hobbes attempts to demonstrate that it is, by suggesting that a woman may choose to care for a child, thereby giving it life, in the hope of securing some future benefit. In the state of nature, this means the hope of securing a future ally:

> If therefore she breed him (because the state of nature is the state of war) she is supposed to bring him up on this condition, that being grown to full age he become not her enemy; which is, that he obey her. For since by natural necessity we all desire that which appears good unto us, it cannot be understood that any man hath on such terms afforded life to another, that he might both get strength by his years, and at once become an enemy. But each man is an enemy to that other whom he neither obeys nor commands. And thus in the state of nature, every woman that bears children, becomes both a mother and a lord.[44]

Hobbes is proposing here that a mother's motivation for raising her child is grounded in self-interest. She gives it life, nourishing and raising it, in the hope that it will not become her enemy as an adult.

As Hobbes depicts it, mothering is a rational activity in several senses: it involves choices, including the choice of not caring for the infant; it entails undertaking to care for the infant as a voluntary act; and it involves a rational calculation of what benefits might accrue to the mother for caring for the infant. Giving birth may occur naturally, that is, as a result of sexual relations, but giving life does not. Mothering is a rational self-interested activity which rests on the power and the capacity to exercise the choice of life and death over another being.

As such, Hobbes portrays mothering not as de Beauvoir describes it, as the mere perpetuation of life, but as an activity that may involve the taking of life. De Beauvoir has argued that women's oppression, their relegation to immanence, is founded on the historical fact that women were excluded from the forays in which men went out to kill.[45] For de

Beauvoir, the sex (male) that risks life and takes it has defined transcendence; the sex (female) that simply perpetuates life by giving birth is confined to immanence.[46] In Hobbes, however, the sex that bears and gives life is also the sex that can first take it away. In de Beauvoir's terms, Hobbesian motherhood is an engagement in transcendence, not immanence.[47]

What is noteworthy in Hobbes' depiction of maternal power is that he does not invoke natural maternal feelings or instincts to explain why mothers would choose to nourish and rear their children. He presents as a serious option that they would choose not to do so, both in the form of abandoning them or giving them up to the care of others (adventuring them to fortune) and in the form of refusing to give them life (exposing them). In the absence of a natural instinct to nourish the child, biological motherhood does not necessarily confer maternal care. At the same time, Hobbes acknowledges the impact of biology – because women bear and give birth to the infant they usually have first contact with it and can attest to its maternity or paternity. But Hobbes does not ground maternal power and dominion in a natural maternal urge to have or care for children. He grounds it in the exercise of the power of life and death over them.

Maternal power, moreover, is analogous to political power. Hobbes' description of the epitome of political power, in the form of the great Leviathan, reveals a being who can exert terror by dint of being able to exercise the power of life and death over subjects. This power is akin to the power that Hobbes attributes to women in the state of nature. Rather than reading this analogy as symptomatic of a typically masculinist fantasy of the mythical powers attributed to women, one might read this as a stark but real evocation of the power that can accrue to women as the givers of life, a power that is grounded not in nature in the form of a natural maternal instinct but in reason in the form of the exercise of self-interested choice and in women's peculiar biological make-up, which gives them first access to the infant.[48] In repudiating a natural maternal instinct to have and care for children, Hobbes also weakens the connection between biological and social parenting. Biological begetting, he emphasizes, does not confer dominion. The rightful parent is the one who first nourishes the child, thereby giving it life, rather than the one who begets it, which of itself does not ensure life.[49] Moreover, being the biological mother of a child, he implies in his discussion of maternal power and dominion, does not mean that one will necessarily or automatically care for it. Biological begetting does not guarantee social parenting. Hobbes leaves open the possibility that there may be advantages to caring for one's own children, over and above caring for a stranger's children. Nevertheless, he has difficulty accounting for the care of children, one's own or another's, in the state of nature where there is no binding common authority to regulate relations between parents and children.

PARENT-CHILD RELATIONS

What would induce women or men to raise children in the state of nature? Very little, given the tenuousness of any natural bond between parents and children; the selfish passions which motivate human beings, male and female alike; the absence of binding covenants and laws, including the Law of Gratitude, which would ensure that children keep their promises to their parents; and the inability of children to exercise reason, which precludes them from engaging in contracts or covenants.

Hobbes refers to the existence of 'the naturall inclination of the Sexes, one to another, and to their children,' in the state of nature.[50] By this he presumably means that the sexes are attracted enough to each other to have sexual relations, the result of which may be children. But his remark about the natural inclination of the sexes 'to their children' must be read in light of the way he presents the relations between parents and children. These show little evidence of any natural desire on the part of men or women to have children, any natural bond between parents and children which would induce the former to care for the latter, or any natural love of parents for their children's well-being.

For example, Hobbes cautions against assuming that children are the 'natural' heirs to their parents' political power. Only where a monarch has not explicitly designated an heir or where there is no established custom to determine who succeeds to the throne can it be assumed that power be passed on to the children rather than to a stranger. If 'men are presumed to be more enclined by nature, to advance their own children, than the children of other men,'[51] this is not because one can presume that parents naturally love their offspring or wish to see them prosper. One can assume, instead, that parents wish to extend or increase their own honour, prestige, and power, at present or in posterity, through their children:

Furthermore, because by natural necessity all men wish them better, from whom they receive glory and honour, than others; but every man after death receives honour and glory from his children, sooner than from the power of any other men: hence we gather, that a father intends better for his children, than any other person's. It is to be understood therefore, that the will of the father, dying without testament, was that some of his children should succeed him.[52]

In this passage, Hobbes explains an act in which parents give something to their children as an act that benefits the parents. He suggests that generosity to one's offspring is motivated by the perception that one will benefit from that generosity, more so than one would benefit from generosity towards a stranger. Parents do not necessarily wish to pass on their goods, possessions, or powers to their children out of concern for the children's well-being. Children are little more than means for enhancing the power and honour of their parents.

If the link between parents and children is tenuous, the link between siblings seems weak as well. A brother or sister may inherit the throne, if the monarch has no children or if there is no declaration to the contrary, 'For those that are nearest to us in nature, are supposed to be nearest in benevolence.'[53] We can suppose that a near of kin ought to be chosen over a stranger, Hobbes advises, not because we can be assured that any natural affection between family members *does* exist but 'because it is always presumed that the neerer of kin, is the neerer in affection.'[54] We can presume that, out of self-interest, an individual prefers to bestow power on his own kin, rather than on a stranger. Bestowing power on his own kin enhances his own reputation, and hence his own power —'and 'tis evident that a man receives alwayes, by reflexion, the most honour from the greatnesse of his neerest kindred.'[55]

As Hobbes describes them, parents have little natural altruistic love for their children. Likewise, children have little love for their parents.[56] Children are naturally selfish and ungrateful; in other words, they are like adults in the state of nature: 'Unless you give children all they ask for, they are peevish, and cry, aye and strike their parents sometimes, and all this they have from nature.'[57] Children are not exempt from wanting to destroy or invade their parents' property, Hobbes implies, when he observes that a man locks his chests against his servants and children.[58] Parents believe they must protect themselves from their children, as from others, who will do them harm if given the opportunity.

Moreover, in the state of nature, as Hobbes describes it, there is no guarantee that the children will not grow up to become their parents' enemies and to kill them as they would any other. Blood relationships are not immune from competition and the desire to appropriate another's power. In the absence of a strong natural bond between parents and children, and in the face of children's propensity to see their parents as simply other beings with whom one competes for power, parents must be assured that they are not rearing an enemy. But this assurance, we must conclude when we examine Hobbes' state of nature, can only be had in civil society where a sovereign authority ensures that individuals keep their promises and covenants.

One of the difficulties of the Hobbesian state of nature is that the so-called Laws of Nature, including the third Law of Nature – that individuals perform the covenants they make – are inoperative in that state.[59] Hobbes tells us that promises and covenants are not binding in the state of nature because there is no guarantee that the party who is to perform afterward will do so.[60] Yet, the parent-child relationship, as Hobbes characterizes it, must rest on a covenant because it requires that children perform later on, as adults, their part of the bargain, or that children repay their parents, in the form of promising obedience to them,[61] for the care the parents have lavished on them. This means, therefore, that parents have no incentive or motivation to nourish and raise children in the state of nature, since there is no guarantee that they will be repaid for their effort by future gain. The keeping of promises and covenants is something that must be legislated by the sovereign authority in civil society. This is precisely why Hobbes must end up advocating the use of sovereign power to legislate parent-child relations.

Even if the state of nature were conducive to the making of covenants, children, lacking reason would be unable to participate in them. Although potentially reasonable creatures, children, Hobbes points out, do not have reason, which is based on the ability to use speech correctly: 'Children therefore are not endued with Reason at all, till they have attained the use of Speech: but are called Reasonable Creatures, for the possibility apparent of having the use of Reason in time to come.'[62] Children's deficiency has repercussions for their ability to consent to their parent's dominion. They can do so only as adults, since only as adults do they become reasonable creatures. One cannot make a covenant with one's children while they are children, since children cannot engage in the necessary transaction until they are adults – until they have reason.[63] Parental dominion over a child then – that is the right to a child's obedience in return for having saved its life – can only be acknowledged by the child when it has become an adult, when its reason tells it that it must obey the one who saved its life.[64]

Moreover, because they do not have the reason to exercise foresight, children are not subject to the law, whether it be natural or civil law. Only as adults do they become reasonable creatures and only reasonable creatures, Hobbes emphasizes, have the ability to follow the law and the ability to recognize that their interest is advanced by doing so:

> Over naturall fooles, children, or mad-men there is no Law, no more than over brute beasts; nor are they capable of the title of just, or unjust; because they had never power to make any covenant, or to understand the consequences thereof; and consequently never took upon them to authorise the actions of any Soveraign, as they must do that make to themselves a Common-wealth.[65]

Furthermore, lacking the ability to make covenants, children cannot 'enter' civil society on their own. Although Hobbes makes provisions for those who have no reason – fools and children can be represented by 'Guardians' until their reason returns to them – these provisions in the form of guardianship can only take place in civil society:

> Likewise Children, Fooles, and Mad-men that have no use of Reason, may be Personated by Guardians, or Curators; but can be no Authors (during that time) of any action done by them, longer then (when they shall recover the use of Reason) they shall judge the same reasonable. Yet during the Folly, he that hath right of governing them, may give Authority to the Guardian. But this again has no place but in a State Civill, because before such estate, there is no Dominion of Persons.[66]

This means that there is no mechanism by which children could leave the state of nature either as their own representatives (since they cannot make covenants) or under the guardianship of their parents (since guardianship exists only in civil society) or under the dominion of their parents (since parents have no incentive to establish dominion over children by saving their lives); yet they have no status in the state of nature.

In Hobbes' framework, children can exist only in civil society,[67] since only in civil society can a bond between parents and children be established, one that is necessary if human beings are to produce and reproduce themselves. Without the care of parents, either biological or social ones, the child cannot survive. Without the survival of the child, the political community cannot reproduce itself. The absence of a civil authority capable of legislating relations between parents and children signals a lapse in continuity or a return to the state of nature in which the life of not only the individual but also of the species is threatened.

What kinds of provisions does Hobbes make for regulating relations between parents and children in civil society? Since Hobbes assumes that civil society does not transform human character, human beings are motivated by the same desires in civil society as they are in the state of nature.[68] This means that the factors which determine parent-child relations in the state of nature (the tenuousness of the biological bond between parents and children, the selfish passions which motivate men and women alike, and the inability of children to exercise reason) are relevant to civil society as well. The difference is that there is a sovereign authority which can ensure adherence to covenants, promises, and laws. Through these, particularly the Laws of Gratitude, Marriage, and Education, civil society ensures that parents have the motivation to rear their children, thereby ensuring the physical and political reproduction of the community.

GRATITUDE

In civil society, the sovereign authority ensures that the Laws of Nature are operative. The most important Law of Nature where parent-child relations are concerned is the Law of Gratitude or the fourth Law of Nature. It stipulates that one who has received a benefit from another must do nothing to make the benefactor regret his goodwill:

> *That a man which receiveth Benefit from another of meer Grace, Endeavour that he which giveth it, have no reasonable cause to repent him of his good will.* For no man giveth, but with intention of Good to himself; because Gift is Voluntary; and of all Voluntary Acts, the Object is to every man his own Good; of which if men see they shall be frustrated, there will be no beginning of benevolence, or trust; nor consequently of mutuall help; nor of reconciliation of one man to another; and therefore they are to remain still in the condition of War; which is contrary to the first and Fundamentall Law of Nature, which commandeth men to Seek Peace. The breach of this Law, is called *Ingratitude*; and hath the same relation to Grace, that Injustice hath to Obligation by Covenant.[69]

Honouring one's parents falls under the Law of Gratitude:[70]

It must therefore be ever understood, that he who is freed from subjection, whether he be a servant, son, or some colony, doth promise all those external signs at least, whereby superiors used to be honoured by their inferiors. From whence it follows, that the precept of honouring our parents, belongs to the law of nature, not only under the title of gratitude, but also of agreement.[71]

Gordon Schochet has argued that the importance of the Law of Gratitude in Hobbes' scheme is that, by ensuring children's consent to the dominion of their parent, their father in particular, it is a mechanism for passing on patriarchal authority.[72] I argue that the Law of Gratitude can be understood less as a means to ensure children's consent to the dominion of fathers or mothers (children, lacking reason, cannot consent to their parents' dominion until they are adults)[73] than as a means for ensuring that parents have an incentive to care for their children. The Law of Gratitude is directed at parents, not children. It gives parents the guarantee that their children, once they become adults, will repay their parents, in a form that promotes the parents' interest, for the care lavished on them. Hence it provides parents with an inducement to raise children.

The Law of Gratitude comes into effect when children become adults, when they are capable of reason and of recognizing that following the law is in their self-interest. In the state of nature, the problem, as Hobbes poses it, is that once children are adults, once they reach the age of reason, they are no longer much weaker than their parents and thus are unlikely to honour their father or mother.

In civil society, once children are adults, they are obligated to adhere to the civil laws which are derived from the Laws of Nature and include the Law of Gratitude. This Law secures for parents the assurance that their grown children will honour them. Honour is simply a sign of power for Hobbes.[74] The Law of Gratitude then functions as a way of obligating children to increase their parents' power, thereby furnishing parents with an incentive to care for their offspring.

What we see in Hobbes is that the laws of civil society do not change the nature of the inducements that parents have for raising children. They confirm and assume that the parent-child relationship is little different from any other relationship – it too operates on the principle of benefit to the self. Directed at parents, the Law of Gratitude presupposes that parents need to be guaranteed a reward for caring for their offspring.

MARRIAGE

Marriage laws in Hobbes's framework can be understood as another mechanism for ensuring that children are cared for. Entering the marriage contract in civil society is one of several ways in which the mother gives up dominion over children to the father (or to another). Hobbes lists a number of them.[75] Except for the first, they concern civil society rather than the state of nature.

First, if the mother abandons the infant in the state of nature, thereby refusing to give it life by nourishing it, she gives up the right of dominion to anyone who may find the child and give it life by nourishing it. According to Pateman, the mother would inevitably abandon the child as a liability.[76] Pateman intimates this is proof that women are in fact the weaker party in the Hobbesian state of nature: that is, they are at a disadvantage because they bear children. A more convincing interpretation is that it is an indicator of women's capacity for rational self-interest. Women are not necessarily weaker than men in Hobbes' state of nature;[77] but they are as self-interested as men. And they have no natural maternal urge to care for children. Consequently they might well decide that establishing dominion over the child, by giving it life, carries no guaranteed rewards. But this is also true of any other person, any man, for example, who finds an abandoned child.[78] Both men and women in the state of nature have little incentive to acquire dominion over children, which requires that they give them life (by nourishing them) and raise them to adulthood so they can reap the rewards for having given them life.

Hobbes seems to say that mothers may contract away dominion over the child in the state of nature, that is they may agree to give children up to the dominion of a particular person, the father for example, rather than simply abandoning them to whoever may find and save the child's life. But the examples he gives of women contracting away dominion (except for the first where they merely refuse to give the child life) involve or take place in forms of civil society rather than in the state of nature. The reason may be this: it is difficult to see how a woman could make a contract, in the state of nature, before the birth of the infant, to give dominion over the infant to the father or another once the infant was born. Such an exchange would entail making a covenant in which the mother promises to 'deliver' her part of the bargain – the infant – at a later date. A woman may contract to have sexual relations, in which the exchange of benefits is simultaneous, but how can she 'contract' away her right to dominion over the child in the state of nature, prior to the birth of the infant? The latter entails making a covenant. Given what Hobbes has said about the lack of validity that covenants have in the state of nature, it is difficult to see how a woman would be able to contract away dominion of the child, to a particular person, before she herself had the opportunity to wield the power of life and death over the infant. Once the infant is born, it is in her power. Once she has the opportunity to wield the power of life and death over it, moreover, she has the opportunity to exercise first dominion over it.

A second way in which the mother contracts away dominion over the children is if she is taken a prisoner. In this case the conqueror who has acquired dominion over her person, and has established a form of civil society based on conquest, 'hath also dominion over all belonging to the person.'[79] The proposal that children be included along with a mother's possessions reinforces the theme that children are not ends in themselves; they are like property which can be passed from one to another.

The third way in which a mother may pass dominion over to another is if she becomes a subject to a supreme authority in civil society: 'Thirdly, if the mother be a subject under what government soever, he that hath the supreme authority in that government, will also have the dominion over him that is born of her; for he is lord also of the mother, who is bound to obey him in all things.'[80] Hobbes raises a number of issues here. If the authority of the sovereign in civil society supersedes the mother's or father's authority over the child, to whom do the children owe their allegiance in civil society? To their parents or to the sovereign authority? Furthermore, is the mother's authority over the children taken away in civil society to the same degree as the father's authority?

The fourth way that the mother passes away dominion over the child is if she gives herself to a man on the condition that he will support her and the child, in which case the father acquires dominion over both the mother and the child. This is done for 'society's sake,'[81] which indicates that it occurs in civil society. Hobbes seems to suggest here that women may have fewer economic means than men in civil society. If they do, however, we cannot assume that it is because they are less rational, capable, or self-interested than men. Women do not, moreover, automatically assume the status of their husbands or the fathers of their children in civil society. Female rulers who have children, Hobbes points out, do not lose their authority or become subject to their husbands. Furthermore, Hobbes is explicit on this point: we may find that either the male or the female has subjugated the other; the children belong to the one who has dominion.[82]

A fifth way that a woman may pass dominion over her children to another is by entering the contract of marriage:[83] 'But in a civil government, if there be a contract of marriage between a man and woman, the children are the father's.'[84] But why does the dominion over the children go to the father and not the mother? Hobbes' explanation – 'because in all cities, to wit, constituted of fathers, not mothers governing their families, the domestical command belongs to the man; and such a contract, if it be made according to the civil laws, is called matrimony'[85] – has been the focus of much criticism. It has been cited as proof that Hobbes does not take seriously woman's maternal power over children in the state of nature. His portrayal of the marriage contract has been taken as evidence that the family, where men are made heads of household, is the source of women's oppression.[86]

Furthermore, Hobbes is attributed with sanctioning the 'naturalness' of the family headed by the father. According to this argument, the Hobbesian state of nature consists of families headed by fathers who have patriarchal control or dominance over their wives, servants, and children. Carole Pateman, for example, suggests that Hobbes' patriarchalism rests on the power of the husband over the wife in the state of nature.[87] From this state, men as heads of families then contract to form civil society. Women are either represented by men or left out altogether in the institution of civil society.[88]

As a theoretical construct, Hobbes' state of nature, I have argued, cannot account for the existence of families constituted of parents and children because it cannot account for why men or women would nourish and care for children rather than abandon them. But what do we make of Hobbes' references to the existence of families in historical periods that seem to resemble a state of nature? Moreover, Hobbes frequently compares families to Commonwealths, in a way that implies they both are regulated by the same kind of authority.[89] In other places he indicates that families are different from Commonwealths, implying that the authority of the father in the family is different from that of the sovereign authority in civil society.

There is much confusion in Hobbes' discussion of families and the state of nature if one assumes that the Hobbesian state of nature is solely a pre-civil state which has historically preceded all forms of civil society. Hobbes' state of nature, as a theoretical construct, is important less as a historical condition which existed prior to all forms of civil government than as a state of being which can occur at any time; it represents a lapse in order which sets off a chain reaction, eventually leading to a state of chaos and death for all.[90]

At the same time, we cannot ignore Hobbes' allusions to a historical process by which families grew into Commonwealths and forms of civil society.[91] We find that women are present as heads of families in Hobbes' historical account. He seems to take seriously the Amazons as a historical example of women having dominion over children and acting as heads of households.[92] The Hobbesian state of nature as a historical condition then would have to be described as one which might have been constituted of families (headed either by the mother or the father) who were at war with each other for lack of a common authority. Some of these families might have operated internally in such a manner that there was a common authority (either the father or the mother) who had enough power to protect members of that family, in which case they operated as if they were in a form of government or a form of civil society.[93]

In referring to the Amazons as an example of the mother's dominion over children, moreover, Hobbes insinuates that women are capable of acting as heads of families and establishing forms of government or civil society as heads of families. The message we get from Hobbes is that women's nature does not preclude them from creating Commonwealths but history has shown that for the most part Commonwealths have been erected by the fathers, not by the mothers of families.[94]

The way that Hobbes describes the founding of Commonwealths by the power of the father, however, suggests that this power is not 'natural' in the sense that it is unchallenged or unquestioned by the children. He compares subduing one's enemy and establishing a Commonwealth by conquest to subduing one's children and establishing a Commonwealth by paternal generation. He describes the latter as 'when a man maketh his children, to submit themselves, and their children to his government, as being able to destroy them if they refuse.'[95] Children, it appears, are not 'naturally' subject to their fathers; they must be *made* to be so. If the father's dominion over the children were 'natural,' why would he need to exert the same kind of force over them as the force one uses to conquer a strange enemy?

Furthermore, in the passages where Hobbes describes the move from the father-headed family to civil society or compares the father-headed family to a form of civil society, he omits any mention of husbands subduing their wives by force.[96] Pateman suggests in an earlier interpretation of Hobbes that this is intentional, a position she later reverses when she contends that Hobbes implicitly subsumes women as wives under the power of the father-husband.[97] Pateman's first interpretation, however, is more compatible with a number of other cues we find in Hobbes: that women as heads of families can establish Commonwealths; that women can inherit the political power of the sovereign authority in civil society; that queens exert political power over their husbands; and that paternal dominion is based more on custom than nature. The failure to mention conquest over wives, moreover, also underscores the greater importance of parent-child relations over and above adult male-female ones in Hobbes' scheme.

The comparison of conquest to generation further amplifies and exposes the antagonistic relationship between parents and children. The family dynamic, it seems, involves the same dynamic as interactions between individuals who live in the state of nature, that is, in a condition without a common power to force them to submit to the laws conducive to peaceful relations (the Laws of Nature). By comparing the family to a Commonwealth, Hobbes intimates that the relations between parents and children need to be governed or guided by the same principles that regulate other (political and social) relations in civil society. This is what makes it so difficult to place the family in the so-called 'private' realm.

Hobbes distinguishes the political realm as a realm designated by the authority of the sovereign. It includes whatever the sovereign sees fit to declare as being conducive to the keeping of the peace. Furthermore, Hobbes distinguishes between political systems, which are regulated by the authority of the sovereign, and so-called private systems, which are regulated by and made by subjects amongst themselves. Only those private systems that are sanctioned by the sovereign are legitimate. The sovereign authority thereby determines the parameters of the private sphere.[98] What distinguishes the private realm, furthermore, is that it is a realm of liberty, that is, a domain where the law is silent and where subjects are at liberty to act as they please.[99]

Hobbes lists the family in civil society as an example of a private body of the regular kind where authority is vested in one person. According to the custom of most civil societies, that person is usually the father. What kind of authority then does the father have in the private realm? In one passage Hobbes suggests that the father's publicly sanctioned authority over the family in civil society is 'natural' because it is based on the authority that fathers had over their children in the state of nature: 'For the Father, and Master being before the Institution of Common-wealth, absolute Soveraigns in their own Families, they lose afterward no more of their Authority, than the Law of the Common-wealth taketh from them.'[100] This implies that the sovereign authority must leave fathers some freedom to exercise authority over their children, an authority which can be distinguished from the sovereign's authority over children as subjects.

Parental authority in the family, however, can be legitimate for Hobbes only as long as it does not conflict with the sovereign's authority in civil society. That the potential for conflict exists is of concern to Hobbes – he warns of the dangers of the authority of the father (or mother) to the peace of the Commonwealth. Families that are too powerful become factions which must be outlawed because they detract from one's allegiance to the sovereign and thereby threaten the peace of the Commonwealth.[101] At the same time as Hobbes warns of the subversive effect of family allegiance, he finds it necessary to allow parents some liberty 'to institute their children as they themselves think fit.'[102] Why? In order to give them some 'harmless liberty,' perhaps,[103] but more importantly to ensure that parents have incentive to raise their children. Hobbes has told us that they will do so only if they derive some benefit from it. And to derive some benefit from it they must be able to exert some power over their children – to view them as means towards the end of increasing their honour and power. This is why Hobbes must propose that parents have some authority over children in a (private) realm left unregulated by sovereign authority. They must have enough authority to give them some power over their children, but not enough so that the power of the family unit challenges the power of the sovereign authority.

The 'private' domain in civil society is supposed to be a sphere in which the sovereign's authority does not intrude. Where the family is concerned, however, this poses a problem. If left to itself, the Hobbesian family, in which the relationship between parent and child is paramount over the relationship between husband and wife, would be guided by the same principles as those which operate in the state of nature. One of these principles is that each is his own judge of what is good and evil. It comes into effect not only in the state of nature or 'the condition of meer Nature, where there are no Civill Lawes,' according to Hobbes, but 'also under Civill Government, in such cases as are not determined by the Law.'[104] But can relations between parents and children be left in the private domain where the law does not determine what is good and evil? If the private domain operates under the principles of the state of nature, then the obligation of children to parents would also be determined by every person's judgment.[105] As a result, parents would have no assurance that their children would be obligated to obey and honour them.

Hobbes places the family in the private domain of civil society, yet he cannot leave it there. In an unregulated sphere where the mechanics of the state of nature operate, what guarantee is there that parents would care for their children, thereby ensuring the physical and political reproduction of the community? The Hobbesian state of nature, I have argued, cannot provide such a guarantee, given that men and women are selfishly motivated and deficient in a natural urge to have and care for children. In civil society, Hobbes locates the family in an arena where selfish passions may clash. This is why dominion over the children, like dominion over subjects, cannot be divided. If relations between parents and children are little different from other political or social relations, as Hobbes indicates they are, then they may require similar forms of regulation in civil society.[106]

Hobbes addresses himself to whether the association of parents and children is distinctive when he asks whether it is a greater crime to kill a parent than to kill another in civil society. His answer in *Leviathan* is: 'For to kill ones Parent, is a greater Crime, than to kill another: for the Parent ought to have the honour of a Soveraign, (though he have surrendred his Power to the Civill Law,) because he had it originally by Nature.'[107] Here Hobbes seems to say that a parent has a unique relationship with a child that is distinct from the association of subject and sovereign and that honour is due to the parent even where there is no civil society. But in a footnote in *De Cive* we get an insight to the real status of parent-child association in the state of nature. Here Hobbes asks: Is it a greater crime for a son to kill his father in the state of nature? He realizes that this is a legitimate question, since he has implied that, in the state of nature, children, when grown, will have no special tie to their parents; they are as likely as strangers to view their parents as enemies and kill them accordingly. Hobbes has also argued that killing another in order to preserve one's life is not a crime in the state of nature. Is it then not a crime for a child to kill a parent in the state of nature?

> It hath been objected by some: if a son kill his father, doth he him no injury? I have answered, that a son cannot be understood to be at any time in the state of nature, as being under the power and command of them to whom

he owes his protection as soon as ever he is born, namely, either his father's or his mother's, or his that nourished him.[108]

In the passage above Hobbes responds to the question by contending that a child is never in a state of nature with its parents because a child is born into the dominion of its parents. It is born, so to speak, into a relationship of allegiance to its parents. Yet that allegiance must be based on a covenant, since a child can only repay its parents in the form of being obliged to them at a later date when it becomes an adult. And only in civil society will those covenants be guaranteed. Although Hobbes appears to say that the parent, the father in most civil societies, has some natural power over the child, in the form of a natural relationship with the child that derives from the state of nature, in fact he is saying that parent-child relations can only be guaranteed in civil society. The 'natural' relations between parents and children, like the so-called Laws of Nature, paradoxically, require civil society in order to become operative.

This is especially the case where custom gives the father dominion over the children, which, according to Hobbes, is prevalent in most civil societies. Why does Hobbes support rather than challenge this custom? Hobbes is adamant that authority over the children ought not to be divided. He notes that mothers have had and in some cases still do have dominion over the children in civil society, but that it has been and still is more customary to grant fathers dominion over the children in civil society. The custom, we can surmise, is based on the perception that men are superior to women.[109] But we cannot assume that Hobbes supports the idea that men are in fact superior to women or that he grounds his endorsement of paternal dominion on the father's superiority. A more plausible interpretation is that he endorses the custom as being conducive to peace. If one parent must have dominion and if it has become accepted practice to give dominion to the father, then there would seem to be nothing to gain by proposing what Hobbes has presented as being more in keeping with nature – maternal dominion.

The paradox, however, is that greater force and regulation are required in adhering to custom against nature. Hobbes is very much aware that it is civil society rather than natural propensities which determines that dominion be given to the father. Natural propensities would give dominion to the mother (since she knows the infant is hers and she is usually the first to have access to it). The link between father and child, concomitantly, is more tenuous than the link between mother and child. When, in his discussion of the maternal dominion, he invokes the importance of maternal certitude and first access to the infant, Hobbes implies that it is more difficult to induce the father to nourish the child, to raise it, and thereby to acquire dominion over it. It may also be difficult to get away from the mother's first opportunity to exercise the power of life and death over the infant.

If paternal dominion is less 'natural' than maternal dominion, this may explain why the father has to make the children his by force. It may also point to a need for greater regulation on the part of a sovereign authority to sustain paternal dominion. Even more than a civil society founded on maternal dominion, one which is founded on paternal dominion or one in which the father has dominion over the children in the family requires extensive laws and regulation to create and maintain a parent-child bond.

In sum, the Hobbesian family has a number of characteristics. (1) The parent-child relationship is paramount to the adult male-female one. (2) Historically, the state of nature may have included families, but the family is not 'natural' in the sense that there is any natural affection or love between parents and children. (3) The bond between parents and children, especially when the father has dominion, is as tenuous in civil society as it is in the state of nature. (4) Either parent, the mother or father, can act as head of the family, defined as the one who has dominion over the children. (5) Most often it is fathers who act as heads of families and who consequently have dominion over children in civil society. (6) The father's dominion over children, which is the custom of most civil societies, is more difficult to sustain than the mother's dominion over the children. (7) The family may be relegated to the private realm in civil society but, given the tenuousness of the parent-child bond and the absence of natural affection between parents and children, it ends up requiring extensive state regulation.

EDUCATION

What makes the family a political matter subject to the jurisdiction of the sovereign authority? The association of parents and children is of concern to Hobbes (and to other thinkers I consider) because it ensures both the physical and political continuity of the human species. It becomes a matter of political concern especially where it is deemed to have no natural affective basis. Moreover, as a contract theorist, Hobbes must be doubly attentive to generational continuity, since it is a way of passing on political obligation to the state from one generation to the next. The challenge is to explain how each successive generation consents to the contract which has been established by its forbears, and thereby sustains the legitimacy of political authority.

Biological continuity or the continuity of the species is problematic in Hobbes' state of nature (because, as I have argued, children have no status in that state). In Hobbes' civil society, political continuity remains troublesome. There is a propensity for human beings in civil society to return to a state of nature. One of the main political concerns of the sovereign authority ought to be keeping the peace not only for the present but also for future generations, by making provisions for the peaceful succession of political power. The sovereign must ensure that a Commonwealth does not revert to a state of nature during the process whereby political power or the power of the sovereign authority is passed on to another.

Hobbes worries that the greatest drawback of his preferred system of government – a monarchy – is that succession is uncertain. He takes great pains to elaborate on how a legitimate heir to the throne is to be determined once a monarch dies. The greatest threat to peaceful succession to power once a monarch dies, Hobbes warns, is when the government goes to an infant. Most often, the infant is put into the hands of adults who would gain by killing it.[110] Here Hobbes reinforces the image that infants or children exist for the purpose of furthering the interest of adults. They are means for increasing the power of adults.

To ensure peace, political power must be passed on from one sovereign to another. Conversely, the allegiance or obligation of subject to sovereign must also be passed on from one generation to the next. The parent-child association in Hobbes' scheme is an important vehicle for transmitting political authority. But it does not necessarily operate in the patriarchal fashion that Schochet, for example, claims it does. Hobbes clearly defends the principle that the dominion of parents over children, whether it be maternal or paternal dominion, be passed on from one generation to the next.[111] He also clearly rejects the patriarchal justification for monarchial government. That is, he dismisses the argument that monarchy is a legitimate form of government because the monarch's power is based on the jurisdiction that God gave to Adam, a jurisdiction that was passed down from father to son throughout successive generations.[112] Hobbes repudiates this form of patriarchalism in a number of ways. He disavows the divine basis of political authority; he acknowledges the legitimacy of maternal dominion over children and presents it as relatively more 'natural' than paternal dominion; and he attempts to base the legitimacy of political authority, including the authority of the father over children, on consent. Schochet emphasizes this last point. What was unique about Hobbes, according to Schochet, was not that he eliminated patriarchal ideology, in the form of the use of the fatherly image as a foundation for a theory of political obligation without historical or moral principles, but that he established patriarchal ideology on the consent of the children, projected into the future through the Law of Gratitude.[113]

As Schochet poses it, the difficulty is accounting for why and how children consent to political allegiance to the civil society in which they are born. According to Schochet, Hobbes' way around the difficulty is the Law of Gratitude. It compels children to obey their parents, and by obeying their parents, Schochet implies, they also obey the power of the sovereign authority. I argue that the latter is not necessarily the case – Hobbes recognizes that obedience to parents can also threaten allegiance to the sovereign authority. Furthermore, preceding the problem of why children as adults would consent to the rule of their parents or to a sovereign authority is the question of why and how parents would raise their children. How does one produce those adults who then owe their allegiance to civil society?

In Hobbes' design, the two motivations adults have for entering and maintaining and remaining in civil society are self-interest and fear, both of which require the exercise of reason. Self-interested individuals are able to exercise reason, which tells them that creating civil society is in their interest. Hobbes sets up the state of nature, in part, to show the logic of self-interested individuals creating society for their own benefit: 'All society therefore is either for gain, or for glory; that is, not so much for love of our fellows, as for the love of ourselves.'[114] Self-interest maintains civil society by telling adults that their interest is best served by not challenging the laws of civil society. To be self-interested, one must have reason, which enables one to recognize the Laws of Nature or what is conducive to peaceful living. As the dictates of right reason, the Laws of Nature inform individuals that in order to fulfil their basic desire, to live, and to avoid their basic aversion, to die, they must enter and remain in civil society. Hobbesian individuals may be naturally selfish as children who think only of themselves but they are not naturally self-interested in the sense of having the ability to recognize that they must consider the effects on others of their actions.[115] Self-interest must be learned, since it requires the reason to know that one's interests are bound up with others.

Fear is connected with the ability to reason. Fear rests on the ability to have foresight, to be anxious about the future. Ultimate fear, Hobbes suggests, is a state of anxiety and insecurity about losses which one may incur in the future. Most important, politically, fear is what gets individuals to keep their word. For example, the power of religion is its ability to instil in humans the fear of God which compels them to keep their word. This power is limited in the state of nature because not everyone believes in the same God.[116] In Hobbes' proposal for civil society, the belief in an absolutely powerful God is replaced by a belief in an absolutely powerful sovereign being or a Leviathan. Hobbes paints the Leviathan in as fearful terms as he does the state of nature. As a terrible, all-powerful, God-like being, the Leviathan is able to instil enough fear in individuals to keep them from breaking the civil contract or from getting out of line.[117] And any disobedience on the individual's part, Hobbes emphasizes, breaks the covenant. Individuals agree to contract into civil society or to acquiesce to a conqueror out of fear not love. The fear of being killed in the state of nature drives individuals to society, whether its origins are derived from compact with one another or from submitting to a conqueror. The fear of the Leviathan or of returning to a state of nature keeps them in society.

Fear also keeps in line those individuals who do not have the reason to recognize that their self-interest is advanced by instituting civil society or by acquiescing to a conqueror (or who may know that their self-interest will not be advanced by doing so).[118] They may not want to consent to the original contract, or to a conqueror, or to the civil society in which they were born. If they decline to, they remain in the state of nature, which is a state of war in which they may 'justly' be killed.[119]

If fear and reason are the principles that operate to keep adults obligated to civil society, how does one ensure that they are passed on to the next generation? Self-interest and fear may account for how civil society maintains itself over one generation, or explain a horizontal arrangement among adults, but it is more difficult to rely on them to account for a vertical arrangement between generations or between parents and children. First, it may be difficult to show, as Hobbes attempts to, that the raising of children operates on the principle of self-interest and fear. One must account for how children are raised, however, since one must explain how adults acquire the sense of self-interest and fear, based on reason, which attaches them to civil society. Second, since children have no reason, how do they become self-interested adults capable of consenting to civil society or acquiescing to a conqueror and recognizing that it is in their best interest to do so?

When Hobbes claims that we are not born as we are but acquire our nature as adults,[120] he addresses the condition of infancy and acknowledges that infants are born with neither reason nor self-interest. Humans may be born with a desire to seek peace, based on their instinct for survival, but not the reason to know how to go about implementing it. That must be acquired through education, 'wherefore man is made fit for society not by nature, but by education.'[121] Children may be selfish, but not self-interested, since they do not yet have a sense of self. Similarly, lacking reason, they would have neither the foresight nor the concern about the future which is a central element in fear. If reason and self-interest induce them to form society, then human beings are not born with the qualities or abilities to create or maintain civil society. These qualities must be instilled through education.

Education becomes important as a way of ensuring the creation of self-interested and rational adults who will consent to civil society by obeying its laws. Education becomes the key in transmitting political continuity over time. And parents play a vital role in providing children with such an education.

Since it is education that makes individuals fit for society, it is important that there are no laws for the education of children, or nothing binding parents to educate their children, in Hobbes' state of nature.[122] This means that the state of nature is incapable of producing or reproducing adults who would be able to institute, submit to, or engage in any form of civil society.

The purpose of education for Hobbes is neither the creation of moral beings nor the promotion of enlightenment, other than 'enlightened self-interest.' Education is a form of socialization which creates obedient subjects who will not pose a threat to the absolute power of the sovereign authority. The kind of education that is conducive to such compliance, Hobbes implies, moreover, is not the kind that entails enlightenment (it is the opposite of what we might call a liberal education). For example, Hobbes remarks that the reading of books or other intellectual activity, especially the 'Reading of the books of Policy, and Histories of the antient Greeks, and Romans,' is dangerous and seditious, being one of the things that, along with dividing sovereign authority, leads to the dissolution of civil society.[123] He recommends a sort of education in 'citizenship' to supplement fear and self-interest as a means of ensuring the allegiance of subjects. Subjects ought to be taught to refrain from loving the governments of other nations, admiring any one of their fellow subjects, and disputing or using the sovereign's name disrespectfully. They ought also to be instructed regularly regarding the laws of civil society.[124]

Education in the form of socialization is also the mechanism whereby rational, self-interested human beings capable of forming any sort of social and political affiliation are created. As Hobbes presents it, a fundamental dilemma of human existence is that human beings require others in order to survive, that is they require a form of society, but they are not born with the ability or desire to create it. They are not even naturally sociable. The fifth Law of Nature, for example, is that men try to accommodate each other, to be sociable rather than unsociable.[125] As a Law of Nature, this maxim is operative only in civil society. It addresses itself to adults, moreover.

The state of infancy, Hobbes emphasizes, is precisely a sign that we are *not* born fit for society.[126] His reasoning at first glance seems circular and nonsensical: the fact that we are born helpless infants cannot serve as a basis for society because by definition society is based on a rational act; infants and children lack reason, therefore they cannot act rationally to create society.[127] Hobbes is aware, however, that infants on their own cannot initiate any form of social or political relationship. Only adults can do that. The predicament is that adults cannot be counted on to initiate a relationship of care with the helpless infant. Even to establish dominion over the infant, to save its life, requires that one give it, by nourishing it, some primary care.

An infant is not born with the skills to create a social relationship, yet, in order to survive, it requires such a social relationship in the form of an association with a 'care-giver.' Without such an association, the helpless infant will not survive and neither will the political community. A central requirement for accounting for any form of society or political community, therefore, is accounting for some form of affiliation between an adult and a helpless infant. This becomes particularly challenging if one spurns the idea that there are natural affective ties between parents and children. Hobbes' state of nature illustrates this difficulty.

He asks us to consider men in the state of nature as if they had sprung up like mushrooms. We cannot account for their being raised and educated by their parents from infancy on; therefore, we must consider them as if they had been born as adults: 'Let us return again to the state of nature, and consider men as if but even now sprung out of the earth, and suddenly (like mushrooms) come to full maturity, without all kind of engagement to each other.'[128] The primary engagement to which

Hobbes refers here, we can surmise, must be the engagement of the helpless dependent infant to the one who has first access to it, usually the mother. This engagement is tenuous, however, since there is no guarantee that the mother or another will nourish, care for, and educate the child without the inducements that civil society provides. This is why the condition of infancy is not evidence that society is natural for Hobbes: the fact that an infant is born helpless and dependent does not mean that someone will naturally, in the sense of 'automatically,' care for it, thereby establishing a (natural) social relation to it or with it. As Hobbes depicts it, the conundrum of the human condition is that we are born dependent and requiring the care of adults, yet that care is not naturally forthcoming. This is the real reason that the infant's helplessness is proof, for Hobbes, that we are born unfit for society.

In the Hobbesian state of nature, without laws on education (coupled with the absence of a marriage law and a binding Law of Gratitude), there is no assurance that adults capable of exercising their reason and self-interest, which are the basis of civil society, would be produced or reproduced. There is no guarantee that the care required to make them into human beings capable of any form of social or political association is forthcoming.

In Hobbes' civil society, the laws on education established by a sovereign authority make parents responsible for educating their children. Once again, however, parents must be convinced that they will derive some benefit from taking the trouble to do something for their children. Hobbes provides for this by proposing that parents teach their children the Law of Gratitude, which persuades children to honour their parents, thereby increasing the parents' power.[129] Most interesting is that Hobbes couples this with another directive – children ought to be taught that their father had original power over them in the state of nature:

> And because the first instruction of Children, dependeth on the care of their Parents; it is necessary that they should be obedient to them, whilest they are under their tuition; and not onely so, but that also afterwards (as gratitude requireth,) they acknowledge the benefit of their education, by externall signes of honour. To which end they are to be taught, that originally the Father of every man was also his Soveraign Lord, with power over him of life and death; and that the Fathers of families, when by instituting a Common-wealth, they resigned that absolute Power, yet it was never intended, they should lose the honour due unto them for their education. For to relinquish such right, was not necessary to the Institution of

Soveraign Power; nor would there be any reason, why any man should desire to have children, or take the care to nourish, and instruct them, if they were afterwards to have no other benefit from them, than from other men. And this accordeth with the fifth Commandment.[130]

Why does Hobbes propose that children be taught that fathers had dominion over them in the state of nature when at the same time he has argued that in the state of nature it is usually mothers who have the first opportunity to acquire dominion over children? The teaching of father-right may be necessary, Hobbes realizes, because although custom has given fathers dominion over children, that custom is not based on nature. Children must be instructed to believe that fathers had original power over them in the state of nature, precisely because paternal power is less 'natural' than maternal power. Even more artificial and tenuous than the mother-child tie, the father-child one must to a greater extent be upheld by law and bolstered by education.

In civil society, where the father has dominion over the child, he has the responsibility for providing for the well-being of the child, including its education. How is he to be convinced to do so? Only by an appeal to self-interest. But it is more difficult to convince the father than the mother to care for and educate the children, since the father, unlike the mother, does not have certainty that the children are his own. Moreover, he may not have the first access to the child.

What Hobbes indicates then is that children must be socialized to believe that fathers have natural absolute rights over them in civil societies in order to make it easier for fathers to elicit honour and obedience (and therefore power) from their children, thereby giving fathers greater assurance that they will benefit from raising and providing an education for their children.

The Hobbesian state or sovereign authority might be read less as a patriarchalist one, sanctioning the natural power and freedom of the father over the children in the family, than as both a 'maternalistic' one, substituting state regulation for a natural maternal urge to care for children, and a 'paternalistic' one, having to buttress that regulation in order to cement the father's unnatural dominion over the children.

The laws on education, established by the sovereign authority in civil society, make parents, the father in most cases, responsible for educating their children, for the benefit not only of the parents, whose honour and power are increased, but also for the benefit of the state, which requires obedient subjects. At the same time as the parent-child relationship can pose a threat to the sovereign authority, it can also be of benefit to the sovereign authority if it ensures that parents educate their children to be obedient subjects.

For Hobbes, society, including the most primary social relationship, the parent-child one, is artificial. The mother-child relationship is influenced by biological considerations – a woman's ability to bear and give birth to the child makes her certain the child is hers and gives her initial access to it – but not by a natural maternal urge to care for the child. This initial access is what makes maternal dominion more 'natural' than paternal dominion. It is also what makes the absence of a natural maternal urge more threatening to the continuation of the community than the absence of a paternal urge.

Berns contends that, for Hobbes, man is naturally neither social nor political; the problem then becomes how to make him so or answer the question of how it is that he does live in society.[131] I argue that, for Hobbes, woman too is naturally neither social nor political. She is as self-interested and as lacking in the natural desire to sacrifice her interests for the benefit of others as man. The problem then becomes to explain how it is that, having first access to an infant, she would give it life rather than abandon it to death, or to explain how it is that any form of human society can perpetuate itself. Woman's self-interestedness is more threatening than man's self-interestedness to the survival of the social and political order. But her capacity for rational self-interest is also what makes her as capable as man of participating in politics, wielding political power, and exercising the rights and duties of citizenship.

Although Hobbes does not address directly the question of women's engagement in political life, we can take the clues he gives us about women's capabilities as well as the way he depicts the requirements for political life, and ask whether there is anything about them that would preclude women from exercising them. In particular, we can ask whether Hobbes' framework makes it difficult or impossible to extend to women the same rights as men.

POLITICAL PARTICIPATION

The most basic form of political participation in Hobbes' scheme consists in consenting to the civil contract which establishes a sovereign authority. Does he depict women as being incapable of doing so? Are women excluded from the contract that creates civil society and therefore from civil society itself? I have argued that Hobbes makes room for women acting as heads of families. Therefore, the contention that Hobbes' framework assumes that men as heads of families consent to civil society for their wives is not convincing.

A more general claim made about Hobbes and other contract theorists is that women are deemed to be incapable of contracting to civil society because their bodies are perceived as making them incapable of rational behaviour. For example, Carole Pateman contends that women are considered to be subject to uncontrollable passions and hence incapable of exercising the reason required to engage in the social contract.[132] The underlying assumption of this kind of argument is that men are considered to be rational, and hence fit for political life. According to Mary O'Brien, for example, Western political thought is characterized by a dichotomy whereby women are identified with the passions, the body, and the private realm and men are identified with reason, the mind, and the political.[133] This kind of argument is inapplicable to Hobbes in two ways. First, Hobbes does not present political man as being wholly rational. Second, Hobbes' discussion of maternal dominion suggests that he attributes to women the capacity to exercise reason.

Hobbes does not simply identify men with reason and the mind, women with passions and the body. Neither does he simply exalt reason in favour of the passions.[134] Human behaviour is motivated by the passions, according to Hobbes, 'for the Passions of men, are commonly more potent than their Reason.'[135] The desires, the greatest of which is the desire to avoid death, include all sorts of physical, mental, spiritual, and emotional wants and needs. The passions may contribute to the chaos of the state of nature, but they are not evil in themselves. Hobbes relies on them as a powerful motivation for human action in both civil society and the state of nature.

If Hobbes supposes that men are motivated by their passions, he also indicates that women, as well as men, are capable of exercising the reason that is required to create and maintain civil society. I have argued that the motivations Hobbes ascribes to adults for creating and maintaining the civil contract are self-interest and fear. Both entail the exercise of reason, which includes the capacity to apprehend the Laws of Nature or what is conducive to peaceful living, to have foresight, and to apprehend how one's actions affect others.

Hobbes presents women as capable of being as self-interested as men when he portrays them as being capable of making a rational self-interested calculation in relation to their children. His discussion of maternal power in the state of nature suggests that women are no more naturally caring or social than men. Women, like men, must be convinced that caring for a child will bring them some future benefits. They are not naturally selfless enough to make caring for their offspring an instinctive act. 'Mothering' as rational activity, then, becomes an indicator of women's ability to exercise reason and self-interest and, consequently, also an indicator of their potential ability to consent to civil society.

The second motivation for creating and maintaining civil society that Hobbes ascribes to adults is fear. Individuals will consent to civil society or acquiesce to a conqueror out of fear for their lives and in order to secure their lives. For Hobbes, consent is not incompatible with fear or lack of choice.[136] To consent to civil society out of fear that one will be killed or because one has little choice, given the undesirable alternative posed by the state of nature, is legitimate. Moreover, Hobbes stipulates that one is bound to honour the civil contract even if one was not one of the original consenting members. If women, or some women, or some men failed to consent to the original contract, they are nevertheless bound by it on an ongoing basis. For women to consent to civil authority out of fear or lack of choice, therefore, would be compatible with the motives that men may have in consenting to civil authority.

The requirements for creating and maintaining civil society in Hobbes' design are that one either exercises reason and sees that one's self-interest can be served by seeking peace in civil society, experiences a fear of being punished for disobedience by a greater power such as the sovereign authority, or apprehends the danger of being left to the mercy of one's fellow beings in the state of nature. As such, the requirements for becoming a subject in Hobbes' design do not by definition exclude women. But what of the requirements for exercising political power?

POLITICAL POWER

In Hobbes' scheme, the greatest political power is held by the sovereign authority in civil society and the ultimate symbol of political power is the image of the Leviathan. The sovereign authority is attributed absolute and undivided power to make and interpret the laws,[137] direct and appoint public ministers, and determine the parameters of the subject's freedom of movement. A central task of the sovereign authority is to regulate power among individuals, the exercise of which in the state of nature leads to chaos and confusion. Hobbes' discussion of the exercise of power in the state of nature includes the following propositions.

Power is the means whereby one fulfils one's desires. Since everyone has desires, everyone requires power in order to fulfil their desires. The problem is that the desires of some are limitless and therefore they desire limitless power. Original or natural power is defined as eminence over others in faculties of body or mind. The second kind of power, instrumental or acquired power, can be secured either by natural eminence or by fortune.[138] But it is best obtained by seizing the power of others, that is, by appropriating the means others have of fulfilling their own desires. In the state of nature, this often entails killing another.

Physical differences in bodily strength are not the key element in being able to exercise this power, according to Hobbes. The fragility of the human body, Hobbes implies, makes such differences irrelevant.[139] Moreover, the physically weaker may use their faculties of mind, such as cunning, to achieve their aim. By proposing that the differences in strength or prudence between men and women are not such that a man can automatically wrest dominion over children from a woman without war,[140] Hobbes suggests that women are capable of killing another (woman or man) in the state of nature, and hence are capable of exercising power and acquiring the power of another in the state of nature.

In civil society, the absolute power of the sovereign authority rests on the appropriation of the power of all subjects. The chaos of the state of nature is due not only to some trying to exert power over others, but also to the absence of an agreement on what constitutes power or what is valued.[141] One of the tasks of the sovereign authority in civil society is to rectify this situation by establishing the criteria for what is to be considered a sign of honour or power.

The best indication that Hobbes presents women as being capable of exercising political power in civil society is his contention that women too can act as and inherit the power of a person who has sovereign authority:

> And likewise where the Custome is, that the next of the Male Kindred succeedeth, there also the right of Succession is in the next of the Kindred Male, for the same reason. And so it is if the Custome were to advance the Female.[142]

Although Hobbes indicates that succession should go to a male before a female, if there are children of both sexes, because 'men, are naturally fitter than women, for actions of labour and danger,'[143] he also advises that this kind of succession take place as a last resort, in the absence of an established custom or knowledge of the sovereign's will. In other passages, moreover, Hobbes suggests that the pre-eminence which is given to male children over female children in succession is based more on custom than on nature:

> Among children the males carry the pre-eminence; in the beginning perhaps, because for the most part (although not always) they are fitter for the administration of greater matters, but specially of wars; but afterwards, when it was grown a custom, because that custom was not contradicted.[144]

We can read Hobbes as insinuating that custom has most often decreed that male rather than female offspring inherit political power, but that women are not precluded by a natural inferiority of mind or body from exercising or inheriting that power.

In another passage Hobbes contends that one can have a well-governed monarchy even with a woman, a youth, or a child, provided that those charged with administrative matters are competent:

> Whence we understand, that the conveniences or inconveniences of any government depend not on him in whom the authority resides, but on his officers; and therefore nothing hinders, but that the commonweal may be well governed, although the monarch be a woman, or youth, or infant, provided that they be fit for affairs, who are endued with the public offices and charges.[145]

He implies in this passage that women, along with children and youths, are considered to be less competent than men in the administration of political matters. He also suggests, however, that whether or not women are in fact less competent than men in this area is irrelevant, since the main requirement of being a sovereign is that one must wield absolute power and authority. One need not necessarily be a good administrator, since that task can be delegated to others. We can interpret Hobbes then as emitting the following message: If women are less capable than men of political administration, of being public ministers appointed by the sovereign authority to administer the civil law, for example, this may be due more to custom than to nature, more to the perception that they are less capable rather than to the deficiency of their natural faculties. When it comes to wielding the power of the sovereign authority, however, women are as capable as men of doing so.

The image of the Leviathan as the ultimate symbol of political power is of a being with God-like attributes which form the psychological basis for its power: 'The End of Worship amongst men, is Power. For where a man seeth another worshipped, he supposeth him powerfull, and is the readier to obey him; which makes his Power greater.'[146] Having power means having the ability to get others to obey us. And getting others to obey us, according to Hobbes, entails making them believe that we have the power to help or hurt them.[147] To be able to wield power is to be able to induce a psychological state of fear in another. To have the power of life and death over another is the ultimate political power. It is based on the ability to instil the ultimate fear in others – the fear of death – and it is one of the powers Hobbes attributes to the Leviathan. One could argue that the image of the Leviathan parallels the image of the mother, who first exercises the power of life and death over the infant in the state of nature, a power which is God-like in the sense that it can facilitate the creation of a new life. It is not clear, moreover, if we extrapolate from Hobbes' description of maternal power in the state of nature, that women lose their potential or capacity to wield maternal power in civil society. I shall return to this point.

A number of indicators suggest that women as Hobbes depicts them are capable of exercising power in both the state of nature and civil society: they can kill another in the state of nature; they can act as and inherit the power of the sovereign authority in civil society; and the power they wield as mothers parallels the power of the God-like Leviathan.

POLITICAL CITIZENSHIP: RIGHTS AND DUTIES

Political citizenship in Hobbes is *not* identified with the warrior hero, who has often been cited as the ultimate symbol of the masculinity of citizenship.[148] The requirements for citizenship in Hobbes' framework are based neither on physical strength nor on an ideal of heroism. As such, they do not, by definition, exclude women. In fact, the Hobbesian citizen more closely reflects what has been viewed as a traditional female concern – survival – than what has been viewed as a traditional male concern – the heroic laying down of one's life. The Hobbesian individual in the state of nature is not so much the strong, solitary, independent 'male' warrior as the sometimes frightened, dependent 'female' who uses prudence and cunning rather than sheer physical strength to outwit the enemy. The human body (male or female), Hobbes emphasizes, is fragile. Human life is easily extinguished. Although Hobbes depicts the state of nature as a state of war, he does not exult in war. His portrayal of life in the state of nature reveals an attempt to show that war is the thing that all beings wish to avoid. The central purpose of Hobbes' theory is to convince men and women to seek peace.

The intermittent references Hobbes makes to women's qualities may hint at male superiority in some areas, but it is a superiority that seems to be based more on custom than on the natural physical and mental superiority of the male sex. For example, Hobbes remarks that women and children are more prone to weeping caused by sudden dejection.[149] But he implies that this is not because they are naturally weaker or more emotional than men but because they are more dependent on others: in Hobbes' words, they 'rely principally on helps externall.'[150] He also refers to women as being more cowardly and timorous than men, noting at the same time that some men too can have these qualities.[151]

More important, Hobbes makes allowance for cowardice in civil society. We ought not to be surprised by it, he intimates. Running away from war is an act that springs out of the desire for self-preservation. As a subject in Hobbes' civil society, one has the right to resist any action, including going to war, which might lead to one's death. At the same time one can rightfully be killed for disobeying the sovereign authority's commands and thereby threatening the peace of the Commonwealth. For all practical purposes, subjects can rightfully be sent to their death in a war which is supposed to defend the Commonwealth, but subjects cannot be commanded to kill themselves or accuse themselves (which might also lead to their death).[152]

In civil society, physical or other kinds of bravery are not valuable in themselves. The sovereign authority may decree them to be necessary for the sake of preserving the Commonwealth, but, from the perspective of the subjects, there is no requirement that they be willing to lay down their lives voluntarily. If women are more timorous and cowardly than men, this would not mean that they would be prohibited from exercising political citizenship, as Hobbes defines it, since the exercise of political citizenship is not tied up with the desire to be the warrior-hero.

Moreover, if women were considered to be more cowardly or to have fewer strengths than men, would this justify treating them unequally in civil society, according to Hobbes' suppositions about equality? When discussing natural differences as a basis for inequality in the state of nature, Hobbes maintains that men are by nature so similar in faculties of mind and body that the differences in strength of mind or body are minimal, not great enough, it seems, to justify inequality in civil society.

The bottom line of equality in the state of nature is that each can kill another by using physical strength or cunning.[153] Hobbes indicates that there is a basis for women being equal to men in the state of nature because of their ability to do so. Men are not naturally superior to women to the extent that men could wrest control over children from women without engaging in war.[154] Men are not so physically or mentally superior to women that a woman could not kill a man.

In the state of nature, individuals are also equal in the sense that they consider themselves to be as good as another. This is what creates the potential for conflict. In civil society, the solution is that the sovereign authority establishes civil laws that ensure all are viewed as equal. Irrespective of whether or not they are in fact equal, treating them as if they were equal in civil society is desirable, according to Hobbes, because it is more conducive to peaceful coexistence:

> If Nature therefore have made men equall, that equalitie is to be acknowledged: or if Nature have made men unequall; yet because men that think themselves equall, will not enter into conditions of Peace, but upon Equall termes, such equalitie must be admitted. And therefore for the ninth law of Nature, I put this, *That every man acknowledge other for his Equall by Nature*.[155]

Furthermore, in relation to the sovereign authority, all subjects in civil society – men and women – become equally inferior. The sovereign authority, whose power Hobbes compares to the Leviathan, ends for all time the question of who is better by becoming the best, by becoming the 'King of the Proud' or 'King of all the children of pride.'[156] Everyone else becomes equally worth less.

Hobbes' argument implies that if women saw themselves as equal to men, their equality ought to be acknowledged by the civil law in order to keep the peace. In this sense, Hobbes' notion of equality, when applied to women, makes irrelevant the debate about whether or not men and women are naturally equal. But that there is a basis in nature for considering them as equal is apparent in the suggestion that a woman as well as a man can kill another.

Considering men and women as equal would include extending to them equally the rights and duties of citizenship. The political rights of the Hobbesian subject are determined by the sovereign, who may cede to them rights, such as the right not to be commanded to kill or accuse themselves, which will not threaten or limit the sovereign's authority.[157] For example, such rights do not preclude the sovereign from commanding the subject to do life-threatening things for the sake of preserving the peace and security of the Commonwealth.[158] As I have argued earlier, as Hobbes presents them, these kinds of rights are not grounded in the desire to be the warrior hero – they are grounded in the desire to preserve one's life.

In addition, Hobbes advocates through the tenth Law of Nature that subjects retain (or attain) in civil society certain rights which are necessary for life, since the end for which individuals give up their supposed liberties in the state of nature is their self-preservation. The tenth Law of Nature suggests that rights in civil society should provide not only security in the sense of bare survival, but also a certain quality of life.[159] The rights necessary to such a life, according to Hobbes, include the right to govern one's own body, and the right to enjoy water, motion, freedom of movement, and everything else 'without which a man cannot live, or not live well.'[160]

Although Hobbes does not explicitly state that these rights be extended to women, he does seem to leave an opening for such an extension. The tenth Law of Nature, which designates the right to things necessary to life, is based on the ninth Law of Nature, which is that everyone be treated as if they were equal. There is little to suggest that women are incapable of exercising such rights. At the same time, however, problems arise in granting the most essential one –the right to govern one's body[161] – to men and women, as if there were no differences between the two.

Given women's unique biological reproductive capacities (which Hobbes is very much aware of, since he uses them to ground his discussion of maternal dominion), the right to govern one's body may entail, for women more than for men, the right to govern another life (before or after birth, we can presume). Hobbes touches on this point in 'De Corpore Politico' when he connects maternal power and dominion to the right to propriety to one's own body:

> And considering men again dissolved from all covenants one with another, and that (Part I. chap. IV. sect.2) every man by the law of nature, hath right or propriety to his own body, the child ought rather to be the propriety of the mother, of whose body it is part, till the time of separation, than of the father.[162]

The child initially belongs to the mother, since the child is initially a part of the mother's body. At the point of separation, at birth, moreover, she has the first access to it and, being the first to wield the power of life and death over it, the first opportunity to acquire dominion over it or to do as she will with it.[163]

It is significant that Hobbes does *not* claim that a woman's unique reproductive capacity to carry another life justifies the right of others to govern her body. In fact he cedes to women the right to govern their own bodies and the products of their reproductive labour when he cedes to them, in the state of nature, the right to exercise the power of life and death over their children, including the right to commit infanticide (or abortion, one can presume). The important question then would be: Do women carry this right over to civil society?

This issue comes to the foreground if women are to have the right to govern their own bodies, as Hobbes proposes men ought to have in civil society. If Hobbes' framework is to include women on an equal basis to men, then the right to govern one's own body should belong to women as well as to men in civil society. In fact it would be compatible with the exercise of maternal power. As Hobbes describes it, moreover, it is not clear that the mother can pass away or forego maternal *power*, or the first opportunity to exercise the power of life and death over the infant, in the same way that she can pass away or forego maternal *dominion* over it, that is the right to its obedience for having saved its life. She can exercise her power over the infant so as to forego dominion over it, but can she forego the initial exercise of power over it that initial access to the infant (either before or after birth) gives her?

Hobbes explicitly states that marriage laws in civil society give the father dominion over the children, but if the mother continues to have first access to the child, then she may also continue to have the first opportunity to exercise the power of life and death over it, a power which precedes the exercise of paternal dominion and which then runs up against the sovereign authority's right to the power of life and death over all subjects. Hobbes says, 'But in a civil state, where the right of life, and death, and of all corporal punishment is with the supreme; that same right of killing cannot be granted to any private person.'[164] But the rootedness of maternal power in women's unique biological access to the infant, coupled with the enjoyment of the right to govern their own bodies, might grant to women right to the power of life and death over another being. On the one hand, Hobbes' scheme leaves an opening for the legitimacy of such a right. The civil laws, which are determined by the sovereign authority, define what is to be considered as 'murder.'[165] They may well define the mother's taking away of life, either before or after the birth of the infant, as a legitimate exercise of maternal power.

On the other hand, Hobbes' scheme illustrates that it is precisely in the right to govern one's own body that the contradictory aspects of treating women as if they were the same as men become apparent. Women's bodily difference from men may be threatening to the community, not because it literally threatens the unity of the body politic, as Carole Pateman maintains,[166] but because, coupled with women's similarity in self-interestedness, it threatens the continuity of the political community. If women are given the political right to govern their own bodies, a right which, like other rights in the liberal framework, is based on the advancement of self-interest, this means that the basis on which they would make a decision about governing the life or death of another is self-interest. Why should or would women therefore exercise their rights for the benefit of others, most fundamentally in order to perpetuate the community and the species?

In Hobbes, the exercise of political rights for the purpose of advancing self-interest takes precedence over the exercise of political duties or obligations to pursue the benefit of others.[167] Abiding by the Laws of Nature represents fulfilling one's duties or obligations to others. And the Laws of Nature can be summed up in the maxim 'Do not that to another, which thou thinkest unreasonable to be done by another to thy selfe,'[168] which as Edward Andrew points out is a negative form of the Christian injunction – do unto others as you have them do unto you.[169]

One's duties or obligations to others, therefore, consist not in any positive action to further their interests, but in inaction, in leaving them alone. For Hobbes, among adults, inaction, including political inaction, is more beneficial to the community than action because action involves the promotion of self-interest and therefore includes the potential for conflict. Passive obedience to the laws of civil society is more compatible with self-interest, Hobbes tries to convince us, than active disobedience, which leads inevitably to the dissolution of the Commonwealth and a return to the life-threatening state of nature.

Since the duty aspect of political citizenship is couched in terms of leaving others alone, or in terms of non-action, it would not as such exclude women. Women would seem to be as capable as men of leaving others alone. Hobbes does *not* depict women as being different from men in the sense of being more willing to sacrifice their self-interest for the benefit of others. But a problem emerges – if women are the same as men in this respect, what guarantee is there that they will care for others, including their own children? Inaction is detrimental to parent-child relations and thus to the continuity of the political community. By attributing to women the same motivations as men, Hobbes puts himself in the difficult position of having to provide for reasons, based on self-interest, why women (or men) would and should raise and care for children.

Explaining why a woman would care for an infant is more important, however, than explaining why a man would do so, because the mother usually has the first power of life and death over the infant. If the exercise of this power is contingent on the pursuit of self-interest, then why would she choose to save and care for the infant rather than abandon it? The absence of a natural maternal instinct to care for children is more of a threat to the survival of the infant and therefore of the species than the absence of a natural paternal instinct, since woman's unique biological capacity usually gives her first access to the infant. A man is as likely as a woman to abandon rather than raise a child in Hobbes' state of nature, but a woman has more opportunity to abandon it. At the same time, however, she has the knowledge that it is hers. Maternal dominion is more 'natural' than paternal dominion, but the care that it entails is not naturally forthcoming.

Since it involves the production and reproduction of the political community, the bearing and raising of children is a political matter. One of the duties of the sovereign authority, Hobbes notes in 'De Corpore Politico,' is to foster and ensure population growth: 'it is the duty of them that are in sovereign authority, to increase the people, in as much as they are governors of mankind under God Almighty, who having created but one man, and one woman, declared, that it was his will they should be multiplied and increased afterwards.'[170] Marriage laws or laws regulating relations between adults must be aimed at ensuring generational continuity. If women are motivated by the same considerations as men, why should they or would they, if they had them, exercise their reproductive rights (resting on the right to govern their own bodies) for the benefit of the political community, to ensure its physical and political continuity, for example? This dilemma is more evident in the next thinker I consider – John Locke.

CHAPTER TWO

John Locke

Unlike Hobbes, who is quite explicit in expounding a degree of natural equality between men and women, John Locke (1632–1704) is ambiguous and contradictory in his depiction of the natural relations between men and women. Most commentators concerned with the position of women in Locke have noted this ambiguity.

According to Zillah Eisenstein, Locke continues to perpetuate and assume the patriarchal bias of Filmer, albeit in a new form.[1] Although Locke differentiates political from paternal rule, this distinction merely serves to liberate the family for freer activity in the marketplace; it fails to liberate women from the power of the father in the family, a power that is exercised through the husband's control over the wife in the conjugal relationship. Eisenstein points out that Locke does not follow through on the implications of his assertion that the mother has a greater role in begetting the child, the logical conclusion of which would be to cede greater power to the mother in the family.[2] Instead, he grants greater power to the father in the family, most significantly in the form of a power to bequeath property and control inheritances.

Eisenstein also notes that Locke 'opens up the conception of individuality for women as well as men,' by attributing to women the faculty of rationality in his theory on education.[3] But Eisenstein gives little weight to Locke's position on women's educability. She maintains that, for all practical purposes, women are prevented from acquiring an education in Locke's framework because they are confined to the home. More importantly, they are excluded (along with the working class) from enjoying the benefits of private property. This, combined with their role and function as mothers, serves to bar them from political life. While Eisenstein criticizes Locke for maintaining patriarchal assumptions which relegate women to an inferior and unequal position in the political and public realm, she admits that he appears to open up the possibility of extending to women, as rational creatures, equal rights in the public sphere. Eisenstein does not explore in detail or offer an explanation for Locke's ambiguous position on women's capabilities.

Melissa Butler suggests that Locke is very much aware of the problem of women's place in the civil and political sphere.[4] She argues that, although Locke perhaps accepts that women are inferior by nature, he does challenge the divine ordination of men's authority over women. Most important, Locke allows women the freedom to overcome their natural limitations. He extends to them the qualifications necessary for political life by believing them to be capable of exercising some natural freedom (as demonstrated in his account of Genesis), acquiring property through the exercise of their own labour, owning property in their own right, making contracts with other individuals (the conjugal one for example), and exercising rationality (signalled by their ability to be educated in a fashion similar to men).[5] Butler concludes that, although Locke is never explicit about women's role in civil society, one can infer from his scattered statements on women that he presents them as being capable of participating in political life. In this sense, Locke is a forerunner of the feminism of the next century.[6]

For Carole Pateman, Butler's is an 'uncritical liberal interpretation of Locke.'[7] Pateman suggests that commentators like Butler refer to Locke as an 'embryonic feminist' on the following grounds: the mother's share of authority over the children; the wife's ability to own property in her own right; and the suggestion that a wife may divorce her husband.[8] Pateman does not address these points in particular. Instead, she focuses on Locke's statements on the conjugal relationship, especially the power of husbands over wives in civil society. According to Pateman, Locke presents women as naturally subordinate to men. Their natural subordination is reflected in the conjugal relationship, which is deemed to be a natural rather than a political arrangement. Locke does not challenge the existence of Adam's power over Eve; he simply changes the character of that power.

Pateman also maintains that Locke considers women to be weaker in strength, mind, and body, all signs of a natural inferiority which is used to justify and account for their inability to become equal members of civil society. In Pateman's words, 'Women cannot be incorporated into civil society on the same basis as men because women naturally lack the capacities required to become civil individuals.'[9] Women's physical weakness is exemplified in their reproductive capacities: 'Physical birth symbolizes everything that makes women incapable of entering the original contract and transforming themselves into the civil individuals who uphold its terms.'[10]

Locke's refutation of Filmer, for Pateman, represents the decline of an older form of patriarchalism, symbolized by the power of the father over the son, and the rise of another more modern and hidden form of patriarchalism, embedded in the power of the husband over the wife. This modern form of patriarchalism is embodied in the sexual contract, which, according to Pateman, logically precedes the parental one. Sexual right and power precede parental right and power. Pateman writes: 'If Adam was to be a father, Eve had to become a mother and if Eve was to be a mother, then Adam must have sexual access to her body. In other words, sexual or conjugal right must necessarily precede the right of fatherhood.'[11]

Pateman argues that the modern social contract, which Locke's contract theory exemplifies, is a fraternal pact of men who are attributed with natural power over their wives. Women can never be included in it as equals to men because its purpose is to legitimate 'men's sex-right over women.'[12] In theory, men's motivation for establishing such a contract derives from their desire to appropriate or at least emulate women's procreative abilities by giving birth to new forms of political society.[13] In practice, it derives from their desire and need to express their masculinity, which in its modern manifestation requires that men have sexual access to and mastery over women's bodies.[14]

I differ with Pateman's insistence that the sexual contract necessarily precedes the parental one. Pateman admits that the mother's rights over her children are important in practice. But in theory, she warns, 'to focus on parents and children suggests that patriarchy is familial and that father-right is the problem.'[15] In my view, examining attempts to link mothers and fathers with children can tell us something about women's place in the conjugal relationship and in the political sphere, both in Locke's theory and in liberal practice.

I also disagree with Patemen's contention that 'there is good reason to confine the term "political" to relationships among adults.'[16] According to Pateman, the infant's helplessness and dependence at birth, which was taken as a fundamental political fact by classic patriarchalism, became less relevant in the liberal thought of Locke. In Locke's civil society, 'the dependence of children has no political consequences,' since, unlike adult associations, parent-child ones come to a natural end.[17]

Contrary to Pateman's claim, however, Locke is concerned with more than the ability of parents to influence their children until the children are of age. The association of parents and children, moreover, fulfils important political ends in Locke's design.

Although Eisenstein and Pateman are correct in identifying an ambiguity in Locke's portrayal of women, this ambiguity does not necessarily derive from his treatment of women as naturally inferior to men. I concur with Lorenne Clark that the conjugal relationship in Locke can be understood in the context of the need to ensure paternity and establish a stable union conducive to the accumulation of property for the next generation.[18] I dissent however, from Clark's contention that women's subjection to their husbands in Locke's framework is rooted in and legitimized by assumptions about their natural inferiority.[19] Locke may allude to women's lesser physical strength when he labels men as the 'stronger and abler,' but he also indicates, as Butler argues, that women have essentially the same capacities as men for political life, capacities that are based on their strength of mind or equal faculty to exercise their reason. Women's capacity for reason emerges as a consistent theme in Locke's treatise on education.

WOMEN AND EDUCATION

As Locke describes it, the purpose of education is to produce practical, virtuous, useful, industrious, obedient citizens who have the ability to govern their desires by reason, who comply with authority and obey the laws of civil society, who recognize the importance of social reputation, who have practical and useful rather than abstract knowledge, and who have the breeding which enables them to take their proper place in society. Free individuals are able to recognize the limits on their liberty and their desires posed by the need to follow the laws, whether they be civil or natural laws. A foremost goal of education ought to be imparting to individuals the capacity to use their reason to govern and limit their desires.[20]

Among those desires that need to be controlled are three which Locke claims are 'natural' to the extent that children tend to exhibit them.[21] The first, the love of liberty or the desire to do as one pleases, must be curbed by parental laws.[22] The second, a love of dominion over others, which children express in their desire to follow their own rather than their parents' will, must be curbed by punishing children for non-compliance and by not allowing them to torment helpless creatures.[23] And the third, a desire for one's own possessions, must be curbed so that it does not become covetousness.[24]

The desires ought not to be eliminated, however. They ought merely to be channelled into purposive action. If coupled with the desire to acquire them by one's own industry, the desire for possessions, for example, is a positive quality.[25] One of the worst faults that a child can have, Locke tells us, is laziness or sloth. The listless child, Locke warns, has neither foresight nor desire, which are the great spurs to action and industry – 'for where there is no Desire, there will be no Industry.'[26]

By instilling the habit of obedience in them, parents accustom their children to curbing and governing their own desires. Locke is adamant that, as a general rule, physical punishment should not be used on children, as it promotes violence in them. He makes an exception, however, for obstinate behaviour. Non-compliance is the one fault for which children must be beaten.[27] Children must not be allowed to have their own way, Locke warns. Otherwise, we can surmise, they might want to have their own way as adults. Locke's prescriptions here provide an interesting contrast or complement to his apparent defence of the right to resistance in civil society.[28] In emphasizing that rebellion, or resistance to authority, in children must be severely punished, Locke seems to be saying that the best way to prevent rebellion against political authorities or the law in civil society is to socialize children into adults who will habitually comply with authority.

Locke offers another way in which compliance to civil authority might be encouraged – teaching children the value of social reputation by instilling in them a desire for the esteem of others.[29] Children may not yet have the reason to understand and hence to follow the Laws of Nature, or the laws of civil society,[30] but they do have enough reason to discern whether they are receiving approval or disapproval.[31] Parents, Locke advises, are to esteem and value children for good behaviour and act coldly and neglectfully when they behave inappropriately. Children learn to expect this from others. They are thereby taught that, in adulthood, 'the Things they delight in belong to, and are to be enjoyed by those only, who are in a State of Reputation.'[32] As adults, moreover, their ability to use their own reason and judgment does not invalidate or supersede the opinion of others or social reputation. Even adults ought to use the 'testimony' of other people's reason as a guideline for what is compatible with both divine or natural and civil law.[33] Instilling in children a concern for the opinion of others is presented by Locke as a way of getting them to behave appropriately as adults. It is also presented as something that begins with the child's first social relationship – that with its parents. In this manner, the parent-child association acts as the foundation for social and political relationships in civil society.

Socialization to societal norms rather than intellectual enlightenment is the aim of education for Locke. He is very critical of the kind of education which focuses on the pursuit of knowledge for its own sake, the pursuit that creates scholars and philosophers. (Scholars and philosophers may challenge social norms; the properly socialized individual does not.) The acceptance of 'plain reason' and the conviction of 'clear arguments' are more important than knowledge of metaphysics. In fact, Locke defines wisdom as the practical ability to manage one's affairs, rather than as philosophical apprehension or knowledge of the truth.[34] Education ought to be useful and practical rather than abstract and esoteric, so that 'most time and application is to be bestowed on that, which is like to be of greatest consequence, and frequentest use, in the ordinary course and occurrences of that Life, the young Man is designed for.'[35] The ability to recognize what one has been designed for is due to what Locke calls 'breeding.' Anyone who is given responsibility for a child's education, Locke specifies, must above all be 'well-bred,' in order that they may impart this quality to their pupil.[36] Breeding gives one a quality which makes social acceptance more likely.[37] It is conducive to success in the world, furnishing one with the knowledge and manners appropriate to one's station.[38]

Although Locke grants that his treatise on education is directed towards bringing up a young gentleman and that the education of daughters perhaps ought to be different from that of sons, he also suggests that this difference is minimal and easily distinguishable: 'though where the Difference of Sex requires different Treatment, 'twill be no hard Matter to distinguish.'[39] Locke rarely addresses himself to exactly what those differences might be. In several places, however, he advises that girls be treated similarly to boys.

When he recommends bodily conditioning as a prerequisite for mental development, for example, one would not be surprised if he emphasized the physical differences between boys and girls. Instead, he highlights the similarities between the two when he directs parents and tutors to accustom both boys and girls to the elements in order to strengthen their bodies.[40] Although concessions to beauty (to the ideal of a pale face) may have to be made, daughters too ought to be exposed to the air and sun as often as possible, since they too can benefit from the kind of conditioning which hardens the body: 'and the nearer they come to the Hardships of their Brothers in their Education, the greater Advantage will they receive from it all the remaining Part of their Lives.'[41] Locke implies here that the physical differences between boys and girls are negligible. Furthermore, he suggests that physical strength is developed by conditioning, which implies that it does not provide an irrefutable natural basis for sexual difference. By proposing that girls as well as boys can undergo and benefit from physical hardship, Locke minimizes the natural physical differences in strength and ability between men and women. He also undermines them as a standard for inequality between the two sexes.

Locke's recommendation that both boys and girls be unconstrained by braces, laces, or tight clothing might be interpreted in a similar fashion – as expanding rather than contracting the potential for equality between men and women in his framework.[42] To be free of constraining clothes is to have freer bodily movement and a self-imposed rather than an externally imposed control over one's body. We might see this recommendation as an indication that girls are not more fragile than boys. We might also see it as a symbol of the applicability of the concept of the ownership of one's own body to women (a concept I shall discuss shortly).

In addition, almost all the references Locke makes to the female sex – to young girls and adult women – in 'Some Thoughts Concerning Education' consist of his upholding them as favourable examples of individuals who have either been educated in the proper manner or who have educated others in the proper manner. Taken together, they disclose that women are able to exercise reason in educating their children, that young girls are capable of acquiring the kind of education prescribed for young boys, and that women seem to have just those characteristics which a proper education ought to instil in young men.

In one example, Locke praises as prudent and wise a mother who, rather than giving in to her daughter's will, whips her little girl for not complying with the mother's commands.[43] This incident tells us several things. First, Locke is saying that little girls, like boys, do have a will of their own and wish to exert that will. Second, he is saying that little girls, just like little boys, need to be taught compliance, even if it means being physically punished for disobedience. Third, Locke is saying that women are not necessarily more emotional or less capable of regulating their passions when it comes to fulfilling their duties as parents, the most important of which is responsibility for their children's education. Locke is worried that parental tenderness might get in the way of carrying out such duties.⁴⁴ This incident illustrates, then, that he deems mothers to be capable of governing, through reason, any fondness they may have for their children for the sake of educating them to govern their own desires. The mother in this case does not let her affection for the child override her judgment, which tells her that the daughter must be taught the hard lesson of compliance.

Locke praises the education of daughters as carried out by women in the home. The results have been so desirable, he intimates, they ought to be emulated in the education of sons.⁴⁵ Daughters educated at home may be a bit more bashful but certainly no less competent than their brothers educated at boarding schools away from home.⁴⁶ Moreover, bashfulness is not an undesirable trait – it may be as useful for protecting against vice in a young man as in a young woman.⁴⁷

Another example that Locke uses to show that education has been properly handled concerns a woman who has instructed her children, at home, in the fundamentals of geography.⁴⁸ Locke applauds the mother for showing good sense in teaching the child what is useful and practical. He commends the plain common sense of women. Their lack of abstract knowledge and training make them more, not less, capable and reasonable. Women, who usually do not learn logic and rhetoric, are often more articulate than men, who have often been versed in both, Locke insists.⁴⁹ He recommends that grammar be spared sons as it is daughters.

Locke cites women's elegance in speaking a language plainly and simply as an example of 'good breeding.'⁵⁰ If breeding consists in the ability to manage one's affairs, to be socially useful, and to deal practically with the outside world, then women, as Locke depicts them, seem to be perfectly capable of acquiring it. The question which Locke does not directly address is whether young girls and women ought to confine the use of their aptitude to the home. What he does disclose, however, is that women are capable of acting in the outside world. Moreover, he elevates rather than disparages the world of women in the home. He portrays it as the realm more conducive than the outside world to the formation of reasonable, prudent, virtuous, capable citizens. The home prepares both sons and daughters to meet the more dangerous world outside.⁵¹ Locke also praises and upholds as worthy of emulation women's involvement with everyday practical matters. In fact, he paints women as having just the kind of practical, useful knowledge which he believes a proper education ought to instil in young men.

The picture of women that emerges through the examples Locke gives of them engaging in various aspects of parenting is of thrifty, virtuous, practical, industrious beings, capable of controlling their desires and full of practical common sense, if not abstract intellectual thought – in other words, the qualities that add up to just the kind of 'gentleman' that a proper education ought to develop and perpetuate. To the extent that such qualities are conducive to becoming a good citizen, women seem to have the advantage over men.

If women have such potential, how and why do they end up in a seemingly inferior position to their husbands in the conjugal relationship? To say that Locke draws on women's supposed natural inferiority to men in making them subject to their husbands is problematic as well as inconsistent with his depiction of women's capacity for reason and education.[52] As Patemen points out, if women's natural inferiority makes them naturally subordinate to men, then why is a formal marriage contract required to make it so? More important, if women are deemed to be inferior and subordinate to men because they lack the ability to exert their will or exercise their reason, then how can they be deemed as capable of engaging in and consenting to a marriage contract?[53]

WOMEN AND CONJUGAL RELATIONS

Locke introduces the question of conjugal relations in his attempts to refute Filmer's argument that the basis of legitimate government is Adam's God-given paternal and conjugal powers.[54] Locke takes pains to examine the biblical passages which Filmer uses as proof that Adam was given divine sovereign rights which were then passed down from one generation to the next. In one of those passages, according to Filmer, God gave Adam dominion over Eve, which in turn reinforced Adam's original political powers. Locke challenges Filmer's interpretation of the relevant passage and its implication for the legitimacy of Adam's political powers.

To refute Filmer, Locke makes the following arguments. (1) The whole incident of Eve's subjection to Adam does not prove that Adam had political power over Eve, since Eve's subjection was meant as a punishment for Eve, not a victory for Adam. Locke notes that both Adam and Eve ate the forbidden fruit, both were banished from the Garden of Eden, and both were deprived of eternal life. God did not intend to reward Adam for Eve's temptation to sin, but to punish both Adam and Eve. (2) At the same time, Locke admits that Eve and representatives of her sex were to be punished more than Adam and representatives of his sex. Part of the greater punishment was that women would bring forth children in pain and, as wives, be subject to their husbands. (3) Locke emphasizes that these two punishments were not ordained by God, that is, God did not stipulate that women would always and necessarily have to bear children in pain or be governed by their husbands. God only 'foretold' or predicted that women would suffer these two punishments. If God had ordained them, then their removal would be considered sins, which they are not, Locke emphasizes. Locke points to instances where women alleviate the pain of childbirth by medicine and where they retain or attain authority over their husbands in the conjugal contract. Queens, for example, have both political and conjugal authority over their husbands. And there is no more obligation that a woman should be ruled by her husband 'if the Circumstances either of her Condition or Contract with her Husband should exempt her from it, then there is, that she should bring forth her Children in Sorrow and Pain.'[55]

The authority of husband over wife, Locke suggests, is based more on custom than on divine ordination. But what are we to make of Locke's remarks about there being a 'Foundation in Nature' for the husband's authority? The relevant passage reads:

> God, in this Text, gives not, that I see, any Authority to *Adam* over *Eve*, or to Men over their Wives, but only foretels what should be the Womans Lot, how by his Providence he would order it so, that she should be subject to her husband, as we see that generally the Laws of Mankind and customs of Nations have ordered it so; and there is, I grant, a Foundation in Nature for it.[56]

Does he mean that women's subjection to their husbands is justified by their natural inferiority to men? We can interpret his remarks as a reference to the Laws of Nature, or the God-given laws of reason which regulate relations among individuals. This would mean then that it is reasonable to have men as husbands exercise authority over their wives. But is it reasonable because women are naturally inferior to men?

Although Locke alludes to women as the weaker sex when he refers to men as 'the abler and the stronger'[57] sex, we cannot assume Locke's message to be that women are necessarily naturally inferior to men. They may on the whole have less physical strength than men, but this does not mean that they cannot condition their bodies or undergo physical hardship, as Locke indicates in his treatise on education. Most important, it does not mean they are naturally inferior in reason.

The theme of women's capacity for reason, which runs throughout Locke's 'Some Thoughts Concerning Education,' is buttressed by the example he uses in his deliberation on the faculty of reason in *An Essay Concerning Human Understanding*.[58] To illustrate that this faculty does not rest on or require the study of the principles of Aristotelian logic and syllogism, Locke describes a woman exercising her reason:

> Tell a country gentlewoman that the wind is south-west, and the weather louring, and like to rain, and she will easily understand it is not safe for her to go abroad thin clad in such a day after a fever: she clearly sees the probable connexion of all these, viz. south-west wind and clouds, rain, wetting, taking cold, relapse, and danger of death, without tying them together in those artificial and cumbersome fetters of several syllogisms that clog and hinder the mind, which proceeds from one part to another quicker and clearer without them; and the probability which she easily perceives in things thus in their native state would be quite lost, if this argument were managed learnedly and proposed in mode and figure.[59]

Women are equal to men in their capacity for reason, it seems. It may be reasonable, however, for husbands to exercise authority over their wives as their natural equals. In other words, it may be reasonable to exert one's will over an equal. But why and in what way? To answer this we might look at the extent of conjugal authority.

Locke indicates that conjugal authority extends mainly to the 'common concernment' or common property of husband and wife:

> If therefore these words give any Power to *Adam*, it can be only a Conjugal Power, not Political, the Power that every Husband hath to order the things of private Concernment in his Family, as Proprietor of the Goods and Land there, and to have his Will take place before that of his wife in all things of their common Concernment; but not a Political Power of Life and Death over her, much less over anybody else.[60]

He further suggests that the wife's acquiescence to the husband's will in disposing of and regulating their common property is necessary because of the potential for a conflict of wills:

> But the Husband and Wife, though they have but one common Concern,

yet having different understandings, will unavoidably sometimes have different wills too; it therefore being necessary, that the last Determination, *i.e.* the Rule, should be placed somewhere, it naturally falls to the Man's share, as the abler and the stronger.[61]

Most of the time, Locke implies, there is no need for the husband to exert his will over his wife, since both have one common concern. Because one is dealing with two wills, however, conflict seems inevitable some of the time. Locke cedes to women the potential of exerting their will to a degree that poses conflict. A clash of wills is more likely to occur between two equals than between a superior and an inferior. If women were deemed to be naturally inferior to men they would likely not have the independence of will that Locke indirectly grants to them here.

Locke also attributes to women the potential and the right to accumulate property through their own labour and to own it in their own right. In his discussion of the rights of a conqueror in a just war, Locke stipulates that a conqueror may justifiably take from the wife and children enough property to serve as reparation, but he may not take the property that is the children's by inheritance or the wife's as a result of her own labours:

> Here then is the Case; The Conqueror has a Title to Reparation for Damages received, and the Children have a Title to their Father's Estate for their Subsistence. For as to the Wife's share, whether her own Labour or Compact gave her a Title to it, 'tis plain, Her Husband could not forfeit what was hers.[62]

He is clear that the husband's control over property 'leaves the Wife in the full and free possession of what by Contract is her peculiar Right.'[63]

Women's potential to accumulate and own property in their own right, coupled with the assumption that property is something that one secures for one's own interest to the exclusion of the interest of others,[64] makes the conjugal union an arrangement of two individuals who may not have a common concern and for whom conflicts over property seem inevitable. But why ought the husband's will to prevail in case of disagreement?

The simplest way to resolve conflict between two independent wills or entities is to give one the 'last determination.' Locke's proposal that it 'naturally falls to the Man's share, as the abler and the stronger'[65] seems to refer to the man's probable greater physical strength rather than to his greater mental faculties. Ultimately, Locke may be saying, sheer physical strength is the final regulator in case of conflict. But we cannot interpret Locke as simply advocating that might is right. We can better grasp why the husband has the final rule by understanding the aim of the conjugal union in Locke's design.

The conjugal authority of the husband, Locke emphasizes, extends neither to the power of life and death over his wife nor to the power to regulate her property.[66] This is proof, Locke wants to claim, that the conjugal relationship is not a political association and that conjugal power, like parental power, is distinct from political power. But a closer examination reveals that the aims of the conjugal union, and hence the exercise of conjugal power, are the advancement of political ends. In what way?

Locke depicts the conjugal relationship as a voluntary contract in which the association of parents and children is more important than the association of husband and wife. The mutual support and assistance aimed at augmenting care and affection between husband and wife are secondary to the community of interest aimed at maintaining the common offspring:

> *Conjugal Society* is made by a voluntary Compact between Man and Woman: and tho' it consist chiefly in such a Communion and Right in one anothers Bodies, as is necessary to its chief End, Procreation; yet it draws with it mutual Support, and Assistance, and a Communion of Interest too, as necessary not only to unite their Care, and Affection, but also necessary to their common Off-spring, who have a Right to be nourished and maintained by them, till they are able to provide for themselves.[67]

Maintaining one's offspring includes both educating them and accumulating property to pass on to them. Once these objectives have been met, the conjugal union might even legitimately be dissolved:

> But though these are Ties upon *Mankind*, which make the *Conjugal Bonds* more firm and lasting in Man, than the other Species of Animals; yet it would give one reason to enquire, why this *Compact*, where Procreation and Education are secured, and Inheritance taken care for, may not be made determinable, either by consent, or at a certain time, or upon certain Conditions, as well as any other voluntary Compacts, there being no necessity in the nature of the thing, nor to the ends of it, that it should always be

for Life; I mean, to such as are under no Restraint of any positive Law, which ordains all such Contracts to be perpetual.[68]

The central purpose of the conjugal union for Locke is to establish and cement parent-child relations. These relations in turn have important political ends. Through them one secures (1) the propagation of the species, by facilitating the care of children, (2) the continuity of the political community, by assuring that children are educated to become consenting citizens, and (3) the vertical accumulation of property, by providing an incentive for individuals to accumulate more property than they need for themselves.

PROPAGATION OF THE SPECIES

Adultery, incest, and sodomy, Locke asserts, 'cross the main intention of Nature, which willeth the increase of Mankind, and the continuation of the Species in the highest perfection, and the distinction of Families, with the Security of the Marriage Bed, as necessary thereunto.'[69] His insistence on stable conjugal relations might be understood, in part, as a response to his concern for the continuation, multiplication, and improvement of the species.

According to Locke, there is often little will or design in the begetting of children. Procreation is most often the by-product of the desire to fulfil sexual appetites rather than the result of a desire to have children.[70] Although men may desire sex, they do not always desire to beget children. But the hand of God intervenes to create an act of conception. This God does 'most commonly without the intention, and often against the Consent and Will of the Begetter.'[71] By making God rather than man responsible for conception, Locke takes the desire to beget children out of the realm of rational deliberation and places it in the realm of 'natural necessity,' a necessity that is determined by God, often against the wishes of the man and often without his knowledge.

Ironically, as Locke depicts it, it is for men rather than for women that reproduction is more subject to natural exigencies. In suggesting that men may beget children against their will and without their knowledge, he is implying that men as fathers are more enslaved than women to natural necessity posed by the invisible hand of God. God may make men fathers without their ever knowing it. It is more difficult (if not impossible) for God to make women mothers without their knowing it. Men's sense of paternal uncertainty contrasts with women's sense of maternal certainty. Women may experience some uncertainty about whether or not a child has been conceived. Eventually, however, this uncertainty disappears. Moreover, women know that the child they have borne is theirs. Uncertainty over paternity for men means that they may never know that they have participated in conceiving a child. Furthermore, once a child is born to them, they may be uncertain that the child is in fact theirs.

Locke also insinuates that men, unlike women, do not voluntarily and deliberately use their labour power to create a child. For women, it is not only a matter of engaging in the sex act, as it is for men; for women, it is also a matter of using their labour power to carry and nourish the child in the womb, to give it birth, and to nurse the child once born. Locke denies that the man is the '*Nobler and Principal Agent in Generation.*'[72] The father, in contributing only the seed in the act of conception, contributes less than the mother, who nourishes the child and carries it in her body:

> For no body can deny but that the Woman hath an equal share, if not the greater, as nourishing the Child a long time in her own Body out of her own Substance. There it is fashion'd, and from her it receives the Materials and Principles of its Constitution;[73]

Women's labour is more necessary than men's to the propagation of the species. It is also more contingent on reason – the knowledge that a being to whom one must apply one's labour power has been conceived and the certainty that the child to whom one ought to apply one's labour power is one's own.

In presenting procreation as an unintentional result of sexual desire, Locke also implies that there is neither a natural paternal nor maternal desire to procreate. He does not invoke a natural desire on the part of women to conceive children or a natural maternal instinct, peculiar to women, to care for them. The problem of parental care, as Locke envisions it, seems to apply to both men and women. Since the conception of a new life is most often the result of divine intervention rather than human choice and since most in fact would choose that it not take place, why would they or should they take care of the children once born? Locke seems concerned that parents might not care for them. This is evident in the seriousness with which he discusses alleged incidents of parents murdering, killing, castrating, and eating their children.[74] He attempts to refute Filmer's claim that such occurrences show that the parent (the father), has the power of life and death over his child, by summoning up God as an intermediary between parents and children. First, Locke claims that it is God, not the parent (the father), who gives the child life; therefore only God, not the parent (father), has the power to take that life away.[75] Second, Locke claims that God has taken care to ensure the propagation of the species by placing in humans (as well as in animals) the principle of wanting to preserve their young:

> He has in all the parts of the Creation taken a peculiar care to propagate and continue the several Species of Creatures, and makes the Individuals act so strongly to this end, that they sometimes neglect their own private good for it, and seem to forget that general Rule which Nature teaches all things of self Preservation, and the Preservation of their Young, as the strongest Principle in them over rules the Constitution of their particular Natures.[76]

Here Locke suggests that the desire to preserve their young is so strong in humans that parents would even sacrifice their own self-preservation or interest to preserve their children.

Yet he admits that the Bible mentions parents sacrificing their children and acknowledges that it may even have become customary and fashionable in some nations and places to do away with one's children.[77] It becomes apparent then that the desire to preserve one's young is not 'natural' in the sense that parents will automatically or necessarily care for their children. Neither is the desire so strong that it has prevented some parents from killing their children at random or some peoples from entrenching the killing of children in law or making it customary.[78] Locke's response is to maintain that what is customary is not necessarily what is right.

What is right is that parents ought to preserve their children. Not to do so, Locke contends, goes against the 'dictates of Nature and Reason, as well as his Reveal'd Command.'[79] Locke is referring here to the Laws of Nature, or the God-given dictates of reason. To know that they must care for their children, then, parents must be aware of these laws or dictates. Preserving one's children is a duty embedded in law rather than in an innate and universal instinct.[80]

As Locke depicts it, caring for a child is not determined by natural necessity to the same degree as begetting it. It is the result of some degree of rational deliberation by which parents recognize, understand, and act on their duty to care for their children, and thereby propagate the species. This means that, despite Locke's attempt to place it in realm of 'nature,' the forum in which the care of children is to take place – the conjugal union – is more a realm of reason.

Locke tries to show that 'natural necessity' dictates that the conjugal union last longer than it takes merely to conceive and give birth to a child:

> For the end of *conjunction between Male and Female*, being not barely Procreation, but the continuation of the Species, this conjunction betwixt Male and Female ought to last, even after Procreation, so long as is necessary to the nourishment and support of the young Ones, who are to be sustained by those that got them, till they are able to shift and provide for themselves.[81]

He compares the human to the animal world. In herbivores, the need to nourish the young does not prolong the male-female union. But in birds and beasts of prey, the male-female union is prolonged because the male must help the female provide food.[82] Locke does not tell us that this is the case in humans, however. He only tells us that in humans the female is capable of conceiving another child before the one is able to nourish itself.[83] This 'natural fact,' Locke concludes, necessitates a longer union in humans than in animals. We cannot assume, however, that Locke is here providing a support, in nature, for women's weakness or their natural inferiority in conjugal relations. It becomes apparent that what Locke wants to do is to make a 'political' case for encouraging population increase, or for encouraging parents to have more children than they might want to have by intention (which is weak) or as the result of sexual desire (which like any other desires would be controlled by reason in the properly educated citizen).

Population increase for Locke is part and parcel of the increase in wealth and property.[84] Increase in wealth depends on labouring to cultivate the earth; increase in population depends on (reproductive) labouring to people the earth. Their advancement, Locke suggests, is what the art of government is all about: 'This shews, how much numbers of men are to be preferd to largenesse of dominions, and that the increase of lands and the right imploying of them is the great art of government.'[85] As well as being the proper ends of the government, the growth of industry and the growth of population are signs of good government. Locke censures Filmer's model of government as working against population increase. Filmer, says Locke, 'takes great care there should be

Monarchs in the World, but very little that there should be People: and indeed his way of Government is not the way to People the World.'[86]

Locke also alludes to the desirability of improving the quality of the species – 'the continuation of the Species in the highest perfection.'[87] In encouraging parents to provide better-quality care to create a better-quality product – a more rational and industrious citizen of civil society – Locke points us more in the direction of social than genetic engineering. What becomes clear, however, is that the aims of the conjugal union become more political than natural.

Natural necessity might dictate that male and female stay together until the children can nourish themselves. But it cannot explain why parents should take care of children until they are at the age of reason (for Locke the age at which they can become consenting members of civil society) or do anything more than provide them with nourishment and safety until they can fend for themselves. Neither can it account for why parents ought to have more children than is necessary to replace them (in order to perpetuate the species) or why the children themselves ought to be improved through the parents' efforts. These are matters of 'political necessity' for Locke, making the conjugal union an arrangement that fulfils political ends more than it fulfils natural ones. Locke's support of a longer conjugal union does not show that women are naturally weaker because they need men to help them care for the children as much as it shows that the aims of the conjugal union are more political than natural. Another most important function of the conjugal union in Locke's design is that it ensures the continuation of the political community, by encouraging a kind of relation in which parents are obligated to educate their children.

CONTINUATION OF THE POLITICAL COMMUNITY: EDUCATION

Locke wants to refute the idea that one owes allegiance to the government to which one is born simply because one's parents may have an allegiance to it. One cannot inherit political power over others, or the right to govern, from one's parents.[88] Neither can one inherit from them political allegiance to a particular form of political power or government.[89] Each generation, when it comes of age, is at liberty to consent or not to consent to any government it wishes.[90] But does the liberty of each successive generation not threaten the continuity and stability of the political community?

Locke's most immediate answer is that the children's wish to enjoy their parents' property provides them with an important incentive to consent to government. Children, Locke insists, can only enjoy the property of their parents if they consent to the rules of their parents' government:

> the Son cannot ordinarily enjoy the Possessions of his Father, but under the same terms his Father did; by becoming a Member of the Society: whereby he puts himself presently under the Government, he finds there established, as much as any other Subject of that Commonwealth.[91]

Being able to bequeath property to them allows parents to elicit from their children some compliance to the parents' wishes.[92] It can also work to elicit from them some compliance to civil society: 'By this Power indeed Fathers oblige their Children to Obedience to themselves, even when they are past Minority, and most commonly too subject them to this or that Political Power.'[93]

But fear of losing the parents' fortune may garner only a temporary obedience from the child. As soon as the child comes of age, at which time it is able to dispose of its property as it wishes, or as soon as it comes into its parents' inheritance, then it has no incentive to comply with its parents' will.[94] Locke writes: 'Indeed, Fear of having a scanty Portion if they displease you, may make them Slaves to your Estate, but they will be never the less ill and wicked in private; and that Restraint will not last always.'[95] Locke is concerned above all with restraints that do 'last always,' restraints which will induce children to oblige themselves both to their parents' wishes and to the government of their parents.

Just as the fear of being disinherited can engender only a fleeting compliance with the parents, so the enjoyment of property can engender only a fleeting consent to government. Enjoying the property of one's parents may force one to tacitly accept and temporarily abide by the laws governing the Commonwealth (rules which regulate property at least), but it does not make one a full-fledged citizen. One who merely follows the regulations of a Commonwealth in order to enjoy his possessions in it is not necessarily a permanent citizen. He is like a foreigner who enjoys only the temporary sanctuary of a Commonwealth.[96] Once he quits his possessions, then he is 'at liberty to go and incorporate himself into any other Commonwealth, or to agree with others to begin a new one, in *vacuis locis*, in any part of the World, they can find free and unpossessed.'⁹⁷ In contrast, one who makes an 'express promise' becomes a permanent, full-fledged citizen whose allegiance is based on more than the transitory enjoyment of property, who expresses a positive desire to abide by the laws of the Commonwealth, and whose engagement goes beyond simple residency.⁹⁸

The forms which such express declarations of consent might take include consenting to the principle of majoritarianism,⁹⁹ voting for or choosing the Representatives who wield the legislative power of government,¹⁰⁰ consenting to any government appropriation of one's property (taxes, for example),¹⁰¹ and pledging oneself to the Commonwealth by 'Oaths of Fealty, or Allegiance, or other publick owning of, or Submission to the Government of their Countreys.'¹⁰² The exercise of these forms of consent requires that one has the reason to understand and acknowledge their benefits, that is, that one be at the 'age of reason.'

For Locke, the central criterion of adulthood is that one is able to use reason to understand and abide by the laws and to recognize that freedom is not the licence to do as one pleases.¹⁰³ The state of maturity is one

> wherein he might be suppos'd capable to know that Law, that so he might keep his Actions within the Bounds of it. When he has acquired that state, he is presumed to know how far that Law is to be his Guide, and how far he may make use of his *Freedom*, and so comes to have it; till then, some Body else must guide him, who is presumed to know how far the Law allows a Liberty.¹⁰⁴

How does one acquire this state of understanding, since, as Locke acknowledges, humans are born with neither the ability to understand the laws of reason nor the freedom that is required to consent of civil society of their own will?¹⁰⁵ Through education is Locke's answer. Education is the mechanism by which they acquire the reason that enables them to use their freedom in an appropriate manner. Education creates adults who are willing and able to oblige themselves to the laws of civil society. In Locke's scheme, property engenders only a partial and temporary allegiance. Education engenders a more permanent and complete one.

Locke gives parents the responsibility for ensuring that, through education, their children become full-fledged consenting members of civil society. He also attributes to parents considerable power aimed at fulfilling this responsibility. As Locke describes it, the parent-child association is defined by a number of characteristics: some degree of natural parental tenderness, a parental duty to care for children, the requirement that parents be able to exercise reason, the primacy of education over nurture, the advancement of parental self-interest, and the need for extensive parental control.

Parental tenderness, Locke writes, tempers the power that parents can exercise over their children:

> God hath made it their business to imploy this Care on their Off-spring, and hath placed in them suitable Inclinations of Tenderness and Concern to temper this power, to apply it as his Wisdom designed it, to the Children's good, as long as they should need to be under it.[106]

Those parents who may not feel any affection towards their children are nevertheless obliged to care for them. After Adam and Eve, 'all *Parents* were, by the Law of Nature, *under an obligation to preserve, nourish, and educate the Children*, they had begotten, not as their own Workmanship, but the Workmanship of their own Maker, the Almighty, to whom they were to be accountable for them.'[107] This God-given duty, as I have shown earlier, is embedded in the Laws of Nature. Not to educate one's children appropriately is to break the Law of Nature. Understanding and acting on the Laws of Nature demands that parents themselves have been educated to become rational creatures.

Parents who care for their children properly will be rewarded with their children's lifelong honour and respect, the degree and amount of which are directly related to the degree or amount of care the parents have lavished on the children.[108] The children's obligation to the parents may vary, Locke suggests, depending on 'the different care and kindness, trouble and expence, which is often imployed upon one Child, more than another.'[109] He implies here that the parent-child relationship resembles a form of contract in which self-interested parties exchange benefits. He also implies that the quality of education parents provide for their children is more important than the quality of nourishment they may dispense. Parents are to be proportionately rewarded for providing the former rather than the latter: 'and the *honour due from a Child*, places in the Parents a perpetual right to respect, reverence, support and compliance too, more or less, as the Father's care, cost and kindness in his Education, has been more or less.'[110]

Locke's concern that parents give their children an appropriate education may explain the degree of power he attributes to them. As Locke describes it, the power that parents can legitimately exercise over their children is quite extensive. It includes the power to command them, chastise them, and elicit absolute obedience from them. In essence it is a form of 'temporary Government.'[111] Yet, Locke is adamant that parental power is distinct from political power.[112] He makes this claim on three grounds. The first is that parental power excludes the power of life and death over one's child. God as the giver of all life holds that power. And only the civil magistrate has the power to make laws that regulate the life and death or the property of members of civil society, powers which are distinctly political. The second is that parental power is temporary because it is only exercised when the child is under age. It is not to be confused with honour, which a child owes to its parents for life. The third is that parental power is 'natural' rather than political – a response to the infant's natural helplessness and inability to care for itself.[113] These grounds become shaky, however, first, when women's contribution to the formation of the child is introduced, and second, when one considers that the aims of parental power in Locke's framework are the advancement of political ends. I will consider the last point first.

How 'natural' is parental power? If we are to believe that the justification for parental power is 'natural necessity,' then that power would consist in enough control over the child to enable the parent to care for its safety and growth needs. It would not consist of the kind of extensive powers that Locke grants to parents. These might be explained as a response to his fear that too little parental control is detrimental to the child's education.

Locke equates the need for parental power with the need for education when he states: 'It [parental power] is but a help to the weakness and imperfection of their Nonage, a Discipline necessary to their Education.'[114] And education, Locke believes, requires extensive control over the child in order to be successful. In 'Some Thoughts Concerning Education,' he refers to the parents' authority over the child as that of a lord: 'I imagine every one will judge it reasonable, that their Children, *when little*, should look upon their Parents as their Lords, their Absolute Governors; and, as such stand in Awe of them.'[115] Being an absolute lord over one's children means that one is neither familiar nor indulgent towards them; one does not spoil them by letting them have their own way. Parents ought to demand that the children be in awe of their powers to prevent them from thinking they can circumvent the parents' will by playing on their affection.

Locke is less concerned that parents might abuse their power over their children by being too strict with them than he is concerned that, where education is concerned, parents will not be strict enough:

> yet God hath woven into the Principles of Humane Nature such a tenderness for their Off-spring, that there is little fear that Parents should use their power with too much rigour; the excess is seldom on the severe side, the strong byass of Nature drawing the other way.[116]

Parental affection might induce parents to care for their children's needs, once they have decided to preserve them. But such affection, Locke warns, may undermine the parents' effectiveness in educating their children: 'Parents, being wisely ordain'd by Nature to love their Children, are very apt, if Reason watch not that natural Affection very warily, are apt, I say, to let it into Fondness. They love their little ones, and 'tis their Duty: But they often, with them, cherish their Faults too.'[117] And the greatest fault children can have is non-compliance. Parental affection is dangerous because it could lead parents to spoil their children by letting them have their own way. This in turn is not conducive to the creation of obedient citizens who recognize that their desires must be limited, regulated, and channelled in an appropriate fashion. Locke is adamant that parents must not release their children from direct parental control or consider them to be of age until they are certain the children are capable of understanding the limits of their freedom.[118]

Proper parenting, as Locke depicts it, rests less on natural love than on rational control. One must govern one's natural fondness for one's children in order to educate them in governing their own desires. The power of parents over children rests less on natural necessity, which might dictate that the helpless infant is nourished and protected, than it does on political necessity, which dictates that the child is educated to become a rational, free, consenting citizen of the civil state.

Education is important in Locke's design as a means for producing an ongoing commitment to civil society and an ongoing allegiance to government. Although Locke claims that parental subjection and power are relinquished once the children come of age,[119] their after-effects, as he describes them, are to maintain control over the children as adults. When successful, education allows parents to let go of their children, knowing that they will choose the path the parents wish them to follow. This path, for Locke, includes the granting of express consent to civil society.[120] The benefits that accrue to parents for educating their children, in the form of honour, are outweighed by the benefits that accrue to the political community, in the form of having educated adults who, by consenting to civil society and to government, ensure the stability and continuity of the political community.

One of the central purposes of the conjugal union, then, is to contribute to political continuity by ensuring that children are educated in an appropriate manner. Women play an integral role in the education of children, Locke suggests in his emphasis on early socialization, in his numerous references to women educating their children at home, and in his depiction of women as having the rational capabilities required for parenting. Once again, Locke makes no particular distinction between mothers and fathers. He does not suggest that parental affection or tenderness are any greater in women than in men, reinforcing the idea that there is neither a natural instinct, peculiar to women, to care for children nor a natural urge to have them.

The care of children is depicted as a rational rather than a natural activity; moreover, it is depicted as a rational activity that fulfils political ends. Women's role in it, therefore, would be an indicator of their capacity for reason as well as an example of their contribution to the fulfilment of political ends. Women's capacity for reason is also evident in the third aim of the conjugal union – the accumulation of property.

ACCUMULATION OF PROPERTY

The desire to pass on one's property to one's children, in Locke's design, provides individuals with an incentive to accumulate property beyond the amount that they could make use of in their lifetime. In destroying the spoilage principle and providing a means whereby excess could be hoarded up,[121] the introduction of money provided some incentive for men to cultivate more land and acquire more property than they could make use of for themselves:' Where there is not something both lasting and scarce, and so valuable to be hoarded up, there Men will not be apt to enlarge their *Possessions of Land*, were it never so rich, never so free for them to take.'[122] But why should they be industrious and accumulate more money than they could use for themselves?[123]

The motive that Locke implicitly attributes to men for applying their labour to the cultivation of the earth or to making use of things, a labour which establishes their original right to private property, is self-preservation.[124] One labours in order to preserve oneself. Locke emphasizes that property is 'for the benefit and sole Advantage of the Proprietor, so that he may even destroy the thing, that he has Property in by his use of it, where need requires'[125] Why would one then not simply accumulate as much as one needs to preserve one's life, enable one to live a life of comfort, or serve one's own needs and wishes? More important, why would one not simply squander what one has accumulated in one's lifetime as old age approaches? The squandering of accumulated property is precisely what Locke wants to avoid. He invokes nature, God, inheritance and bequest to argue against it.[126]

Locke tries to connect the human desire to continue the species with the need to pass on property to one's children. Since the continuation of the species requires that children be cared for as well as conceived, one could argue that parents need some property to nourish their children until they are of age and able to fend for themselves. But how does this justify the children's right to inherit property when they are adults and able to care for themselves? Locke's answer rests on two problematic assumptions – the first that children are extensions of their parents, the second that parents have a God-given duty to accumulate property for them.

If the earth was given to men in common,[127] Locke asks, why should the possessions they accumulate not simply revert to the common lot after their death? He replies:

> The first and strongest desire God Planted in Men, and wrought into the very Principles of their Nature being that of Self-preservation, that is the Foundation of a right to the Creatures, for the particular support and use of each individual Person himself. But next to this, God planted in Men a strong desire also of propagating their Kind, and continuing themselves in their Posterity, and this gives Children a Title, to share in the *Property* of their Parents, and a Right to Inherit their Possessions.[128]

Locke here tries to equate the desire to preserve oneself with the desire to preserve one's children. But this connection only works if the children are viewed as extensions of the parents, as being parts of the parents. If property is for the advantage of the individual who accumulates it, excluding what may benefit others, then children cannot be viewed as 'others.'[129] Otherwise, why would parents have the desire or motive to pass property on to them? Why would the parents not simply accumulate enough property to live well themselves or dissipate in old age what they had amassed? Locke's explanation suggests that parents must be convinced they are benefiting themselves – that they are preserving themselves in their children.

But if the children are parts or extensions of the parents, if they belong to them, can the parents do as they wish with them? Can they legitimately buy, sell, or even do away with them? (One can dispose of one's property as one wishes, including property in one's person, Locke emphasizes.)[130] Locke seems aware of this problem. He calls on God as an intermediary. God gives life to the child; only God has the right to take it away.[131] Do parents, however, have the right to sell their children into enforced labour, for example, as they might be able to do to themselves?[132]

To separate parental from political power, Locke insists that parents cannot make laws that regulate property. This is the task of those who govern. Neither can parents dispose of their children's property: 'The Power of the Father doth not reach at all to the Property of the Child, which is only in his own disposing.'[133] Children have property rights, it seems. But their right to dispose of their own property comes into effect only when they are of age. Prior to that, the parents simply act as guardians of the children's property: 'And though a *Father* may dispose of his own Possessions as he pleases, when his Children are out of danger of perishing for want, yet *his power* extends not to the Lives or Goods, which either their own industry, or anothers bounty has made theirs.'[134] Here Locke suggests that children may acquire property on their own – either through the generosity of others or through their own labour – which the parents cannot touch. Parental power can only be exercised 'for the Benefit of their Children during their Minority, to supply their want of Ability, and understanding how to manage their Property. (By *Property* I must be understood here, as in other places, to mean that Property which Men have in their Persons as well as Goods).'[135] If guardianship includes a temporary power over the children's persons, as Locke implies it does here, then presumably it includes a power over the children's labour power. Locke reinforces this idea when he recommends that parents exercise their power for the good of the children by making them 'most useful to themselves and others; and, if it be necessary to his Condition, to make them work when they are able for their own Subsistence.'[136] While the child is a minor, the parent's power over the child's person may not extend to power over its life, but it seems to extend to the power to dispose and make use of its labour power.

Locke introduces a temper to the power that parents may exercise over their children as extensions of themselves: a God-given duty to care for them. He also tries to establish that this duty obliges parents to pass on property to their children and that it is grounded in nature – the fact that children are born weak, dependent, and requiring the care of adults.[137] The obligation to care for them, however, as Locke describes it, extends far beyond 'nature' in the form of the need to nourish and protect them when young:

> For Children being by the course of Nature, born weak, and unable to provide for themselves, they have by the appointment of God himself, who hath thus ordered the course of nature, a Right to be nourish'd and maintained by their Parents, nay a right not only to a bare Subsistance but to the conveniences and comforts of Life, as far as the conditions of their Parents can afford it. Hence it comes, that when their Parents leave the World, and so the care due to their Children ceases, the effects of it are to extend as far as possibly they can, and the Provisions they have made in their Life time, are understood to be intended as nature requires they should, for their Children, whom after themselves, they are bound to provide for.[138]

In this passage, the first inducement Locke gives parents to accumulate excess property is a (God-given) duty to provide their children with more than bare subsistence, to give them the 'conveniences and comforts of life.' The second and more important one is the obligation to provide for the children after the parents' death. Although, practically speaking, parental obligations cease (as do all obligations) when the parents are dead, parents have an obligation, while they are alive, to ensure that they can continue to provide for their children after their own death. They can only fulfil this duty, Locke suggests, by passing their accumulated property on to their children. The implications of doing so, however, are that, with the exception of instances where the parents die young and thus die before the children are independent or able to take care of themselves, the parents are taking care of children beyond the age at which the children are able to provide for themselves.

What Locke is doing here is presenting as 'natural necessity' the duty of parents to care for their children when their children are independent adults, perfectly capable of taking care of themselves. One could argue that 'natural necessity' dictates that parents are obligated to bequeath some property to their children, to be used if the parents die while the children are dependent. This argument, however, would not be sufficient for what seems to be of great concern to Locke – assuring that property as a whole accumulates from one generation to the next by being passed from parents to their adult 'children.'

His concern with such vertical accumulation is evident in his discussion of property relations between generations. Locke maintains that parental duties and obligations are simply carried forward to the next generation. Generational continuity is secured by children paying back the debt to their parents (for caring for them and passing their property on to them), in part, by caring for and passing property on to their own children.[139] Locke emphasizes that property ought to move forward not backward. If the son should die, the children, rather than the father, should inherit the property. Only where there are no children does the father have the right to inherit his son's property before a stranger. Parents, Locke contends, have a God-given duty to accumulate more property than they can use up in a lifetime in order to pass it on to their children and thereby facilitate the total, vertical accumulation of wealth in society (as well as provide children with an incentive to consent to the political system in which they are born).

This is the context in which Locke champions the stable, conjugal union as an economic unit conducive to industry or the accumulation of excess property:

> Wherein one cannot but admire the Wisdom of the great Creatour, who having given to Man foresight and an Ability to lay up for the future, as well as to supply the present necessity, hath made it necessary, that *Society of Man and Wife should be more lasting*, than of Male and Female amongst other Creatures; that so their Industry might be encouraged, and their Interest better united, to make Provision, and lay up Goods for their common Issue, which uncertain mixture, or easie and frequent Solutions of Conjugal Society would mightily disturb.[140]

A stable conjugal union is conducive to industry because it encourages parents to accumulate more than they need in order to pass it on to their children. A monogamous union, Locke implies, is desirable, for the same reason. If parents are motivated to pass property on to their children as extensions of themselves, then they must be convinced that the children do in fact belong to them. Paternal uncertainty, to which Locke indirectly refers,[141] might threaten the passage of property to the next generation.

WOMEN AND CONJUGAL RELATIONS: RIGHTS AND DUTIES

Does the need to establish certainty over paternity explain women's subjection to men in the conjugal relationship? Lorenne Clark has argued that it does. In her words, 'If Adam does not own Eve, how can he be sure who his descendants are and, hence, on whom his apples ought properly to devolve?'[142] According to this interpretation, the husband must be given control of the wife in the conjugal relationship in order to ensure that there is no outside access to her reproductive capacities.

There is no doubt that establishing certainty over paternity is essential in Locke's design (in light of the importance Locke places on the movement of property from one generation to the next and in light of assumptions about what might induce parents to accumulate excess property) and that monogamy is a means of establishing paternity. It is less certain, however, that Clark's argument in itself adequately explains why Locke makes the husband the one whose will prevails in case of a conflict over property or why Locke's framework makes it difficult to grant the wife the final determination. First, both men and women, Locke suggests, are capable of controlling their desires through reason. Both are capable of voluntarily contracting to a monogamous conjugal union in which their desires are regulated according to the rational ends of the union. This means that there may be little need for men to control women to ensure that they do not have access to other men. Second, even if there were a need to restrict women (as mothers) in order to ensure paternity, why not simply rely on strict sanctions for adultery or on the stipulation that women be confined to the home? Third, if control over conjugal property is to function as a mechanism for restricting women's sexual activity, then why allow women any right to accumulate and hold property on their own?

If the importance of certainty over paternity is insufficient in explaining the husband's say in the case of a conflict over property, the importance of making the father's rather than the mother's will prevail in regulating the children may provide a more satisfactory explanation. The regulation of property can refer not only to the regulation of one's possessions in the form of goods and lands, but also to the regulation of one's children as extensions of oneself.

Why does Locke not uphold the mother's over the father's will and power in regulating the children? He emphasizes that either parent can exercise parental power.[143] He invokes the legitimacy of maternal right to challenge Filmer's contention that the father alone has dominion over the children. The biblical injunction to honour one's parents, Locke points out, applies to both the mother and the father.[144] And in case of a separation the children may go to either the mother or the father, depending on the civil laws in place.[145] Either parent may act as head of the family, Locke indicates, when he describes it as a unit 'wherein the Master or Mistress of it had some sort of Rule proper to a Family.'[146] In fact, it would make more sense to give the mother greater power over the children, in light of Locke's acknowledgment that the mother has a greater role in producing the children and in light of his propositions on the origins of property – the labour one attaches to something is what makes it one's property. But, as Eisenstein points out, Locke does not follow through on the logical implications of these propositions.[147] We might not be able to determine whether this oversight is deliberate or unintentional. But we can ask what would happen, in Locke's framework, if women did have the final determination. We can see that it might be problematic. It might entail acknowledging the implications of applying to women Locke's propositions on rights over one's body, property, and labour power.

I agree with Pateman that Locke's concept of the ownership of one's body and labour power cannot easily be extended to women, but I disagree with the emphasis in her explanation of why this is so. According to Pateman, the owner of the body is an 'individual' who is male and who desires to control women in order to have guaranteed sexual access to them;[148] women's labour power cannot be separated from their bodies because it is precisely to women's bodies that men want access. The idea that women own their bodies in a Lockean sense, moreover, lends itself to the support of prostitution and surrogacy contracts.[149] Pateman cites Locke's reference to 'a Communion and Right in one anothers Bodies, as is necessary to its chief End, Procreation'[150] as proof that Locke supports the husband's right to sexual access to his wife's body.[151] But undermining Pateman's interpretation is Locke's suggestion that the man and woman have a right 'in one anothers bodies.' This indicates some degree of equality between the two participants in the conjugal relationship.

Moreover, Pateman focuses on the sexual contract – men's desire and need to exert their control over women in order to define themselves as men. In Locke, however, the parent-child contract is more important than the sexual one. Sexual access to women is important as a means of ensuring the propagation of the species and the continuity of the political community rather than as a means for exercising sexual power for its own sake.

At one point, Locke states that the conjugal union, or the relation between man and woman, is the most basic unit of society.[152] Yet he also suggests that the notion of the primacy of the male-female association hinges on a founding myth. He invokes the biblical one, which explains that Adam and Eve came into the world as full-blown adults, fully rational and capable of parenting future generations:

> *Adam* was created a perfect Man, his Body and Mind in full possession of their Strength and Reason, and so was capable from the first Instant of his being to provide for his own Support and Preservation, and govern his Actions according to the Dictates of the Law of Reason which God had implanted in him.[153]

Adam and Eve were born capable of understanding and abiding by laws which directed them to fulfil their obligation of preserving their children and thereby ensuring the continuation of the species.

Locke's assumptions direct us to consider this: common sense tells us that human beings are not born as reasonable adults, capable of forming contracts of marriage or of propagating the species. The propagation of the species not only requires that children be conceived but also that they be cared for, which requires that parents have the reason to know that they ought to preserve, nourish, and educate their children. One must account for how adults acquire the reason that makes them capable of such of a task. Locke may state that the conjugal union is the most basic unity of society, thereby implying that the sexual contract precedes the parental one, but he ends up suggesting the opposite – that the parental contract is more important than and precedes the sexual one. In other words, Locke takes the opposite stance from the one Pateman claims he does on the chicken-and-egg question. At the same time, however, it is precisely women's right to govern their bodies and, attached to it, their labour power that is difficult to acknowledge in Locke's scheme.

Locke grounds property in bodily labour: 'every Man has a *Property* in his own *Person*. This no Body has any Right to but himself. The *Labour* of his Body, and the *Work* of his Hands, we may say, are properly his.'[154] Having a right to one's body by extension entails having a right to the product of one's bodily labour. Private property originates in the use of one's labour power to appropriate what then belongs to oneself, exclusive of the rights of others.

What would it mean if this concept were applied to a woman's right over her body and the products of her labour, if one considers reproductive labour as part of that labour? Locke indicates that women do in fact labour with their bodies in the creation of a product – a child – when he grants that women make the greater contribution to generation.[155] Since a woman puts more of her labour into the child, would the child belong to her, exclusive of the claims of others or the common good? If Locke's theory of the ownership of one's person and one's labour power means that each is 'the absolute proprietor in the sense that he owes nothing to society for them,'[156] then this could mean that women, as the proprietors of their body and reproductive labour power, would owe nothing to society in the use of either. To give women maternal power over the child as property might be to concede that women have the right to own their children and dispose of them freely as the products of their reproductive labour, a conclusion which would be unacceptable if one were concerned, as is Locke, with population increase.

One could argue that Locke does limit the right of any individual to exercise the power of life and death over another in a number of ways and that these would apply to women's power over their children as well. First, on the grounds that human life belongs to God, Locke emphasizes that one's freedom in the state of nature does not include the freedom to take another's life or even one's own life.[157] The liberty to dispose of one's person and possessions does not include the liberty to destroy oneself.[158] Second, the right to property does not justify letting another perish for want: 'And therefore no Man could ever have a just Power over the Life of another, by Right of property in Land or Possessions; since 'twould always be a Sin in any Man of Estate, to let his Brother perish for want of affording him Relief out of his Plenty.'[159] Third, Locke emphasizes that the right of property is separate from the right of life and death over another. Thus, one cannot pass on political power, which includes the power of life and death over another, to one's children.[160]

A woman's right over her own body or her property right in her own person need not translate to a right over the life of her child in Locke's scheme. The problem, however, lies less in her right over her own body than in her right over her reproductive labour power. Exercising the latter can mean that she is in fact exercising a power which effects the life and death of a potential or actual human being. For a woman, more than for a man, *not* attaching her labour to a newly conceived life can mean taking away that life. This comes into play in a woman's decision not to attach her labour to a new life in the womb.[161] Abortion, like infanticide, Locke insists, goes against one's duty to abide by the God-given laws of nature: 'When it shall be made out that men ignorant of words, or untaught by the laws and customs of their country, know that it is part of the worship of God not to kill another man; not to know more women than one; *not to procure abortion*; not to expose their children; not to take from another what is his though we want it ourselves.'[162] But a woman's right to govern her own (reproductive) labour power, as an extension of the right to govern her own body, may undermine that duty. Why? Not because women are deemed incapable of using reason to abide by their duties, but because they are deemed capable of using reason to pursue their own interest.

As Locke describes it, the desire to use one's labour power to create and accumulate property derives from the aspiration to advance one's own interests, rather than and even against the interests of others or the common good. Since women are rational creatures, capable of accumulating property and of exercising independent wills, they may be influenced by these kinds of considerations. Moreover, the 'labour' men bring to the creation of a new life, Locke suggests, is less intentional and less essential than what women contribute. Men do not voluntarily and deliberately use their labour power to create a new life to the same extent as women, for whom it is not only a matter of engaging in the sex act but also a matter of carrying and nourishing the new life in the womb, giving it birth and nursing it once born. Women's labour is more necessary than men's to the propagation of the species, the continuity of the political community, and population increase, ends which are vital in Locke's construction. Yet, in the absence of a natural maternal instinct, women's labour is also more contingent on rational deliberation involving considerations of self-interest. Acting on self-interest, women may decide not to use their bodies in labouring for the next generation. They may not regard the products of their reproductive labour – the fetus or the child – in ways that support the common good, most fundamentally by ensuring the continuity of the species and the political community.

Locke is concerned that both parents 'labour' for the next generation, but he might be more concerned that women be induced to do so because of their greater contribution to generation. Extending to women the right to do as they will with their bodies and reproductive capacities might result in women having the right to decide not to nourish and carry the fetus in the womb, give birth to it, or nourish it after birth. Or, if we consider Locke's claim that the laws in civil society are not intended to force individuals to take care of their bodies – 'Laws endeavour, as far as possible, to protect the good and health of subjects from violence of others, or from fraud, not from the negligence or prodigality of the owners themselves'[163] – such a right would preclude laws forcing pregnant women to take care of their bodies for the sake of the new life.

I am not suggesting that by giving the father control over conjugal property in the form of the children[164] Locke believes he will force women to make use of their reproductive labour in ways that support the political ends of the conjugal union. I am suggesting, instead, that Locke may implicitly recognize, and we can recognize, that giving women as mothers that control, in the context of Lockean assumptions about property and labour in one's person, might entail acknowledging the legitimacy and paramountcy of women's reproductive rights, rights which are potentially subversive to the fundamental political ends of the conjugal union.

WOMEN AND THE POLITICAL REALM

Locke's failure to acknowledge women's unique reproductive rights translates into a failure to grant them the right to govern their bodies and their labour power to the same extent as men. This in turn undermines their political status as free and equal members of civil society in Locke's blueprint. Freedom of bodily movement is an important element in the enjoyment of liberty, Locke suggests: 'If freedom can with any propriety of speech be applied to power, it may be attributed to the power that is in a man to produce or forbear producing motion in parts of his body by choice or preference; which is that which denominates him free and is freedom itself.'[165] It is connected to the freedom to govern one's own body: 'Every Man is born with a double Right; *First, A Right of Freedom to his Person*, which no other Man has a Power over, but the free Disposal of it lies in himself.'[166] And freedom over one's body is related to equality – the equal right not to be subject to the will of another.[167] Enjoying the right of liberty to dispose of and order one's actions, person and property, within the bounds of the law, according to one's own will and without being subject to the will of another, is what makes one equal to another in the state of nature and in civil society.[168] Freedom is connected to reason. One must have the reason to know the bounds of freedom in law, both natural and civil law.

What makes the extension to women of freedom to govern their own bodies and labour power to the same degree as men problematic is not the perception that they are incapable of using reason to govern their body or labour power, or make use of their freedom, but paradoxically, as I have suggested, precisely the perception that they do have such capacities for reason. Women seem to be caught in the bifurcation, evident in Locke, between rights, conceived as resting on the exercise of rational self-interest in the pursuit of one's own interest, and duties, conceived as resting on an apprehension, through reason, of what actions benefit others, the carrying out of which furthers the common good. In conjunction with their unique bodily reproductive capacities, women's use of their capacity for reason in exercising the rights of citizenship potentially conflicts with the use of their reason in exercising the duties of citizenship.

The duty aspect of political citizenship as Locke formulates it consists in being able to comprehend the Laws of Nature which regulate behaviour towards others. The Law of Nature stipulates, for example, that one must preserve the lives of others as well as one's own life.[169] Women are portrayed as being capable of reason and of acknowledging the Laws of Nature in the exercise of their parental duties. As parents, both men and women engage in fulfilling duties towards others. In preserving their children, caring for them, accumulating property for them, and educating them in order to propagate the species, increase population, and ensure the continuity of the political community, parents are also thereby fulfilling duties which have political ends.

But this duty towards others is threatened by women's potential right over their reproductive labour, a right which might presuppose that, motivated by considerations of self-interest exclusive of the interests of others, women can do as they will with the products of their reproductive labour or decide not to attach their reproductive labour to a new life in order to ensure its well-being and along with it the well-being of the political community.

In conjugal relations, the husband's will prevails in case of a conflict over property whether in the form of goods or offspring. But this does not necessarily imply, as Pateman maintains, that husbands consent to civil society for their wives.[170] Although the position of women, especially married women, in civil society is ambiguous, this ambiguity is not, as Pateman assumes, grounded in the perception that women are naturally inferior to men. Nor is it grounded in the perception that their bodies, especially their reproductive capacities, make them incapable of regulating their desires through reason. As Locke describes it, women's role in reproduction is an indicator of their capacity for reason. But their unique relation to reproduction, coupled with the assumption that self-interest is what may motivate them to make use of their reproductive abilities, makes their capacity for reason seem threatening to the political continuity.

Locke portrays women as having reason enough to comprehend the Laws of Nature when it comes to parenting. Presumably, then, they would be able to judge whether the Laws of Nature were broken, what means are to be used to punish the offender, and what means, within the bounds of the Law of Nature, are most effective in preserving their property (which they are capable of accumulating). In other words, women have the capacity to exercise the powers that Locke attributes to men in the state of nature.[171] Does women's greater physical weakness, to which Locke alludes when he designates men as the stronger and abler, put them at a disadvantage when it comes to the power to punish those who transgress the Laws of Nature? According to Locke, 'every Man in the State of Nature, has a Power to kill a Murderer.'[172] Perhaps, but not greatly so since the power is given up in civil society, except in cases where there is no time to appeal to a common authority. I shall return to the question of women's physical weakness.

According to Locke, these powers of judgment are transferred to the government or to common authority in civil society. Wielding the legitimate powers of the state, or holding the power of the magistrate in civil society, as Locke describes it, involves making laws that may include the death penalty, making laws for preserving and regulating property, and employing the force of the community in executing the laws and defending the Commonwealth.[173] The executive power of carrying out the laws ought to be separated from the legislative power of making them, Locke advises. But the executive ought to exercise the power to make war and defend the Commonwealth (the federative power). Women are qualified to wield executive prerogative, Locke intimates, when he acknowledges the legitimacy of the power of queens.[174] What about women's participation in a legislative capacity? We can get clues about this by examining how they fare in Locke's account of consent.

Participation in politics in Locke's scheme is exemplified in giving consent, both tacit and express, to civil society and government. He comes close to combining the two forms when he suggests that individuals cannot be considered to have consented to a government until either they are put in a full state of Liberty to chuse their Government and Governors, or at least till they have such standing Laws, to which they have by themselves or their Representatives, given their free consent, and also till they are allowed their due property, which is so to be Proprietors of what they have, that no body can take away any part of it without their own consent.[175]

And the two main criteria for consent are property and reason. Since women can own property in their own right, presumably they would have some incentive to tacitly consent to civil society or to a particular form of government.[176] At the same time, their enjoyment of property is less certain, since they have less control than men over property in the conjugal relationship and since they do not have property in their own persons and over the products of their labour to the same extent as men. If the enjoyment of property provides an incentive to consent to civil society or to a particular form of government, then women might be less motivated than men to do so.[177]

Since women are described as being capable of being educated to become obedient citizens of the state, presumably they would be capable of engaging in some forms of express consent such as choosing representatives and giving oaths of allegiance, activities which constitute some of the political rights of citizenship.[178] The power of the people to choose representatives who make laws for them is a way of consenting to those laws.[179] Locke relates this to the right not to have one's property taken away, through taxation for example, without one's consent.[180]

Although there was some debate in Locke's time over the question of women's suffrage,[181] Locke does not directly address the question in his *Two Treatises of Government*.[182] But he does present women as having the capacity to exercise democratic forms of consent. By deeming them to be capable of exercising reason and owning and accumulating property, he depicts them as having the qualities compatible with his account of political participation.

But what of Locke's apparent support for the political right to resist an aggressor?[183] If the prince or executive abuse their power by using unjust force against the people, Locke suggests, they are responsible for instigating a state of war: 'For wherever violence is used, and injury done, though by hands appointed to administer Justice, it is still violence and injury, however colour'd with the Name, Pretences, or forms of Law.'[184] And in a state of war there is no appeal to a common authority. The right to resist government may come into play here. It is not simply a matter of exercising sheer physical force, however. It is a matter of exercising one's reason, since a most important component of the right to resistance is judging whether the prince or executive have in fact abused their trust through the use of unjust force. The people may judge that they have: the prince may, however, ' decline that way of Determination.'[185] When this happens, as it surely would in almost all cases, then 'the Appeal then lies no where but to Heaven.'[186] But a state in which the government has put itself in a position to have its authority challenged is 'easie to be avoided.'[187] Individuals will put up with a great deal of government wrongdoing without responding to it with armed conflict, Locke notes.[188] His emphasis on forming law-abiding citizens through education, by punishing children for non-compliance in particular, reinforces that he seems more concerned with preventing resistance or rebellion than encouraging it.

And what of fighting in a war, just or unjust? Locke seems to assume that women, along with children, do not engage in battle. A conqueror has no right over the life or property of the wife with children, since 'They made not the War, nor assisted in it.'[189] Yet he indicates that women are capable of being responsible for negotiating war and peace in their capacity as queens. The 'federative power,' as Locke calls it, which is to remain in the hands of the executive, includes the power to deal with members of other Commonwealths, to make war and peace, and to use force in their execution.[190]

Does Locke in his apparent support for the use of force present a notion of citizenship that would exclude women on the basis of their lesser physical strength? Would women have trouble meeting its requirements on the grounds that they do not have the physical courage or strength to do battle for the Commonwealth or to exercise their right of resistance? Not necessarily. Women may be at some disadvantage when it comes to armed conflict, whether it be the right to kill a murderer in the state of nature, engage in a just war, or participate in armed resistance, Locke implies when he refers to men as the 'abler and stronger.' But this must be considered in light of the following: (1) his references to women's strength of mind or faculty of reason; (2) his suggestion that girls as well as boys can benefit from hardening their bodies and that physical strength is in part a result of conditioning; (3) his portrayal of women as mothers being no more prone to be governed by their emotions than fathers or more reluctant to use physical force on their children (the image of the mother whipping her daughter for non-compliance); (4) his allusions to women's competence in wielding the federative (war-making) power as queens; (5) his suggestion that exercising the right to resistance requires the reason to make judgments, not mere physical strength; (7) and his expression of concern for preventing rather than encouraging citizens to resort to physical violence. The main requirements for citizenship in Locke are property and reason rather than physical strength.

The focus on property and reason leaves a mixed legacy for women. Women are depicted as being rational enough to be able to accumulate property and are even presented as models of industry and virtue. But when it comes to property in their person, their very rationality, coupled with their differential reproductive powers, also makes extension of equal status to them problematic.

Locke neither explicitly supports nor rejects equal political status for women. His depiction of women's role in education and in conjugal relations suggests that they have the capacity for political life. They have the potential to become educated to become freely consenting citizens of the state. This capacity is easily translated into such activities as wielding the legitimate power of the state and exercising such political rights as the right to choose representatives. But it does not easily translate into the enjoyment of such civil rights as the right to own, govern, and dispose of property in one's person and, attached to it, one's labour power. In other words, it does not easily translate into the enjoyment of reproductive rights for women.

In fact, against the background of Locke's assumptions about property, labour, and the bifurcation of reason into rational self-interest and the apprehension of one's duties towards others, introducing the idea of women enjoying equal (reproductive) rights does the following: it magnifies the tension between rights and duties in Locke's framework, places women in an ambiguous position at the centre of that tension, and sets up a potential conflict between reproductive rights, formulated as the right to do as one pleases with one's body without accountability to society, and reproductive duties, formulated as the duty to further the welfare of society by attaching one's labour to the production of new life. Women end up in an equally ambiguous and uncomfortable place in the final theorist I consider – John Stuart Mill.

CHAPTER THREE

John Stuart Mill

Unlike Thomas Hobbes or John Locke, John Stuart Mill (1806–1873) addresses directly the question of women's participation in the political sphere. Mill's active and public support of suffrage for women, his political involvement in the movement to extend greater legal rights to women, and his close personal and intellectual relationship with two champions of women's rights – Harriet Taylor and Helen Taylor – are well documented.[1] In *The Subjection of Women* he expresses considerable concern for the plight of women. He also makes a number of recommendations for changing their political and social status.[2] While acknowledging his good intentions, feminist commentators have criticized Mill's analysis on several counts; in particular, his depiction of women's 'nature,' his seeming distinction between exceptional and ordinary women, and his assumptions about women's role in the family.

There is some debate about whether Mill emphasizes the similarities between men and women or attributes to them different and perhaps complementary qualities.[3] Mill has been criticized for doing both. According to Julia Annas, Mill depicts women and men as having different faculties and tendencies – women for intuition and men for reason.[4] This distinction, she maintains, is incompatible with his advocacy of equal treatment for women in the public sphere. Moira Gatens attributes to Mill (and Harriet Taylor) the perception that what is distinctive about women is that their domestic functions – childbearing and rearing in particular – are 'natural' to them, a perception that puts women at a disadvantage in Mill's design for human emancipation.[5]

For Christine Di Stefano, it is Mill's attempts to treat women as if they were the same as men that lead to difficulties.[6] He ends up attributing to women experiences and values associated with a masculine bias (she interprets Mill as exhibiting a typically modern masculinist preoccupation with self-sufficiency, liberty, autonomy, and individualism) and denying them experiences and values reflective of a female perspective. Ultimately, Mill's proposals require that women become masculinized to benefit from public life.[7] Diana Coole joins Di Stefano in concluding that Mill's vision of emancipation for women 'promotes women's conformity to prevailing norms of masculinity.'[8]

Mill's prescriptions for women have also been deemed 'elitist.' Zillah Eisenstein argues that Mill's individualism is applicable to only the exceptional few – women as well as men.[9] According to Diana Coole, emancipation as Mill describes it is likely to be enjoyed by only a minority of women.[10] There may be a connection between Mill's perspective on differences between the sexes and his distinction between exceptional and ordinary women, Nadia Urbinati implies.[11] She interprets Mill as supporting androgyny or a move towards the disappearance of distinctive feminine and masculine characteristics in the sexes. It seems, however, that this is favoured or deemed possible mainly for the exceptional women (and men) of the 'higher ranks.'[12]

Mill's failure to challenge women's role as wife and mother, a number of commentators suggest, undermines his proposal for their equal treatment in public life. According to Carole Pateman, Mill is inconsistent in advocating more equality for women in the sexual contract, in the form of greater freedom to make and break contracts of marriage, at the same time as he assumes a division of labour in which the man works outside and the woman inside the home.[13] Susan Okin applauds Mill for bringing to light the political uses and abuses of arguments that draw on 'nature' to explain women's social and political position and praises him for suggesting that the inequality of women in the family is subversive of justice on a wider scale.[14] But she criticizes him for not recognizing the division of labour within the home as detrimental to women's enjoyment of equal rights in public life or as contributing to their subordinate status within the family.[15]

Zillah Eisenstein is also critical of Mill for maintaining a distinction between the private and public realm and for assuming that most women would choose marriage and motherhood over a role in public life.[16] According to Barbara Cameron, Mill may leave women's traditional role in the family intact because he recognizes that the full-time mother plays an important political role in educating children in citizenship.[17] Critics who accuse Mill of inconsistency in advocating equality of opportunity for women while assuming a sexual division of labour within the family are assuming, Mary Shanley maintains, that Mill's goal is something which it is not.[18] Mill's main concern is not necessarily the complete liberation of women in the public and political sphere. It is achieving marital friendship. Greater male-female equality may be a means to the latter for Mill, but not an end in itself. Or, as Susan J. Hekman emphasizes, there may not be a correlation for Mill between the idea that women and men have the same capacities and the notion that they ought to be treated the same or given the equal benefit of the laws on political participation.[19] Mill may see no contradiction between arguing that women are both equal and different.[20]

These three aspects of Mill's analysis – the 'nature' of women, the distinction between ordinary and exceptional women, and the importance of women's role in the family – are fundamentally connected in Mill's position on women. His argument for extending the same rights and opportunities to women in the public and political realm, I suggest, rests on the notion that (although there are exceptions to the norm) most women have different tendencies and capacities, leading them to make different choices which have important social and political implications. A most significant of these is that most women choose domestic over public and political life. Moreover, if we look at the structure of his arguments, the principles of emancipation he sets forth, the speculations he makes about the likely outcome of changes to women's legal and political status, and the different capacities and tendencies he attributes to women, the picture that emerges is one where women are extended equality of opportunity, but are unlikely to achieve equality of outcome.

WOMEN'S 'NATURE': DIFFERENCES

Mill defines as 'natural' that which cannot be attributed to education or environmental conditions. Of the differences between the sexes, he writes: 'Those only could be inferred to be natural which could not possibly be artificial – the residuum, after deducting every characteristic of either sex which can admit of being explained from education or external circumstances.'[21] He emphasizes that it is difficult to discern what is in fact 'natural' to women (or to men). What at first seems natural is quite often the result of conditioning or training. Moreover, the dominating presence of men has distorted women's development:

> What is now called the nature of women is an eminently artificial thing – the result of forced repression in some directions, unnatural stimulation in

others. It may be asserted without scruple, that no other class of dependents have had their character so entirely distorted from its natural proportions by their relation with their masters.[22]

The difficulty of discovering 'woman's nature' is further compounded by our ignorance of the things that form human character, although the study of psychology can help in this respect,[23] and by the fact that women themselves have written little about the subject.[24] By looking at women as they are, Mill contends, we can only conjecture what the natural differences between men and women might be.

In his own conjectures, Mill clearly rejects the notion that women are different from men in the sense of being naturally fit for subjection or that women's subordination in society is justified by a natural inferiority.[25] But he does not necessarily reject the idea that women may have different 'natural' tendencies and capacities, that is, differences which would remain in the face of similar environmental conditions.

Mill often expresses the idea that it is superfluous to have laws forcing women to do what is deemed to be 'natural' to them. If there are real differences between men and women, they need not be legislated. They will emerge on their own: 'If nature has established an ineradicable and insuperable difference in the capacities and qualifications of the two sexes, nature can take care of itself. What nature has decided may safely be left to nature.'[26] But we find him making two contradictory arguments. On the one hand, as Jennifer Ring notes, Mill is proposing an open-ended experiment in which the results may be unknown: let us remove protective and restrictive boundaries on women and see what happens; we cannot tell what differences or similarities in character and station might emerge.[27] The principles of competition in the marketplace, freedom of choice, and equality of opportunity are central to this argument.

Competition in the marketplace and freedom of choice, according to Mill, are the most efficient means of ensuring that positions in society are filled by those who are most capable and that those with exceptional capabilities have the opportunity to exercise them.[28] Mill supports the principle that one be at liberty to use one's faculties in competition with others to achieve a position in society, in place of having it ascribed either by law or by opinion, as peculiarly suited to the modern world. He proposes that it be applied to women: give women equal or the same opportunity as men to compete freely in determining their position in society, a position based on their true natural capabilities rather than on the artificial ones attributed to them by men's prejudices and societal restraints. This requires that any legal restriction or protective measures on women's activities be removed. Mill writes:

> If women have a greater natural inclination for some things than for others, there is no need of laws or social inculcation to make the majority of them do the former in preference to the latter. Whatever women's services are most wanted for, the free play of competition will hold out the strongest inducements to them to undertake. And, as the words imply, they are most wanted for the things for which they are most fit; by the apportionment of which to them, the collective faculties of the two sexes can be applied on the whole with the greatest sum of valuable result.[29]

We can discover and make the best use of women's natural faculties, Mill suggests, by experimenting with open competition.

On the other hand, Mill tries to make the case that the results of this experiment can only be beneficial, implying that we can predict its outcome. The present situation of women is detrimental to society on the whole, he argues. Their legal subjection within the marriage contract contributes to injustice within the family and in society as a whole. Their exclusion from the public realm leads to an inefficient use of human resources. Their debarment from political participation deprives society as a whole of the most efficient use of women's faculties for governing. And their inadequate access to education contributes to the paramountcy of private over public interests. Extending to women the same opportunities and rights as men, Mill speculates, will rectify these damages, making an important contribution to the greater public good, as well as to the individual happiness of women and men.[30]

Moreover, emerging out of this second argument are two related themes: that women's differences, arising out of their natural tendencies, choices, and situation, are likely to remain, and that equality of opportunity is unlikely to result in equality of outcome (I shall return to the question of inequality of outcome). Women's difference from men becomes visible in Mill's discussion of their mental faculties; their failure to have made an original contribution in art, philosophy, or science; their gravitation towards domestic life; and their moral sensibilities.

Mill dismisses the supposition that women's smaller brain is a sign of lesser intelligence.[31] Instead, he suggests that women's mental faculties exhibit a talent for practical reasoning, which is more intuitive and involves more insight to present fact. Women are more talented in applying general laws to individual cases than in coming up with scientific laws or moral principles. In contrast, men's mental faculties incline them to speculative reasoning, which is more amenable to the creation of general principles.[32]

In his attempt to explain why women have not produced a great original work in philosophy, art, or science, Mill draws on their experience of living in a male-dominated culture, their differing mental capabilities, and their confinement to domestic life.[33] Mill speculates that men may have inhibited women's efforts at originality by appropriating their ideas. Most likely due to their differing circumstances, men may also be more willing than women to make the sacrifices necessary for their ambitions to fame and honour.[34]

Women's mental faculties, Mill intimates moreover, are not conducive to creating anew. Women are better at applying thoughts and styles created by others (men): 'Women's thoughts are thus as useful in giving reality to those of thinking men, as men's thoughts in giving width and largeness to those of women.'[35] Perhaps this is why Mill suggests that women need men to judge the quality of their ideas and make up for their inability to think in abstract general principles. The absence of such men, Mill implies, works against success: 'But they [women's ideas] are mostly lost, for want of a husband or friend who has the other knowledge which can enable him to estimate them properly and bring them before the world.'[36]

Furthermore, women's duties in the home along with their social obligations leave them little time for creative endeavours:

> Whoever is in the least capable of estimating the influence on the mind of the entire domestic and social position and the whole habit of a life, must easily recognise in that influence a complete explanation of nearly all the apparent differences between women and men, including the whole of those which imply any inferiority.[37]

On the whole, women's situation in the home is not conducive to the development and exercise of the kind of speculative reasoning required for original work. Mill does not rule out the possibility of women creating a work of the first rank.[38] But his explanation of why they have not done so in the past indicates that their experiential situation – defined by their domestic duties – as well as their mental tendencies would likely prevent them from doing so in the future. This seems even more certain when we consider that Mill assumes that most women are likely to choose domestic over public life.

A most important way in which Mill depicts women as being different from men is by supposing that most women will choose the care of the family as their prime occupation.[39] Opening up public occupations to women would increase the pool of mental powers available for public service, Mill says, but 'It is true that this amount of mental power is not totally lost. Much of it is employed, and would in any case be employed, in domestic management.'[40] Mill expresses a number of related ideas – women are more responsible than men for the care of family; they have a greater predilection than men to choose such a responsibility; and these responsibilities are incompatible with undertaking outside occupations. He writes:

> Like a man when he chooses a profession, so, when a woman marries, it may in general be understood that she makes choice of the management of a household, and the bringing up of a family, as the first call upon her exertions, during as many years of her life as may be required for the purpose; and that she renounces, not all other objects and occupations, but all which are not consistent with the requirements of this.[41]

Mill does not rule out the possibility of a few exceptional women choosing to participate in public activity at the expense of a life of motherhood and marriage. Removing legal barriers to public participation for all women in order to give these few the opportunity to use their unusual capabilities 'for the higher service of humanity' would only benefit society on the whole, he argues.[42] Implicit in the following passage is the idea that the first choice of most women is marriage and motherhood, the 'cares of a family' providing an outlet for their faculties, but that circumstances beyond their control may deny some that option. Engaging in an outside profession or occupation would provide these women with a legitimate alternative:

> There is nothing, after disease, indigence, and guilt, so fatal to the pleasurable enjoyment of life as the want of a worthy outlet for the active faculties. Women who have the cares of a family, and while they have the cares of a family, have this outlet, and it generally suffices for them: but what of the greatly increasing number of women, who have had no opportunity of exercising the vocation which they are mocked by telling them is their proper one?[43]

Outside work would also be suitable for women with grown children whose domestic duties had diminished.[44] But the result of opening competition in the public professions to women and men equally, Mill speculates, 'would be that there would be fewer women than men in such employments; a result certain to happen in any case, if only from the preference always likely to be felt by the majority of women for the one vocation in which there is nobody to compete with them.'[45] Men may choose to have families, but they do not compete with women in choosing the care of the family as their main vocation. Most women, given the option, would choose the role of wife and mother over an outside profession or occupation.

Women's assumed tendency to gravitate towards domestic life fits in with the differing moral sensibilities Mill attributes to them. He does not directly assert that women have a different moral sensibility from men. He strongly suggests, however, that their influence in the moral sphere, both private and public, has been different from men's and has led to the support of different kinds of goals and values. Women have brought men chivalry. In the private realm they have tended to encourage the 'softer' virtues and discourage the 'sterner' ones. In the public realm they have directed their activities in support of philanthropy and in opposition to war. And on the whole women have been more prone to support private (family) interests over public ones.[46]

The results of women's moral influence, according to Mill, have been mixed. He warns that their predilection for the 'softer' virtues is not necessarily a sign of moral superiority.[47] But he applauds chivalry, for which he holds women responsible, as 'one of the most precious monuments of the moral history of our race.'[48] Chivalry induced women to admire and encourage in men warlike pursuits. And it discouraged them from engaging in warlike pursuits themselves. Women, Mill suggests, have been more prone to support peaceful means for settling conflict. In the following passage, he attributes their predilection for peace both to their experience – unlike men, women for the most have not been trained to fight – and to their physical weakness – their lesser physical strength, having made them more the victims than the perpetrators of violence, has also given them a greater aversion to violence:

> First, it [women's moral influence] has been a softening influence. Those who were most liable to be the victims of violence, have naturally tended as much as they could towards limiting its sphere and mitigating its excesses.

Those who were not taught to fight, have naturally inclined in favour of any other mode of settling differences rather than that of fighting.[49]

Women's moral influence in favour of peace has been beneficial. But their engagement in philanthropic activities such as charity work and religious proselytism has had less favourable consequences. Religious proselytism, Mill remarks,

> at home, is but another word for embittering of religious animosities: abroad, it is usually a blind running at an object, without either knowing or heeding the fatal mischiefs – fatal to the religious object itself as well as to all other desirable objects – which may be produced by the means employed.[50]

The outcome of women's charity work has also been somewhat undesirable:

> The great and continually increasing mass of unenlightened and short-sighted benevolence, which, taking the care of people's lives out of their own hands, and relieving them from the disagreeable consequences of their own acts, saps the very foundations of the self-respect, self-help, and self-control which are the essential conditions both of individual prosperity and of social virtue – this waste of resources and of benevolent feelings in doing harm instead of good, is immensely swelled by women's contributions, and stimulated by their influence.[51]

The problem, Mill proposes, is that women's education reinforces their tendency to exercise the kind of reason that is practical and concerned with immediate and everyday matters. Where charity work is concerned, the result is that they look only to the immediate effects of relief – the alleviation of suffering – rather than to its long-term effects – dependence:

> the education given to women – an education of the sentiments rather than of the understanding – and the habit inculcated by their whole life, of looking to immediate effects on persons, and not to remote effects on classes of persons – make them both unable to see, and unwilling to admit, the ultimate evil tendency of any form of charity or philanthropy which commends itself to their sympathetic feelings.[52]

Women's habit of looking to immediate effects, Mill implies, might also stem from their experience of daily domestic life, an experience that is particularly relevant to their bias in favour of private or family interests.[53]

Women's proclivity to favour private over public interests, Mill insinuates, is related to their differing mental faculties as well as their experience in the home. Exercising and acquiring practical reason and knowledge are compatible with a focus on immediate, practical, and private concerns, whereas exercising and acquiring speculative reason and knowledge, more prevalent in men, is compatible with a focus on long-term, general, and public concerns.

If women's moral influence has been somewhat unfavourable, this can be rectified, Mill argues, with a proper education and more exposure to public life. Their mental faculties can be 'improved' by cultivation. Their proclivity for practical reason, their focus on immediate concerns, their bent in favour of the particular and the private can be countered by an education that induces them to consider the larger public good. The result, Mill speculates, is that women's greater predilection for the 'softer' virtues may still predispose them to charity work, for example, but they may have a greater sense of the long-term effects of their actions: 'For charity many of them are by nature admirably fitted; but to practise it usefully, or even without doing mischief, requires the education, the manifold preparation, the knowledge and the thinking powers, of a skilful administrator.'[54]

It seems that women's particular bias in moral matters, including their tendency to favour private interests, can be corrected to some degree but not eliminated. Implicit in Mill's criticism of women's inordinate concern with 'private interests' is the notion that most women conceive of their 'self-interest' as being the interest of their family as a whole – the welfare of husband and children – rather than their interest in themselves as individuals.[55] He does seem to attribute this, in part, to social circumstances that perpetuate women's dependence and which do in fact tie women's well-being to their families' welfare. But he also implies that women have a 'natural' tendency (that is, one that will remain in the face of altered circumstances) to give up their own interest, by subsuming it to the welfare of others, particularly their family.

Granted, the desire to sacrifice one's interests for the welfare of others is not something that Mill attributes to women alone. He applauds it as the highest virtue, a sign that one has cultivated one's nobler faculties.[56] And one way of making men more self-sacrificing, Mill speculates, is to take away their legislated dominance over women:

If women are better than men in anything, it surely is in individual self-sacrifice for those of their own family. But I lay little stress on this, so long as they are universally taught that they are born and created for self-sacrifice. I believe that equality of rights would abate the exaggerated self-abnegation which is the present artificial ideal of feminine character, and that a good woman would not be more self-sacrificing than the best man: but on the other hand, men would be much more unselfish and self-sacrificing than at present, because they would no longer be taught to worship their own will as such a grand thing that it is actually the law for another rational being.[57]

Mill makes several observations in the above passage: at present women sacrifice themselves for their own families more than men; women are taught that they are by nature self-sacrificing; and giving them equality of rights would likely undermine the artificially exaggerated ideal of feminine self-sacrifice. But we also find a tacit suggestion that women's so-called self-sacrifice in the family is not as problematic as men's. Men need to be taught to give up their individual interests for the well-being of the family. But only exceptional men, only the 'best' men, would be as self-sacrificing as a 'good' women, or most women, if the legislated dominance of men over women were removed. For most women, domestic life would continue to be a chosen occupation; the duties within would not require of them enormous self-sacrifice, since their 'natural' tendencies incline them both to choosing such duties and to conceiving of their interest as tied to having and caring for a family.

Mill may advocate getting rid of the excessive element in women's self-abnegation in its present form, but he is not necessarily suggesting that women no longer sacrifice their individual interests for those of their family. The observation that women have done so more than men in the past, the suggestion that most women would continue to choose domestic life once the public and political domain were open to them, and the presumption that domestic responsibilities are such that they would exclude women from holding a public office profession add up to the likelihood that most women, by assuming responsibility for the care of the family, would continue to be more self-sacrificing than men. As a quality that would likely remain under changed environmental conditions, women's disposition to self-sacrifice comes across as a 'natural' one.

Fitting in with the notion of women being more self-sacrificing than men is the idea that they are by predisposition more caring of others than men, especially of their family. This is the tacit message of Helen Taylor and John Stuart Mill's remarks on nursing as something for which women are peculiarly suited by inclination, temperament, and physical constitution:

> But the reasons why women are called upon to do the nursing of the sick lie deep in the constitution of human nature. In the first place, the soft voice, the light step, the delicate hand are physical, as the quick intelligence, and the indomitable perseverance the warm sympathies are moral & intellectual qualifications which specially fit women for the task.[58]

They propose that women be trained in nursing so that some may become professionals, but more important, so that all may become more adept at caring for family members. If women have a natural predilection for caring for others, education in the form of training is fundamental in improving the way they carry it out: 'women cannot even exercise a duty so peculiarly fitted to them and so peculiarly encumbent upon them as nursing, without undergoing a course of training to fit them to exercise it well.'[59]

Given equal or the same conditions, Mill speculates, women might perhaps be no different from men in their character, capacities, and choices. But the culmination of his remarks on their different sensibilities, tendencies, experiences, and circumstances points in the opposite direction. Overall, the picture that emerges from Mill's discussion in these areas is one of women having certain tendencies which maybe curbed and re-channelled but not necessarily eliminated through environmental changes such as improved education. Indeed, conjecturing on possible differences in feeling and inclination between married persons, Mill says: 'It would of course be extreme folly to suppose that these differences of feeling and inclination only exist because women are brought up differently from men, and that there would not be differences of taste under any imaginable circumstances.'[60] The central message of *The Subjection of Women* is that society ought to make environmental changes directed at making women's 'natural' tendencies become assets rather than liabilities.[61]

Since Mill warns that much of what is called nature is often the result of circumstances and situation, it is noteworthy that Mill and Harriet Taylor agree that good laws would allow women (and men) to class themselves not only according to the influence of their 'natural or acquired gifts' but also according to the influence of 'all the other peculiarities of their situation.'⁶² One most important peculiarity of women's situation is that they are attributed greater responsibility for the care of the family and the predisposition to freely choose that responsibility.

FAMILY RELATIONS

The family, according to Mill, has been incorrectly viewed as the arena in which individuals ought to have maximum liberty. But the state is justified in intervening in relations both between parents and children and between husbands and wives, on two grounds. The first is that these relations involve power. The second is that the exercise of power in the family has implications for its ability to carry out two functions of political importance – education and the regulation of reproduction.

Implicit in Mill is a tension between education as 'socialization' and the need for social conformity on the one hand, and education as 'enlightenment' and the need to challenge societal norms on the other. The former, I would argue, is geared mainly to the masses, whom Mill depicts as being selfish but malleable, since they tend to be overly concerned with and easily swayed by public opinion and their social reputation. This desire for conformity can be used to socialize them, to inculcate socially desirable traits in them. A most important quality for Mill is a conviction that one's own interests are tied up with those of others: 'a feeling of unity with all the rest; which "feeling," if perfect, would make him never think of, or desire, any beneficial condition for himself, in the benefits of which they are not included.'⁶³

Education as enlightenment, I would argue, is mainly directed at and equated with those who have the cultivated and superior mental faculties that Mill associates with the 'higher' ranks or classes and the exceptional few.⁶⁴ Mill depicts them as being more public-minded to begin with than the selfish masses or 'lower classes,' more likely to know what is better for the whole, and less concerned with and easily swayed by public opinion. For them education takes the form of enlightenment, encouraging them to challenge societal norms, to be creative and original, and to rise above the mediocre masses. This is the theme pervading Mill's *On Liberty*.⁶⁵ A third kind of education is training individuals to perform particular tasks or occupations in society. All three are central to the well-being of society in Mill's model. The first socializes individuals into believing that their own interests are tied up with those of others, an important means for overcoming the contradiction between private and public interests and advancing the public good. The second, which enables the few to challenge social norms accepted by the masses, is vital to progress since it is these few individuals, for Mill, who are responsible for the advance of civilization. The third function of education – training – is important in increasing the ability of individuals to compete in the marketplace, thereby contributing to a more efficient use of human resources.

When Mill refers to the family as a 'school of moral cultivation,' he is emphasizing its role as a vehicle for 'political socialization' inside the home. The decline of public life, a characteristic of the modern world attributable in part to increasing democratization and the general mediocrity of the masses, makes the family more important than the public realm, Mill contends, as a training ground for citizenship or public virtue. Since individuals first learn to interact with others in the family and carry that lesson over to their relations with others in the wider public sphere, what they practise at home will be easier for them to practise in public. Mill writes: 'Citizenship in free countries, is partly a school of society in equality; but citizenship fills only a small place in modern life, and does not come near the daily habits or inmost sentiments.'[66] The reform of the family is vital, Mill insists, if it is to provide its members, both adults and children, with an education in civic virtue.

Reproduction, according to Mill, also has important social and political ramifications. Population size is related to economic well-being by affecting the labour supply and the number of mouths to feed.[67] Unlike Locke, Mill associates progress and economic well-being with population decrease. Moreover, Mill addresses the question, in part, as a problem of supply and demand, governed by marketplace considerations. In supplying society with children, parents need to take into account the demand for their 'product.' The decision to have a child, Mill implies, ought to be based on a calculation of one's means in providing for the child and a consideration of the economic impact of adding another body to the labour pool:

> The fact itself, of causing the existence of a human being, is one of the most responsible actions in the range of human life. To undertake this responsibility – to bestow a life which may be either a curse or a blessing – unless the being on whom it is to be bestowed will have at least the ordinary chances of a desirable existence, is a crime against that being. And in a country either over-peopled, or threatened with being so, to produce children, beyond a very small number, with the effect of reducing the reward

of labour by their competition, is a serious offence against all who live by the remuneration of their labour.[68]

But Mill also suggests that individuals cannot be entrusted to follow the laws of supply and demand in this matter, that reproduction is too important to be left to individual calculations and the ordering principles of the marketplace. Moreover, Mill seems to say, parents cannot be relied on to move beyond selfish considerations to more public ones – the impact of population increase on the well-being of society on the whole. State encroachment on individual liberties for the purpose of preventing births is therefore warranted. Mill favours such indirect means of controlling populations as preventing marriages between adults who do not have the means to care for future children.[69] On the whole, Mill's message is contradictory. He implies that the decision to have a child is a private one, governed by individual choice and the workings of the marketplace. At the same time, however, he indicates that the production of a human being has such important effects on the well-being of others that it cannot be left to the vagaries of the marketplace and that we must consider it to be not a private but a public matter justifiably subject to state regulation.

Intervening in relations between husband and wife is warranted, according to Mill, because these relations involve power, at present power that is unjust. Men's legislated authority over women in the marital relationship engenders in men an inflated perception of their worth which tends to make them more selfish: 'All the selfish propensities, the self-worship, the unjust self-preference, which exist among mankind, have their source and root in, and derive their principal nourishment from, the present constitution of the relation between men and women.'[70] It also furthers in men the perception that they deserve such power and authority on the basis of ascription or birth. This notion, Mill contends, is detrimental to and incompatible with modern notions of justice, according to which 'conduct, and conduct alone, entitles to respect: that not what men are, but what they do, constitutes their claim to deference; that, above all, merit, and not birth, is the only rightful claim to power and authority.'[71]

Mill argues in favour of removing the wife's legal subordination and husband's unjust power by giving women the same rights as men in both the private and public sphere:

> The almost despotic power of husbands over wives needs not be enlarged

upon here, because nothing more is needed for the complete removal of the evil, than that wives should have the same rights, and should receive the protection of law in the same manner, as all other persons; and because, on this subject, the defenders of established injustice do not avail themselves of the plea of liberty, but stand forth openly as the champions of power.'[72]

Making men and women more equal before the law will encourage greater justice in the family, Mill predicts.[73] It is likely to diminish men's perception of their superiority, making them less selfish and less convinced that they deserve authority by birth rather than by merit. And, most important, it can offer an example to children of relations based on equality (of opportunity) rather than on legislated domination and inferiority, thereby socializing them to accept the value of such virtues:

> What is needed is, that it should be a school of sympathy in equality, of living together in love, without power on one side or obedience on the other. This it ought to be between the parents. It would then be an exercise of those virtues which each requires to fit them for all other association, and a model to the children of the feelings and conduct which their temporary training by means of obedience is designed to render habitual, and therefore natural, to them. The moral training of mankind will never be adapted to the conditions of the life for which all other human progress is a preparation, until they practise in the family the same moral rule which is adapted to the normal constitution of human society.[74]

If Mill supports freeing women and men from restrictions (legal ones) in their adult relations with one another – removing the barriers that predetermine the husband's dominion over the wife, for example – he favours placing restrictions on their freedom when it comes to their capacity as parents – preventing them from marrying if they do not have the means to care for the children, for example.

Parents' most important obligation, Mill emphasizes, is to ensure that their children are educated, both in the sense of being 'socialized' to take their place in the social and political order and in the sense of being 'trained' to develop their capacities in preparation for their entry to the work world: 'Hardly any one indeed will deny that it is one of the most sacred duties of the parents (or, as law and usage now stand, the father), after summoning a human being into the world, to give to that being an education fitting him to perform his part well in life towards others and towards himself.'[75] Mill grants that outside institutions also play an important role in what we might call 'political socialization.'[76] He warns of the dangers of state indoctrination if the state were allowed to have a monopoly on educational institutions. But he favors the state requiring parents, out of their own means, to provide their children with a formal education outside the home, in addition to socializing them within the family:

> It still remains unrecognised, that to bring a child into existence without a fair prospect of being able, not only to provide food for its body, but instruction and training for its mind, is a moral crime, both against the unfortunate offspring and against society; and that if the parent does not fulfil this obligation, the State ought to see it fulfilled, at the charge, as far as possible, of the parent.[77]

Mill goes further, considering that parents who do not have the means to provide for their children with such an education might be prevented from marrying. Of laws forbidding such marriages, Mill says: 'Such laws are interferences of the "State" to prohibit a mischievous act – an act injurious to others, which ought to be a subject of reprobation, and social stigma, even when it is not deemed expedient to superadd legal punishment.'[78] Having and caring for children, educating them in particular, are matters of such social and political consequence, Mill is saying, that it is legitimate to impede the freedom of adults if such care is not forthcoming. Parent-child relations, it seems, are more important than relations between men and women *per se*, important enough to justify something that Mill is in principle opposed to – restricting the liberty of association or 'combination' of adults.[79]

Mill also supports state intervention in parent-child relations on the grounds that they entail the exercise of power. Any power parents may have over their children in the form of rights over their persons or conduct is legitimate only as a means to fulfilling their obligation to care for their children or as a reward for caring for them well.[80] Parental power over children cannot be removed – 'It [the family] will always be a school of obedience for the children, of command for the parents'[81] – but the state ought to see to it that it is not abused.[82]

Fathers in particular, however, Mill suggests, are likely to believe that they have the power to do as they will with their children (a notion that the laws tend to reinforce) and to resist such intervention:

> It is in the case of children, that misapplied notions of liberty are a real

obstacle to the fulfilment by the State of its duties. One would almost think that a man's children were supposed to be literally, and not metaphorically, a part of himself, so jealous is opinion of the smallest interference of law with his absolute and exclusive control over them.[83]

Fathers, especially in the lower ranks, according to Mill, are more likely to abuse their power over their children (and wives) in a most physical and brutal manner. This has a particularly debilitating effect on the family as a vehicle for cultivating moral virtues. Children who are witnesses to 'the tyranny of physical force in its coarsest manifestations' grow up to be 'incapable in their turn of governing their children by any other means than blows.'[84] Mill calls for harsh penalties on anyone, 'a man or a woman,' found mistreating children. But he also indicates that along with children, women are most often the victims of such violent abuse perpetrated by men, rather than the perpetrators themselves.[85]

The theme of Mill's observations on parent-child relations is that when it comes to fathers, especially in the lower classes, the important thing is to prevent them from abusing their children and wives, through laws that severely punish offenders. When it comes to mothers, the important thing is to acknowledge their greater contribution and predisposition to the care of the children, through laws ceding them greater rights over the children. Fitting in with the differing moral sensibilities he attributes to women are assumptions about women being more suited to the moral and physical care of children. Being predisposed to the 'softer virtues,' women are the most natural caretakers of the children and therefore ought to have greater rights over them than fathers, Mill implies.[86] He remarks that laws which fail to presume that the mother has greater rights over the child than anyone else are 'an outrage on the most universally recognized and strongest tie of nature.'[87] The difference between mothers and fathers, it seems, is that women are the more 'natural' caretakers of children and fathers the ones more likely to abuse their power over them.

Mill not only supports greater rights over children for mothers and criticizes laws which grant them to the father, he also criticizes laws that permit husbands to claim sexual access to their wives' persons or bodies.[88] Moreover, he opposes the Contagious Diseases Act, which would allow women suspected of prostitution to be apprehended by the police, physically examined for signs of venereal disease, and possibly committed for medical treatment, on the grounds that it undermines a woman's bodily integrity, her rights over her own person and her security of personal liberty.⁸⁹ Furthermore, he favours laws expanding women's rights to own property and dispose of it as they wish, especially when they marry.⁹⁰ And he supports women's rights over their own labour power when he argues against protective legislation limiting their work hours.⁹¹ In other words, Mill comes out strongly in favour of increased property rights for women over their own persons, labour power, goods, earnings, and children. In addition, Mill advocates giving women more choice in consenting to or ending marriage contracts, greater access to education, and the right to engage in any public occupation or aspect of political life.

In Hobbes' and Locke's framework, I have argued, since women are attributed the same capacities as men (for rational self-interest, for example), extending to them equal political rights, especially property rights in their own person and over their reproductive labour power, seems problematic. It comes across as potentially undermining the political ends of the family. In Mill's framework, however, assumptions about women's difference (for one, Mill does not depict women as being rationally self-interested to the same degree as men) make the extension of such rights, as well as access to the educational, the public, and the political sphere, appear much less threatening. Indeed, in Mill's design, they seem to improve the family's proficiency in fulfilling its political ends – educating its members and regulating reproduction. For example, an improved education, Mill hints, would allow women to make better use of their moral sensibilities and mental faculties in educating their children. Mill supports women being elected to school boards, noting that the 'principal domestic teachers [women] have more experience, and have acquired more practical ability in the teaching, at least of children.'⁹² Rather than being suited to instructing in particular branches of knowledge, however, which could be done more efficiently by a hired teacher, women's peculiar abilities, Mill seems to say, are most suited to providing moral training:

> But *this* most precious, and most indispensable part of education, does not take up *tim*; it is not a business, an occupation; a mother does not accomplish it by sitting down with her child for one or two or three hours to a task. She effects it by *being* with the child; by making it happy, and therefore at peace with all things; by checking bad habits in the commencement; and by loving the child, and by making the child love her.⁹³

Mill also associates greater access to education and public and political life for women with population decline. Such opportunites might draw some away from focusing exclusively on child-bearing and rearing.[94] And, presumably, a likely consequence of their greater participation in public life would be a greater concern with the public interest. Encouraged to consider the impact of population increase on the general welfare, more women might conclude that the socially responsible thing to do was to have fewer children. If more women did choose not to marry and have any children at all as a consequence of social and political reforms, this would only contribute to something that Mill finds beneficial to the public – limited population growth.

The enjoyment of rights and opportunities for women is depicted as enhancing rather than undermining or clashing with their political duties or contribution to the public good as carried out either in the family or in the larger political arena. Women's differences, as Mill describes them, suggest that most would continue to choose marriage and motherhood as an outlet for their faculties, to be more caring than men and to conceive of their 'self-interest' as the interest of their family as a whole. Added to that, women's different moral sensibilities, turned outwardly into public life, would encourage them to support moral reforms aimed at the plight of others.

If in Hobbes' and Locke's design, suppositions about women's sameness to men cause potential problems in extending to them the same political rights as men, in Mill assumptions about their difference from men also cause some difficulties, but of a different sort. Women are easily granted equality of opportunity, that is the same opportunity as men to exercise equal political and property rights that the law might grant them in Mill's design. But if we consider Mill's references to what distinguishes women from men and his speculations on the likely consequences of freeing women from restrictions, the results of equal opportunity in Mill's design are likely to be inequality of outcome for women, both in the family and in the larger public and political sphere. For instance, Mill proposes giving husband and wife the same or equal opportunity to work out for themselves who has authority in the marital relationship. Since he is likely to be of greater age, income, and mental ability, however, the outcome in most cases would favour the husband, Mill speculates:

> The mere fact that he is usually the eldest, will in most cases give the preponderance to the man; at least until they both attain a time of life at which the difference in their years is of no importance. There will naturally also be

a more potential voice on the side, whichever it is, that brings them means of support. Inequality from this source does not depend on the law of marriage, but on the general conditions of human society, as now constituted. The influence of mental superiority, either general or special, and of superior decision of character, will necessarily tell for much.[95]

According to Mill's principle of equality of opportunity, the distribution of authority in the marital relationship ought to be determined not by legal restrictions which impose artificial constraints and powers on women and men but on the 'natural' exigencies, of individual capacities, tendencies and situations. But because, according to Mill's description, the situation, experiences, and faculties of most ordinary men and women are different, the result is likely to be inequality of outcome, favouring men over women. A similar difficulty emerges in the political realm.

WOMEN AND THE POLITICAL REALM

Mill advocates that women be given the same political rights as men, including the right to vote and hold office. He refutes the idea that women's difference is a sign of a 'natural inferiority' making them incapable of political participation in such activities as voting, running for office, and assuming positions of leadership. In *Considerations on Representative Government* he argues that women have proved themselves capable of having independent thoughts, business interests, and governing abilities as queens, all of which indicate they are capable of voting as well.[96] When he claims that 'I have taken no account of difference of sex,' considering it to be as 'entirely irrelevant to political rights, as difference in height, or in the colour of the hair,'[97] he is not necessarily refuting the idea that there are differences between men and women. He is insisting that differences should not count as a reason for disqualifying women from voting, since, like other physical criteria such as height or hair colour, they are not a sign of incapacity. In fact, he suggests that women's different tendencies might make them particularly suited for participation in politics. For instance, that a 'nervous sensibility' is found more often in women than in men, Mill remarks, is no reason for disqualifying women from politics.[98] Signalling a temperament which has passion, such a sensibility is well suited to those who want to sway public opinion.

Moreover, Mill reasons, women's adeptness and experience in household management may be valuable and even necessary to government: 'If home is a woman's natural sphere (and I am not at all called upon to contradict the assertion) those departments of politics which need the faculties that can only be acquired at home, are a woman's natural sphere too.'[99] Their talent in regulating household expenditures makes them especially competent in controlling government expenditures: 'there are important matters of public administration to which few men are equally competent with such women; among others, the detailed control of expenditure.'[100] Increasingly, Mill says, politics is less exclusively a matter of coming up with grand designs or schemes – suited to men's mental faculties – than it is a matter of carrying plans out in detail – suited to women's mental faculties.[101] Women's more practical bent and experience in dealing with everyday matters in the domestic realm may give them an advantage when it comes to the political domain, a large part of which entails the administration of everyday matters. Women may even have a 'natural capacity for government,' Mill considers, when he describes the political competence exhibited by Asian princesses formerly excluded from all public contact.[102]

It is ironic, Mill remarks, that women are not barred from doing what they have never distinguished themselves in – art and philosophy – yet they are barred from doing what they have consistently shown they can excel in – politics.[103] Politics, it seems, does not require abstract thought or the exercise of speculative reason, requirements for making an original contribution to art and philosophy. Underlying Mill's remarks is the notion that women can now be included in the political sphere because their differences are not a liability in a society where the political domain has fallen from its pedestal. Women's capabilities in the domestic realm may make them adept at politics because the political domain itself has become an extension of the domestic one. No longer is politics an arena for the exercise of intellect and wisdom and originality. Increasing democratization, which Mill thinks is inevitable, has made it an arena dominated by the 'mediocre masses.' Women's differing mental faculties, their tendency to exercise practical rather than speculative reason, and their experiences in the domestic realm may make it unlikely that they will produce great works of art or philosophy but it may make them particularly suited for the changed nature of politics.

Women's greater participation in domestic life and their differing moral and mental faculties may also account for the divergent interests Mill attributes to them. Women and men of the same class are likely to have similar political opinions, Mill notes, but not necessarily the same interests:

> The majority of the women of any class are not likely to differ in political opinion from the majority of men of the same class, unless the question be one in which the interests of women, as such, are in some way involved; and if they are so, women require the suffrage, as their guarantee of just and equal consideration.[104]

To ensure that women's interests are represented, interests which are different from and even incompatible with men's interests, women need such political rights as the right to vote. They might use their political rights to protect their property rights over their persons and children, to protect themselves from domestic as well as governmental abuses of authority, and to change laws that favour men – such as regulations restricting women's entry to public professions or rulings that impose few penalties on men who beat their wives.

Implicit in Mill's reasoning on representating women's interests are two kinds of arguments. The first is that male legislators deliberately ignore women's concerns because they have no political incentive to listen to them. Giving women the vote can rectify this problem, we can surmise, making it advantageous for male or female representatives to address women's concerns: 'the representation of women's point of view whether through male or female representatives is part of what would be gained by admitting women to the suffrage.'[105] The second kind of problem Mill alludes to would be more difficult to address simply by giving women the vote. Male legislators, he hints, may unintentionally neglect women's interests, finding them difficult to understand or apprehend. They may pass legislation favouring their own (male) interest 'simply because their [women's] interest is not so near to the feelings of the ruling half as the ruling half's own interest.'[106] This problem points to the need for a more direct form of representation. Male legislators, it implies, cannot represent women's interests as well as women themselves; because they are women, female legislators would be better able to apprehend, understand, and therefore represent women's differential interests and concerns.[107]

Mill supports the idea that women's distinctive interests and concerns are legitimate and can best be represented by women holding office. Yet, he speculates that only exceptional women would gravitate towards political office, in contrast to his suggestion that women's distinctive capacities and experiences make them on the whole suitable for politics. Barriers preventing women from assuming positions of political responsibility such as a seat in Parliament or in Cabinet ought to be removed. But the result, Mill conjectures, would be fewer women than men actually occupying such positions. Women who had families would be unlikely to undertake office. Since most women, we have been told, are likely to choose marriage and family, the majority of women would be eliminated as potential candidates. Only those older women whose domestic duties had been fulfilled, those few women who would choose public life over domestic life, or those who had the means to have their domestic duties undertaken by paid help (I will return to this group) would likely take advantage of the opportunity:

> if such trusts [membership in Cabinet or Parliament] were confided to women, it would be to such as having no special vocation for married life, or preferring another employment of their faculties (as many women even now prefer to marriage some of the few honourable occupations within their reach), have spent the best years of their youth in attempting to qualify themselves for the pursuits in which they desire to engage; or still more frequently perhaps, widows or wives of forty or fifty, by whom the knowledge of life and faculty of government which they have acquired in their families, could by the aid of appropriate studies be made available on a less contracted scale.[108]

Most women, it seems, would not take advantage of the opportunity to participate in higher levels of political activity. Giving all women the opportunity to do so, however, according to Mill, would benefit society and promote 'good government' by making available to it the unique capabilities of those exceptional women who may have a special talent for public office: 'As long therefore as it is acknowledged that even a few women may be fit for these duties [holding public office], the laws which shut the door on those exceptions cannot be justified by any opinion which can be held respecting the capacities of women in general.'[109] It may be particularly important to recruit exceptional women to politics, since unexceptional men, Mill worries, are increasingly gaining power in representative institutions.

Women's situation as it is depicted here is beset by contradiction and paradox. Their activity and experience in the domestic realm may make them particularly suited to participating in politics and may lead them to have interests that require political representation. At the same time, their domestic responsibilities also prevent them from engaging in political life at a meaningful level. Voting, Mill emphasizes, is compatible with women carrying out their domestic responsibilities as wives and mothers.[110] But holding office is not, it seems. Paradoxically, women's difference makes it important that they have direct representation in legislative assemblies but their differences also seem to exclude most from engaging in politics at this level.

The differences between men and women in Mill's framework do not suggest that women are inferior to men in the sense that they are incapable of exercising suffrage or even holding office. But they do suggest that equality of opportunity in the exercise of political rights and duties leads to inequality of outcome. Mill may of course be unconcerned with securing equality of outcome for anyone. This is evident in the example he uses to illustrate what he means by an individual's 'rights.'[111] Society ought to defend individual rights to earn what they can in 'fair professional competition' but not their rights to earn a certain sum.[112] Mill supports the former – equality of opportunity – while acknowledging that it does not necessarily lead to the latter – equality of outcome. For women, inequality of outcome takes a particular form. They are asked to settle for less power but to undertake a greater share of political duties. Moreover, the position of working-class women is more contradictory than that of upper-class women.

If having political power is being able to advance one's interests in the political sphere, despite obstacles posed by the will of others, and ultimately being able to determine the political agenda itself, then, according to Mill's assumptions and speculations, women are likely to end up with less political power than men. First, they are likely to have less of the political power that accrues from holding leadership positions, since only the exceptional few, it appears, would be likely to hold office. Second, if, as Mill recommends, their eligibility for voting were to be determined by the same criteria as men's, their vote would have less impact on the political agenda. Mill's criteria exclude those who are illiterate, those who do not pay taxes, and those who are recipients of parish relief.[113] Furthermore, he proposes that plural votes be given to those who have greater mental ability, using in the absence of standardized tests their 'occupation' in society as a criterion for this ability.[114] Since, according to Mill's conjectures, women are less likely to work outside the home (and pay taxes) or have public occupations, even as a result of reforms directed at opening up public life to them, more women than men would likely be excluded from voting and fewer women than men would likely have plural votes. As a result women would be less able to influence the political agenda.

Third, we can extrapolate from Mill's speculations on whether women would bring something unique and original to the field of literature. The kind of creative power that is responsible for great achievements in both literature and politics is similar, Mill indicates.[115] At the same time, increasing democratization has made the political arena less and less a realm in which speculative or creative powers are exercised. He speculates that women might contribute something distinctive in literature.[116] In exceptional women, what distinguishes them from men might eventually be eradicated so that women of genius, like men of genius, would be highly individualistic.[117] But since he supposes that women on the whole would be likely to first accept and measure themselves by the male tradition, it seems unlikely that their contribution would be original in the sense of redefining literature itself.[118] Similarly, in the political realm, Mill's speculations and assumptions point to women bringing their differences to bear on politics – placing certain 'women's issues' on the political agenda – but not necessarily redefining the agenda itself, or redefining what constitutes the political.

The situation of working-class women in Mill's framework is even more ambiguous and fraught with contradiction than that of women as a whole. If, as Mill indicates, only exceptional women would be likely to take advantage of increased opportunities for public and political life, these exceptional individuals, it seems, would for the most part be women of means. As a general rule, Mill proposes, a woman who marries (and most would choose to marry) chooses to devote herself to family and household first. And working outside the home is incompatible with this first priority and responsibility. However, there ought to be some latitude for exceptions, provided they ensure that their domestic duties are fulfilled:

> there ought to be nothing to prevent faculties exceptionally adapted to any other pursuit, from obeying their vocation notwithstanding marriage: due provision being made for supplying otherwise any falling-short which might become inevitable, in her full performance of the ordinary functions of mistress of a family.[119]

Presumably, one could ensure that one's domestic duties were fulfilled by hiring paid help, an option available only to women of some means or property.

For women who live in families without property, Mill thinks it best they remain at home: 'When the support of the family depends, not on property, but on earnings, the common arrangement, by which the man earns the income and the wife superintends the domestic expenditure, seems to me in general the most suitable division of labour between the two persons.'[120] His reasoning is that the household duties (including the care and education of children) of women who have too few means to hire domestic help are likely to be left undone:

> If she undertakes any additional portion, it seldom relieves her from this [care of children and household], but only prevents her from performing it properly. The care which she is herself disabled from taking of the children and the household, nobody else takes; those of the children who do not die, grow up as they best can, and the management of the household is likely to be so bad, as even in point of economy to be a great drawback from the value of the wife's earnings.[121]

In working-class families where the husband blatantly abuses his power over his wife, working outside the home might appear to benefit the wife – increasing her value in the husband's eyes. More likely, however, Mill warns, it can be used as an excuse for the husband 'still farther to abuse his power, by forcing her to work, and leaving the support of the family to her exertions, while he spends most his time in drinking and idleness.'[122]

Those who already have some property or come from wealthy families would be the main beneficiaries of laws expanding women's property rights, Mill admits.[123] Those who have no property to begin with would presumably benefit from Mill's proposed reforms granting women the freedom or 'right' to earn their living: 'The *power* of earning is essential to the dignity of a woman, if she has not independent property.'[124] Yet, once again, Mill indicates that it is unlikely and undesirable that they actually make use of it:

> It does not follow that a woman should *actually* support herself because she should be *capable* of doing so: in the natural course of events she will *not*. It is not desirable to burthen the labour market with a double number of competitors. In a healthy state of things, the husband would be able by his single exertions to earn all that is necessary for both; and there would be no need that the wife should take part in the mere providing of what is required to *support* life: it will be for the happiness of both that her occupa-

tion should rather be to adorn and beautify it. Except in the class of actual day-labourers, that will be her natural task, if task it can be called which will in so great a measure, be accomplished rather by *being* than by *doing*.[125]

The right to the power of earning, we can surmise, would be used only by working-class women whose marriages had broken up or who were as yet unmarried.[126]

Upper-class women may have the advantage because they can obtain paid help, but this does not absolve them from ensuring that their domestic duties are carried out appropriately, if not by themselves then by others. Hired staff cannot be entrusted to perform their task efficiently and honestly without supervision, Mill implies when he explains why domestic obligations leave women little time for accomplishment in the arts.[127] Moreover, the duties expected of women may expand with their station, women of greater property and rank having greater social obligations:

> If a woman is of a rank and circumstances which relieve her in a measure from these cares [superintendence of a household], she has still devolving on her the management for the whole family of its intercourse with others – of what is called society, and the less the call made on her by the former duty, the greater is always the development of the latter.[128]

What upper- and lower- (working-) class women share, we can surmise from Mill's descriptions and recommendations, is *responsibility* for the care of the children and household. It is the 'one vocation in which there is nobody to compete with them.'[129] Mill does not conceive of men taking on domestic duties. When women fail to carry them out themselves or hire others (women) to take over, they are left undone, Mill assumes.

The potential impact of Mill's proposals on reforms to family, public life, and education, considered in light of his depiction of the situation of working- and upper-class women, would be to exacerbate the contradictory situation of women of the 'lower ranks.' If we take seriously the suggestion that the cost of educating children be borne by the parents, women of the labouring poor would have less access to education. Yet an improved education coupled with participation in public and political life, according to Mill, is the means whereby women can counter their bent in favour of children and family and become more inclined to have fewer children.

And when it comes to reproduction, the higher classes, Mill implies, can be relied on to regulate themselves. More socially minded to begin with, they are more inclined to consider the interests of the community as a whole and to refrain from having children for the sake of restricting population growth. For the lower classes, however, not as concerned with the greater good of the community and prone to have more children, direct state intervention is called for. This is the idea underlying Mill's support for state laws which would prevent those adults from marrying who out of their own means could not afford to care for and educate future children. Such laws would have a greater impact on those of fewer means – the working poor. Working-class women, it seems, are more subject to state impingement on their liberty as parents. This theme also emerges in Mill's remarks on parental rights over children. These rights ought to go to the mother over the father, he advises, but to the state over either where parental obligations go unfulfilled. The latter is most often the case in poorer families, Mill assumes:

> If any limitation of her exclusive parental control could be allowable, it is not by or for the man, but by that which we should be glad to see exercised, not only in cases of this kind [where the father abused both the wife and children], but in many others – the tutelary intervention of a public authority, to see that the children of the miserable are not brought up to be miserable, or a source of misery to others.[130]

Furthermore, it is in the 'lower' or 'labouring' classes, in general more brutish and prone to violence, according to Mill, that men are more likely to abuse their power over women.[131] Men of the upper ranks, more inclined to show affection and concern towards others, may tyrannize over their wives in a more subtle and indirect way. But it is in the lower ranks that one finds the most blatant and physical abuse of women.[132]

Overall, the picture that emerges in Mill's framework is one where upper-class women, wealthier and more educated, are more able and more likely to counter their bent in favour of children and willingly have fewer of them. They are freer to choose public life, not because they are freer from responsibility for the domestic realm but because they have the means to hire household help. But it is less necessary for them to work outside the home. The option of choosing to stay home and make the having and care of children a 'rational' activity or project is more open to them. Working-class women, in contrast, with less education to balance their natural predilections, are likely to have more children. Without the means to pay for domestic help, they are less able to take advantage of opportunities in the public and political world. Yet their very lack of means also makes it more necessary for them to work outside the home to supplement their family income. The option of staying home and having and caring for their children as a freely chosen project is less open to them.

In addition, it is in the 'lower ranks' that the interests of women are most blatantly ignored – where they are most often the victims of domestic violence without recourse to protection from the law: 'At present it is very well known that women, in the lower ranks of life, do not expect justice from a bench or a jury of the male sex. They feel the most complete assurance that to the utmost limits of common decency, and often beyond, a tribunal of men will sympathize and take part with the man.'[133] Women can expect little sympathy from male jurors, Harriet Taylor and Mill note: 'Is it because juries are composed of husbands in a low rank of life, that men who kill their wives almost invariably escape – wives who kill their husbands, never?'[134] Working-class women, it appears, have even a greater need than upper-class women to have individuals in positions of political power who can sympathize with their plight and attend to their concerns. Yet, poorer women of the labouring classes would be even less likely than women on the whole (compared to men) either to vote or to hold political office, according to Mill's criteria and recommendations. We might surmise that women of the working class would be better represented by women of means than by men either of the upper or lower classes, an assumption that is buttressed by the idea that women are more caring and compassionate of the plight of the poor than men of either class.

This brings me to the other form inequality of outcome takes in Mill's framework. Women end up with less political power or less influence in furthering their own interests as individuals, but they are asked to undertake a greater share of political duties or greater responsibility for the care of others than men. In support of the principle that individuals are not obligated to society for anything that concerns only themselves, Mill notes that this does not exempt them from fulfilling certain duties which benefit others, such as intervening to save another's life, giving evidence in court, or contributing to the common defence of society.[135] The last example is especially worthy of consideration when it comes to women. Does Mill conceive of them as defending the Commonwealth? In *The Subjection of Women* he refers to Spartan women 'being trained to bodily exercises in the same manner with men,' and to women of the privileged classes in feudal ages being of 'manly character, inferior in nothing but bodily strength to their husbands and fathers.'[136] These comments are made in the context of an observation that Englishmen 'feel it unnatural that women should be soldiers or members of Parliament.'[137] Mill is not advocating that women be soldiers, however. He is proposing that they be free to become members of Parliament, at the same time as he assumes that only a few would take advantage of the opportunity.

Mill alludes to women being physically weaker than men. And he implicitly presents this difference as having social and political implications. First, it seems to make it easier for husbands to abuse the power the law gives them over their wives in a most brutal physical manner. Second, it is responsible in part for women's propensity to support peace and oppose war. But women's physical weakness is not a liability in politics, Mill wants to say, largely because 'the law of the strongest seems to be entirely abandoned as the regulating principle of the world's affairs.'[138] As modern representative democracies demonstrate, progress has entailed moving away from the importance of physical strength.[139] Women's lesser ability and desire for war does not make them ineligible for citizenship or hinder them from performing its duties. If their physical weakness coupled with their disposition to the softer virtues exempts women from soldiering, it also predisposes them to caring for others. In Mill's design, citizenship for women entails not the duty to defend the Commonwealth, but the duty to care for the welfare of others, increasingly outside of as well as inside of the family.

In the family, they are expected to undertake the greatest share of the domestic responsibilities which contribute to the advancement of the political ends of the family. Moreover, in exercising their political rights, it is expected that women both continue to represent the interests of their family, but directly rather than indirectly through their husbands, and expand their concern for others to the greater political arena. Having the vote, Mill supposes, would make it unnecessary for women to rely on their 'feminine attractiveness' to influence their husbands.[140] And being no longer susceptible to the undue influence of their wives, husbands would be freer to consider the public interest. Furthermore, women would be encouraged to pay attention to the public interest by being forced to discuss public matters in preparation for voting. This would likely engender a concern for the greater good in the family as whole. It is not that women will now ignore the interests of their family in favour of their own, Mill comes close to saying, but that they will encourage all family members, husband and children, to consider the public interest:

> It is only by being herself encouraged to form an opinion, and obtain an intelligent comprehension of the reasons which ought to prevail with the conscience against the temptations of personal or family interest, that she can ever cease to act as a disturbing force on the political conscience of the man. Her indirect agency can only be prevented from being politically mischievous, by being exchanged for direct.[141]

Changing women's situation by opening up education and public and political life for them, Mill insists, would benefit women themselves, making them freer and happier. It would also benefit men by making their wives better companions. But most significant, Mill claims, it would benefit society on the whole.[142] In particular, giving women the right to represent their interests, Mill assures us, will not undermine their responsibilities to consider the good of others or their 'political duties.' How so? First Mill tries to reconcile in principle the exercise of political rights such as the vote, directed at advancing one's own interests, with the carrying out of political duties, directed at advancing the welfare of others or the public good. He distinguishes between property and political rights in this respect. Whereas one may rightfully consider selfish interests alone in wielding the former, one ought to consider one's duty to advancing the public good in wielding the latter.[143] This would apply to both men and women, we can assume.

But in emphasizing women's different moral sensibility Mill also suggests that women are more likely than men to wield their rights out of consideration for the welfare of others. Although he seems to say here that the differences women would bring to politics are temporary – 'And I am now speaking, not of women as they might be – not as some improved mode of education would make them – but of women as they now are, and of the capacities which they have already displayed'[144] – in other places he strongly suggests that women would continue to bring different sensibilities and concerns to politics in the face of changed circumstances such as an improved education.

If their past education, in the form of socialization, has contributed to their enslavement – convincing women that they are by nature fit to be men's slaves or that their central duty is to be attractive to men – improved access to education in the form of enlightenment, Mill notes, is already inducing women to challenge these social norms and contributing to their liberation.¹⁴⁵ But it is unlikely to undermine the carrying out of what turn out to be 'political' duties or work against the greater good of society. In Mill's scheme, educating women in the sense of enlightening them does not come across as potentially subversive of the social and political order or the political ends of the family. For one, he emphasizes that education is also what we might call 'socialization.' In particular he stresses the importance of instilling in individuals the idea that they ought to set aside an exclusive concern with their own interests in favour of taking into account the interests of others and the public good. Moreover, becoming more 'enlightened,' it seems, is unlikely to eradicate women's tendency to gravitate towards domestic life, to consider the interests of their family, and to bring their 'softer' moral sensibilities to politics.

The idea that women will continue to bring a more sympathetic influence to bear on politics surfaces consistently in Mill's speculations. He supposes that the effect of opening up political life to women 'would be to infuse into the legislature a stronger determination to grapple with the great physical and moral evils of society.'¹⁴⁶ Women will not become 'hardened' by politics, we are assured by Helen Taylor and Mill (I would substitute the word 'self-interested'); they are more likely than not to use their expanded rights in a most kind and generous way, in support of 'philanthropic legislation,' for example.¹⁴⁷ Overall, they would likely support and initiate legislation concerned with peace, the poor, family matters, social improvement, and moral reform. The underlying message is that it is not dangerous or potentially subversive to give women political rights to further their own interests, since it will not induce them to give up their (political) duties directed at the care of others. Indeed it will only expand them.

There is some merit to the argument that Mill's emphasis on women's differences, on their softer moral sensibilities and on their continuing to bring to government a concern with the welfare of others, was prompted by the anticipation that his proposals would be ill received. Recognizing that he was speaking and writing for an audience which might be hostile to what he was endorsing – equality of opportunity for women in the public and political realm – Mill may have tailored his arguments to their prejudices.¹⁴⁸ He explains in the opening of *The Subjection of Women*: 'In every respect the burthen is hard on those who attack an almost universal opinion ... If they do exhort a hearing, they are subjected to a set of logical requirements totally different from those exacted from other people.'¹⁴⁹ Nadia Urbinati warns against reading *The*

Subjection of Women as a theoretical document. It is a political treatise, she argues, addressed to a particular place and time in which Mill prudently 'wanted to assure his Victorian readers that even without formal obligation, women would choose to raise a family.'[150] Jennifer Ring agrees that Mill wanted to convince men in particular that opening up public and political life to women would benefit all. But she adds that Mill was a man of reason who wanted his arguments to convince and to ring true on rational as well as strategic grounds.[151]

Whether Mill truly believes that women are more caring of others than men or merely suggests that they are, as a strategic device aimed at making his proposals appear less threatening or more acceptable, the dynamic is similar. If Mill felt it was strategic to say that, given equal rights, women would continue to be more caring of others than men, this reinforces what we find in Hobbes and Locke – assumptions that women are as rationally self-interested as men make the extension of equal political rights come across as threatening to the political ends of the community. In Hobbes' and Locke's model, women get caught between rights and duties and the splitting of reason into rational self-interest and duty towards others. In Mill we find that this tension is addressed by proposing that women have a different sensibility from men which predisposes them to use their rights in ways that are compatible with their duties and consequently the well-being of society. If the tension is reconciled, it is in favour of greater duties for women.

CHAPTER FOUR

Reproduction and Politics

Paying attention to how Hobbes, Locke, and J.S. Mill account for parent-child relations, depict women's role in reproduction, and attach political importance to generation is useful in clarifying the controversy surrounding the issue of reproductive rights for women in modern liberal societies. Increasingly vociferous debates over women's right to abortion and to the use of 'new reproductive technologies' such as *in vitro* fertilization and pre-natal screening attest to the difficulties that emerge when one attempts to extend to women the right to govern their own bodies and reproductive labour power in the context of liberal assumptions and projections. The controversy over the new reproductive technologies also brings to the forefront some of the problems that arise in accounting for the care of children on liberal terms.

THE LIBERAL LEGACY: PARENTS AND CHILDREN

In Hobbes' account, self-interest is paramount in forging a tie between parents and children. This tie is formulated as a kind of contractual exchange, requiring state regulation and legislation. For example, the state must establish laws obliging children when grown to repay their parents for the care lavished on them. Without such inducements, there is the danger of activating a state of nature in which women and men are more likely to abandon their children or refuse to give them life than raise them to adulthood. The assumption is that parents will care for their children only if convinced they will benefit from it. To buttress parents' perception that they have something to gain by caring for their children, the state must also leave them the impression that they have some room to manoeuvre or some freedom to exercise power and authority over their children. Having control over one's children becomes part of the benefit of raising them.

Neither men nor women, according to Hobbes, have a natural predilection to have or raise children. Biological ties, on the one hand, have little meaning. The adult who decides to give the infant life by nourishing it is the rightful parent in the state of nature. On the other hand, knowing the child is one's own may give one a greater incentive to save its life. Mothers have the advantage here. Implicit in Hobbes is the idea that one might derive more benefits, more power or honour, from one's own children than from another's.

To avoid conflict, authority over the children must be undivided, Hobbes insists. Either parent may hold legitimate rights and powers over the children in civil society. But Hobbes supports 'father-right' as being more compatible with the prevailing custom. He also indicates, however, that it is more 'artificial' than mother-right, that is less compatible with the state of nature where the one who bears the child has the first opportunity to exercise the power of life and death over it. The state in Hobbes becomes a 'maternal' one, introducing state incentives in place of a natural maternal instinct to induce women to care for children. It also becomes a 'paternal' one, maintaining father-right by ensuring children are taught that it is indeed 'natural.'

In the Lockean account, parents are motivated to care for their children, and, most important, to accumulate excess property for them, as extensions of themselves. Parents need an assurance then that their children are indeed their own, their 'property' so to speak. Because she bears the child, the mother has an advantage here. It becomes problematic, however, to extend to parents rights over their children as products of their reproductive labour or as their 'property' to 'buy' and 'sell' or do with as they will. If the state acts as an intermediary in securing a form of 'contractual exchange' between parents and children in Hobbes, God is invoked as an intermediary in Locke's account, directing parents to fulfil their (God-given) duty to care for their children in appropriate ways. The belief in such God-given obligations prevents parents from abusing their extensive power over their children and ensures that children as adults will honour their parents. This may be why atheism cannot be tolerated in Locke.[1] Among other things, it leaves parent-child relations to the vicissitudes of parental self-interest. For similar reasons, it is the non-interventionist state that cannot be tolerated when it comes to family relations in Hobbes.

As Locke describes it, it is more necessary for women to apply their reproductive labour power to the creation of a new life before and after birth. As in Hobbes, there is no indication, however, that women are any different from men in the sense of having a natural instinct to have and care for children. Locke's assumptions support the logic of ceding to women rights over the children as the products of their greater reproductive labour. Yet these rights cannot be fully acknowledged. They potentially confirm women's rights to the ownership of their bodies and their reproductive labour power, which pose a threat to what Locke considers an important political and economic good – population increase.

In Mill's account, men are more likely to abuse their power over the children. More 'caring' than men on the whole, women have a greater 'natural' predilection to have and care for children and to associate their own interests with the well-being of their families. Women ought to have greater rights over their own bodies, labour power, property, and children, the underlying assumption being that they will wield them in ways that are beneficial to others. Moreover, reproduction is considered to be a 'private matter,' on the one hand, best left to the laws of supply and demand and the individual judgment of adults. On the other hand, it is deemed to have such important social and political consequences that the state is asked to 'intervene' on individual freedom to limit population growth. Such intervention, moreover, seems to be directed mainly at the 'poorer classes.'

In all three thinkers, having and caring for children advance what they consider to be important 'political' ends such as the perpetuation of the political community, the creation of adults who will consent to civil society, the accumulation of excess wealth, and the regulation of supply and demand in the labour force. They lead us to consider that 'generation' continues to be imbued with considerable political importance in modern liberal societies such as Canada. For example, Locke's concern with population increase and Mill's with population decrease, flip sides of the same liberal coin, are evident in the early birth control movements in Canada.[2] Propelled by a desire to limit the growth of the 'undesirable classes' or lower classes and to foster the growth of the more 'desirable classes' or 'middle classes,' the leaders of the movement were particularly worried about the 'high' birth rate in French Canada. The relative growth or decline of the French and English populations continues to be a political matter, often a contentious one. Concerned about the declining birth rate in Quebec, the government of Quebec implemented a program of 'baby bonuses' in the late 1980s in the hope of spurring an increase in 'French numbers.' The proposal to guarantee Quebec 25 per cent of the seats in the House of Commons irrespective of population decline became one of the more controversial issues in the debate over the 1992 Charlottetown Accord on amending the Canadian Constitution, contributing to the Accord's demise. Moreover, there is increasing concern over the political implications of a declining birth rate and aging population in general, which it is feared will result in increased pension and health care costs and decreased revenues. The issue brings up the question of what rewards respective generations expect to enjoy and the obligations they are expected to fulfil. What emerges, for example, is the idea that children are a valuable resource in providing support for aging parents, albeit indirectly through their contribution to state revenues.

In modern liberal societies such as Canada, the alternatives that Hobbes, Locke, and J.S. Mill point to are assumed or invoked to regulate, maintain, and account for links between the generations. The wide discrepancy between the extensive investigations on parental suitability that are part of adoption procedures and the absence of any such regulations governing the suitability of natural parents (except in child custody cases) attests to a theme we find prevalent in the liberal account – that it is difficult enough to explain why parents would care for their own children, but more inconceivable that they would care for another's. Foster parents contend that the amount they receive from the state is inadequate as compensation for the extensive care their charges require, warning that further cuts will make it increasingly difficult to find people willing to undertake such care. This is an insoluable sort of situation beset by liberal assumptions. A cost-benefit analysis, which one encourages by posing the issue in terms of monetary compensation, is likely to show that, even with increased payments to the foster parents, it cannot be demonstrated to be in their 'interests' to undertake the care these children require.

Reports of parents abusing their children and children when grown abusing their parents ('elder abuse') paint a picture of a Hobbesian state of nature, a condition where, without state incentives and supports, parents are more likely to abandon, neglect, or cause the death of their children than care for them adequately, and where grown children are as likely to harm their parents as a stranger. Hobbes' model leads us to consider that the contractual model of parent-child relations in which self-interested parties exchange benefits may not work without extensive state regulation or support, but that there is considerable resistance to the state 'intervening' in such relations when it comes to challenging parental authority. The latter is evident, for example, in the dispute over laws making it illegal for parents to 'spank' their children.[3] In a very Hobbesian fashion, the state is increasingly pressured to regulate parent-child relations, to prevent parents from abusing their power over their children for example, at the same time as it is compelled to advance the idea that parent-child relations are 'private' matters in which parents have the freedom to do with their children as they see fit.

Locke's model indicates that we ought not to be surprised that the revival of classical liberalism in the form of 'neo-conservatism' is associated with the rise of groups such as the Moral Majority.[4] The more the 'right' supports the principles of contract and self-interested exchange in the economic and political marketplace, and opposes state intervention and regulation in general, the more it may be compelled to invoke a Lockean solution to the fear of the breakdown of political and social order – the belief in a God-given duty to have and care for children as a way of securing generational continuity. If one rejects the Hobbesian option – state intervention – yet retains a framework in which rational self-interest is the main secular motivation for human behaviour, it may become necessary to call on God as an intermediary directing parents to carry out their (God-given) duties to have and care for children. Moreover, these duties most heavily fall on women, a point I shall return to.

Another way of accounting for the care of children in the liberal framework, if one rejects or questions what Hobbes points to – state regulation – or deems as implausible or undesirable what Locke points to – the revival of a shared and perhaps state-supported belief in a Christian God – is to awaken the Millian alternative – a sort of 'maternalism' which assumes that women have a greater predilection than men to have and care for children, to associate their own interests with their families, and to be more 'caring' of others in general. This notion pervades what has become prevalent in much recent feminist discourse – an emphasis on women's association with an 'ethic of care.' We also find this emphasis in the feminist response to the conflict over abortion and the use of the new reproductive technologies. Perhaps this is to be expected. The debate over reproductive rights for women in modern liberal societies, I suggest, takes place on liberal grounds. It is coloured by liberal assumptions about women's role in reproduction, especially Hobbesian and Lockean ones.

THE LIBERAL LEGACY: WOMEN AND REPRODUCTION

If we add up Hobbes and Locke's depiction of women's role in reproduction, we find that it is a 'rational' more than a 'natural' activity. It can be understood as 'rational' in several senses. First, it is not influenced by a natural maternal instinct or an innate desire to have and care for children. Second, it entails the exercise of reason. Moreover, reason is associated with self-interest. This is most predominant and blatant in Hobbes, where 'mothering' is the result of considerations of what benefits or costs might accrue from saving an infant's life. In Locke, self-interest comes into play as a motivation for applying one's reproductive labour power to make something one's own. But the exercise of reason in Locke also entails apprehending and following through on one's God-given duty to care for a 'new life.' Third, women's role in reproduction is described as 'rational' in the sense of entailing the choice of whether or not one will 'care' for a 'fetus' before birth or an infant after birth. Caring for a fetus is not a 'natural,' or automatic outcome of recognizing that one has conceived it. Similarly, caring for an infant is not a 'natural' in the sense of 'automatic,' outcome of bearing it. Fourth, exercising the power of the decision of whether or not one to apply one's reproductive labour power to 'care' for the fetus or the infant translates into the power of life and death over it. This is made most explicit in Hobbes' depiction of the state of nature.

Although 'rational' in the sense I have described above, reproduction is also characterized as being influenced by biological factors having important implications for the differences between 'mothers' and 'fathers.' First, conceiving and bearing the fetus in her body does not mean that a woman has a natural maternal urge to care for it, either before or after birth, or a greater attachment to it. It does mean, however, that she usually has the first opportunity in the state of nature either to apply her labour to it, thereby maintaining and giving it life, or to withdraw her 'care' from it, thereby inducing its death. In other words, carrying the fetus gives her the first opportunity to exercise the power of life and death over it. Moreover, it is not clear that women lose this power in civil society. Hobbes' model leaves open the possibility that they carry over to civil society the power deriving from their first access to a 'new life.' Hobbes' model also illustrates that, by giving them first access to the fetus or infant, women's biological capacity to carry the fetus is what makes the absence of a natural maternal urge come across as more threatening to the perpetuation of society than the absence of a natural paternal urge. A second biological difference which we find in Locke has a similar effect. In carrying it and feeding it with her body, the woman must contribute more of her reproductive labour power to the creation of a new life than the man. As a result, the woman's refusal to apply her reproductive labour to its care may seem and in fact be more threatening than the man's.

A third difference between 'mothers' and 'fathers' deriving from woman's biological reproductive capacities is maternal certainty versus paternal uncertainty. This takes two forms. The first is that women know that the infant they have given birth to is their own. This knowledge may give them a slight edge over 'fathers' when it comes to having the incentive to care for it. Since they are not certain, as mothers are, that the infant is indeed 'their own,' it may be more difficult to convince fathers that they are caring for 'themselves,' that is extensions of themselves. Second, men may not be aware that they have contributed to the conception of a 'new life.' As Locke describes it, ironically, it is men more than women who are subject to 'natural necessity' or 'the invisible hand of God,' who can make men 'fathers' without their knowing it. Because conception takes place inside their bodies, women usually know sooner than men that a fetus has been conceived. More aware that they must apply their labour to continue and maintain it, women are more subject to 'rational' necessity.

At the same time as they present reproduction as entailing choice and self-interested deliberation, Hobbes and Locke also assume that conception is more a by-product of sexual desire than a result of rational thought or intention. In fact, it seems that rational deliberation would work against adults choosing to have and care for children, the 'costs' easily outweighing the 'benefits.' Paradoxically, the more 'rational' parenting becomes, the more easily it becomes 'irrational' to choose it.

An additional biological imperative which comes to the forefront in Hobbes' account of the state of nature is that infants are born helpless, requiring the care of adults. We can reformulate this to encompass the pre-birth stage: a fetus is conceived requiring the 'care' of adults to maintain it. Yet, in the absence of natural maternal or paternal instincts, that care is not naturally or automatically forthcoming.

According to Hobbes and Locke then, men and women have different biologically based reproductive capacities but the same capacity for reason, including rational self-interest. In addition there are certain biological imperatives to reproduction such as the infant's helplessness at birth. Moreover, having and caring for children advance important political ends. As a result, the issue of reproductive rights becomes a political matter. It also becomes a contentious matter which places women in the centre of a rift between 'reproductive rights,' resting on the pursuit of their own interests, and 'reproductive duties,' resting on the advancement of the interest of others. Mill's model addresses this tension, I have suggested, by presenting women as being more 'caring' of others than men, more likely to a subsume their interests to the well-being of others and more prone to wield their 'rights' in ways that benefit the larger community. Formulated in Hobbesian and Lockean terms, the debate over reproductive rights for women in modern liberal societies brings forth a similarly Millian response.

WOMEN AND REPRODUCTIVE RIGHTS: ABORTION

The feminist movement introduced the liberal language of 'rights' to the debate about abortion in Canada in the 1970s.[5] As Janine Brodie observes, feminists made use of a rationale 'firmly lodged within classical liberal rights discourse,' claiming the right to abortion for women 'on the fundamental liberal principles of "bodily integrity" (i.e., citizens have a right to make decisions about their own bodies free from state interference) and "individual conscience" (i.e., women are autonomous, rational, and moral agents capable of exercising choice).'[6] In 1988 the Supreme Court of Canada struck down Section 251 of the Criminal Code (which prohibited women from having an abortion without the approval of a 'therapeutic' abortion committee) on the grounds that it violated a woman's security of person, thereby implicitly accepting the liberal terms on which the abortion issue was posed.[7] Explaining his decision, Chief Justice Brian Dickson wrote:

> Section 251 clearly interferes with a woman's bodily integrity in both a physical and emotional sense. Forcing a woman, by threat of criminal sanction, to carry a foetus to term unless she meets certain criteria unrelated to her own priorities and aspirations, is a profound interference with a woman's body and thus a violation of security of person.[8]

The ruling confirmed that the right to abortion for women is about securing for them the same right to govern their own bodies that other citizens expect to enjoy in a liberal polity, a position that feminist activists and thinkers embrace. Christine Overall sums it up: 'A woman's body does not belong to the state; it does not belong to physicians; it does not belong to the woman's husband or partner, or to the father of her children; and, most important, it does not belong to the foetus.'[9] By limiting women's right to abortion, Overall goes on to say, we are asking them to 'sacrifice their independence and accept limits on their autonomy and bodily integrity that are required of no other group of citizens.'[10] We are also 'obliging' them to apply their 'reproductive labour' to the generation of new life.

A woman who is being asked not to have an abortion once a fetus has been conceived, Martha Bolton observes, is being asked not simply to refrain from taking the life of the fetus; she is being asked to engage in the possibly extensive care that is required to maintain its life: 'For any pregnant woman, the only way to avoid killing a foetus is to take responsibility for nurturing and giving birth to it; for some, the alternative is undertaking to care for and raise a child.'[11] Section 251, according to Overall, did more than violate some women's security of person; it also implied that they 'had a legal obligation to procreate; it sentenced them to forced reproductive labour.'[12] Securing the right to abortion confirms that 'Women do not owe their reproductive products or labour to any person or institution, including their male partners or the state.'[13]

The right to abortion is presented as something that women can exercise for any reason they wish, carrying with it no obligation to consider or act in the interests of others, whether the fetus, the father, the family, the community, or the state. As Campbell and Pal put it, 'But if abortion is a right, then it is hard to consider limits to that right, and any reason for aborting has to be accepted as the expression of that right.'[14] Highlighting that the right to abortion exempts women from any obligation to use their reproductive labour for the benefit of others, Overall deems it to be part of women's 'right not to reproduce' – 'To say that women have a right not to reproduce implies that they have no obligation to reproduce.'[15] It means that women cannot be obligated to use their bodies or their reproductive labour to preserve, maintain, or enhance the condition or life of the fetus.

It is not surprising, if we heed the status of women in Locke and Hobbes, that talk of women's right to govern their own bodies and labour power conjures up another side of the liberal equation – an emphasis on women's (God-given) duty to 'care' for a new life after birth or to 'care' for a fetus before birth. Although on opposite sides of the abortion debate and the political spectrum, both the 'pro-choice' and the 'pro-life' lobbies draw from the same liberal well, the former from Hobbes, the latter from Locke. In Locke we find the groundwork for the position many opponents of abortion take; implicit (and sometimes explicit) in their stance is the notion that women have a (God-given) obligation to apply their reproductive labour power to the generation of new life. In

Hobbes' conceptual model we see the groundwork for the position initially, although not exclusively, taken by feminists in securing for women the right to abortion, articulated as extending to them the right to govern their own bodies and labour power. We also see why granting women such a right in civil society has such radical implications and why it might be perceived as such a threat.

For one, as Hobbes shows, it potentially entails the right to make decisions about the life or death of another 'being.' This is brought home when we consider the following issue: some have suggested that a woman's right to abort a fetus simply entails the right to have it removed from her body, but not the right to end its life.[16] Once the fetus is removed from her body it no longer violates her bodily integrity; another might 'save' it and care for it, becoming its rightful parent. Advocates of the right to abortion usually reject this argument, maintaining that the right to abortion entails the right to determine the disposition of the fetus after it is removed from the woman's body, which includes the right to determine its death and the right to prevent others from 'saving' it. This has led some to the observation that 'The quest for abortion rights for women is not merely a quest for control of one's body, though it is surely this in part. The quest for abortion rights is also a quest for the right to terminate the development of an unwanted foetus[,] which can not be accomplished without killing it.'[17] This description underscores the Hobbesian implications of extending to women the right to govern their own bodies and labour power, manifest in the right to abortion: it potentially cedes to women the first opportunity to exercise the power of life and death over another 'being.'

Furthermore, as we see in Hobbes and Locke, granting women such rights comes across as particularly threatening when they are perceived to be as rationally self-interested as men. Janine Brodie misconstrues the nature of the problem when she maintains that the pro-life lobby conceives women as incapable of rational thinking and behaviour and therefore incapable of wielding rights. She attributes to them the assumption that women 'are also closer to nature and thus less rational and less morally responsible for their behaviour than men. Men are capable of objectivity: women are governed by their irrational subjectivity.'[18] Paying attention to Hobbes and Locke can alert us to a more probable explanation. Underlying the opposition to ceding to women the right to abortion is precisely the perception that women are rational and therefore capable not only of apprehending their duties (Locke) but also of knowing and acting on what is in their interest (Hobbes).

And it is difficult, as Hobbes and Locke illustrate, to show that it is in women's interest to have and care for children. Without adequate state incentives to make it rewarding (the Hobbesian directive) or without a belief in one's (God-given) duty to do so (the Lockean directive), a weighing of the benefits and costs is likely to result in women deciding it is not 'worth their while' to attach their labour to the generation of new life. Reports on the rising abortion rate in Canada in the wake of the 1988 Supreme Court ruling, which has been linked to persisting economic recession, may indicate just that.[19] A recent Statistics Canada report shows that more women are delaying childbearing and choosing to be childless. It suggests that 'having children has become less rewarding economically and psychologically in developed societies.'[20] Susan A. McDaniel puts forth a similar explanation to explain the rise of voluntary childlessness in Canada: 'The rewards of motherhood for women may not be as large as they once were, or were perceived to be.'[21] Commenting on an analogous phenomenon in other Western countries, Germaine Greer writes: 'Common morality now treats child-bearing as an aberration; there are practically no good *reasons* [my emphasis] left for exercising one's fertility.'[22] Rational considerations may make mothering 'irrational.'

Brodie is more on the mark when she suggests that the pro-life lobby constructs abortion as being 'selfish.'[23] It seems that women are as caught between 'Hobbesian self-interest' and 'Lockean duty' in liberal practice as they are in liberal theory. Their capacity for rational self-interest, it is feared, may undermine the fulfilment of their (political) duties. Laurie Shrage captures this dimension of the abortion debate in summing up the attitudes expressed by the 'pro-choice' and 'pro-life' lobbies. The former 'see continuing an unwanted pregnancy not as a socially beneficial or altruistic sacrifice that a woman (or couple) can make, but as a decision that is likely to make it difficult for a woman to balance different life opportunities and to pursue economic and vocational security.' The latter 'view continuing an unwanted pregnancy as a worthy sacrifice a woman makes for the greater social good' and contend that women who fail to do so 'demonstrate selfish and materialistic values.'[24]

Extending to women rights over their bodies and labour power comes across as more threatening when they are depicted as rationally self-interested (Hobbes and Locke) than when they are presented as more inclined to equate their own interests with the interests of their families. Mill points to another option that can be summoned as a response to the threat the right to abortion poses – emphasizing that women are more caring and other-oriented than men and implying that as a consequence they are likely to wield their right to do as they please in ways that are beneficial to others, including the larger community. A variation on this theme – that the interests of the woman and the fetus are very much intertwined[25] – has become a prominent motif in the feminist literature on reproductive rights, perhaps an attempt to 'soften' the radical Hobbesian implications of women's right to abortion. But the new reproductive technologies make this increasingly difficult.

ABORTION AND THE NEW REPRODUCTIVE TECHNOLOGIES

The new reproductive technologies include a wide and growing range of technologies and practices aimed at monitoring, assessing, and facilitating the generation of new life.[26] Pre-natal genetic testing and diagnosis, pre-natal sex selection, donor insemination, *in vitro* fertilization, and surrogacy arrangements are examples. The new reproductive technologies have not spurred new formulations of parent-child relations. They reinforce old liberal ones. This is evident both in the way individuals themselves approach the new technologies and in the way that theorists account for their approach. Explaining why individuals will undergo the often lengthy and arduous procedures that are entailed in *in vitro* fertilization challenges us to explore the meaning and significance of having children, Kenneth Alpern observes.[27] He introduces the topic of having children by stating: 'We may now turn to *reasons* [Alpern's emphasis] for desiring to have or for valuing having children.'[28] He then goes on to use an analogy which suggests that children are like other goods or products one may wish to acquire: 'to help clarify exactly what it is about having children that is desired and valued – just as by setting out reasons for wanting a car (for status, for a sense of power, in order to get from place to place, for a sense of freedom), one acquires a better understanding of what the desire is for and how it is best satisfied, as well as its justification.'[29] He identifies the reasons commonly cited for having children, most of which explain it in liberal fashion by referring either to the parents' interests, needs, and desires or to the perception that they have a duty or obligation to have offspring.[30] Moreover, he points out that the demand for access to such services as *in vitro* fertilization which assist couples in conceiving and bearing genetically linked children attests to the desire to have one's own children: 'an adopted child, it is generally felt, is just not, in the fullest sense, one's *own*; one is not a *real* parent of the child.'[31] We might add that support for such technologies reinforces the notion that individuals are motivated to care for children as extensions of themselves.[32] Alpern's discussion reveals the pervasiveness of liberal assumptions both in the way that adults approach the matter of having children and in the way theorists account for how individuals decide to become parents.

As Locke and Hobbes make us consider, to see children as extensions of oneself, as one's own, lends itself to seeing them as one's property or possession. The new reproductive technologies, critics have pointed out, 'commodify' children, treating and perceiving them as if they were products that can be bought, sold, and improved. This is not surprising. The liberal legacy lends itself to such formulations. Surrogacy arrangements (also known as pre-conception agreements) highlight the way in which the new reproductive technologies reinforce liberal assumptions about parent-child relations and, connected to that, women's role in reproduction. Surrogacy arrangements reinforce the separation between biological and social parenting, a separation to which Hobbes subscribes when he proposes that the biological parent who 'abandons' the infant loses parental rights to the one who 'finds' it. Some commentators have suggested that the new reproductive technologies 'challenge the sanctity and increasingly mythological image of the biologically linked nuclear family as normative.'[33] It might be more accurate to say that they increasingly confirm and show how the family resembles the artificial contractual arrangement described by Hobbes.

Surrogacy arrangements assume that women will apply their reproductive labour to the creation of a new life in the hope of securing tangible rewards and benefits, which are set out in the terms of the contract between the woman who carries the child and the couple for whom it is being carried. They bolster the idea that the production of children, like the production of other goods, can be regulated to improve saleability; contracts often stipulate that only if the surrogate mother produces a baby in 'good condition' will she be considered to have upheld her end of the contract and be paid for her services. Surrogacy arrangements also entail what Mill's model offers for women of means – they can pay other women to help them carry out their domestic duties, an important component of which is their reproductive labour. Furthermore, since surrogacy contracts assume that the mother who has borne the child will simply give it up after birth according to the terms of the contract, they support a Hobbesian/Lockean supposition – we cannot assume that because a woman bears the child she has a natural maternal urge to care for it (although she may have a greater incentive to care for it than the father). And surrogacy arrangements also invoke a (Millian) response which emphasizes women's 'maternal qualities,' illustrating the kind of contradictions that characterize women's situation in liberal thought and practice. As Rona Achilles observes of surrogacy arrangements:

> The very success of the procedure is dependent on women conceiving, gestating, and relinquishing their children without any messy emotions like attachment, bonding, affection and/or love. Yet these are precisely the qualities generally required of women to be good mothers; women who leave their child(ren) wear this century's scarlet letter. One mother's virtue, in other words, is another mother's crime.[34]

There is much concern that the new reproductive technologies such as *in vitro* fertilization play up what I call the Millian side of the liberal equation, which expects most women to choose the having and care of children as their main occupation. In a study of twenty-two women who had applied for or undergone *in vitro* fertilization, Linda Williams intimates that women may be responding to something that is socially imposed in going to such great lengths to have children: the notion that having children is what defines them as women.[35] But the demand for access to such technologies also attests to the Lockean and Hobbesian considerations that women and men undergo. The use of fertility clinics does not contradict what I have suggested earlier – that the decision to have children for women, influenced by cost-benefit considerations, is leading more and more women to decide that it is not in their interest to have and care for them. Many who visit fertility clinics are women who have delayed childbearing for reasons similar to those given by women who choose childlessness – the costs are perceived as being too high, threatening such benefits as economic security and career advancement. According to the Royal Commission on New Reproductive Technologies:

> The opportunity costs of having children – lost career opportunities, lost income during pregnancy and child care leave – together with the cost associated with raising children (which has been estimated conservatively at more than $150 000 to raise a child to the age of 18) and the shortage of high-quality, low-cost child care constitute major financial and social barriers that lead many women to delay the birth of their first child.[36]

On the whole, the new reproductive technologies potentially make the having and care of children, including 'mothering,' more rational in the Hobbesian and Lockean sense that I have described, less determined by a 'natural,' in the sense of 'automatic,' progression from conception to birth to care for an infant. By separating sex and procreation, they remove the element of 'natural necessity' in reproduction as envisioned by Hobbes and Locke, making it more influenced by rational deliberation, intention, and choice. Yet they leave intact some of the biological differences between men and women, such as women's greater contribution to generation. Providing the egg for *in vitro* fertilization, for example, may require the use of fertility drugs and numerous attempt to 'harvest' the eggs for implantation. The woman's 'bodily labour' continues to be more extensive than the man's.[37] The new reproductive technologies also leave intact some of the fundamental biological exigencies of reproduction as envisioned by Hobbes and Locke, such as the dependency of a fetus and a newborn on adult 'care.' They may increase the degree to which an infant is born requiring the care of adults. Technological intervention can prolong the life of a fetus or infant that would not have survived without aid, often resulting in the need for prolonged post-natal care.

By augmenting the scope for 'rational choice' while retaining the need for women's greater contribution to generation as well as a 'new life's' dependence on adult care, the new reproductive technologies exacerbate the conflicts that emerge in the debate over granting to women the right to govern their own bodies and labour power, especially the tension between rights and duties that the abortion issue engenders. For one, they intensify the conflict because they highlight the radical Hobbesian underpinnings and implications of the right to abortion. The image of the fetus as a 'human life' is becoming increasingly powerful as technologies such as ultrasound and fetal surgery give it more visibility. New advances in 'neo-natal' technology allow fetuses aborted in late term to survive. Moreover, as Overall notes, these 'fetuses' very much resemble a 'premature newborn.'[38] As the distinction between a 'fetus' and a 'premature newborn' becomes increasingly difficult to maintain, the distinction between abortion and infanticide blurs.

In the advent of new reproductive technologies, women's right to govern their own bodies and labour power, which is at the bottom of the demand for a right to abortion, comes to resemble what Hobbes implicitly cedes to women in the state of nature – the first opportunity to exercise the power of life and death over a 'new life.' At the same time, the new reproductive technologies, by introducing new players into the game, so to speak, threaten to diffuse women's first access to the 'new life,' dispersing it among physicians and medical researchers. This may explain why there is so little support among feminist activists and thinkers for the new reproductive technologies.[39] The fear is that they threaten to undermine women's right to govern their own bodies and labour power – which is secured by women's right to abortion. It may also explain why many feminists simultaneously reject greater access to the 'new reproductive technologies' and reaffirm women's access to what has become the 'old reproductive technology' – abortion.

Paradoxically, in reaffirming women's right to abortion in the face of the threat posed by the new technologies, they show up its Hobbesian underpinnings. For example, Judy Rebick, spokesperson for the abortion lobby in Canada in the 1980s, opposes the new reproductive technologies on the grounds that they take control over their bodies from women and place it in the hands of doctors and scientists. She supports women's right to abortion as securing for women that control. Indeed, she suggests that the term 'pro-choice' is a misnomer: 'While using the term "pro-choice" was important to winning the abortion debate, I am now convinced that the framework of our position on reproductive rights must be the right to control our bodies and reproduction rather than freedom of individual choice.'[40]

The higher visibility of the fetus, facilitated by the new reproductive technologies directed at changing and improving its condition, makes it more difficult for proponents of the right to abortion to respond to the argument that the fetus is a 'person' with rights requiring public protection (and that the decision to abort therefore cannot be a private matter which concerns a woman alone).[41] The arguments feminists tend to make in opposing the 'new technologies' are similar to the ones they use in responding to the opponents of abortion. But the difficulties that emerge in the abortion debate simply resurface, in heightened form.

The feminist response to the claim that the fetus is a person with 'rights' requiring protection usually takes three forms, all of which raise more difficulties. The first is to point out that 'personhood' is open to interpretation and that it is not clear that a fetus is in fact a 'person.' But it is becoming increasingly difficult to deny that the 'fetus' may be a human life with interests. (Indeed the emphasis feminists increasingly place on the connection between the 'mother' and the fetus buttresses this impression.)

A second response is to affirm that women's right to govern their own bodies and labour power supersedes any 'rights' or interests the fetus may have: 'Neither the physician nor the spouse has any rights over the woman's body, and that fact should take priority over any claims about the alleged rights of the foetus.'[42] Patricia Spallone, for instance, argues against both the new reproductive technologies and the anti-abortion position on the grounds that they do similar things – raise the status of the fetus over that of the woman.[43] The impetus for both is a 'fetal-centred thinking' which favours the interests of the fetus over the interests of the woman. A 'women-centred' perspective, in contrast, according to Spallone, takes the interests of the woman to be of prime importance; it opposes intervention in a woman's body for the sake of protecting the fetus. But by taking the kind of position that Spallone and others take, one ends up pitting the interests of the woman against the interests of the fetus, thereby accentuating that the right to abortion is premised on women's right to govern their own bodies and labour power as they see fit, irrespective of the interests of others, whether the fetus, the father, the community, or the state. It adds fuel to the opponents' side which then emphasizes women' duty to forgo selfish considerations and act on the well-being of others such as the fetus.[44]

Perhaps this is why a third response has become so prominent, usually accompanying the second one. This is to maintain that pitting the interests of the woman against the interests of the fetus is the result of an artificial construction of the situation which separates the mother and the fetus. Such a separation is often deemed to be a 'masculinist' perception or way of thinking that denies women's unique relation to reproduction: 'The conceptual split between woman and fetus comes from a Western, male intellectual view of reproduction; it is enhanced by the new artificial reproduction technologies which *literally* split woman and embryo/fetus, a "logical" progression from the mental split between woman and fetus in masculinist thinking.'[45] A 'woman-centred' approach, according to Spallone, is based on two principles: (1) that women's interests take priority, including priority over fetal interests and (2) 'the principle that the welfare of mother and child are intertwined.'[46] The second principle seems to me an attempt to deal with the very real conflicts (not necessarily artificially constructed ones) that arise out of supporting the first principle.

Accentuating the interconnectedness of the woman and the fetus emerges out of the 'ethic of care' approach which has had a considerable influence on feminist discourse since the publication of Carol Gilligan's *In a Different Voice*.[47] The 'ethic of care' approach has come to mean focusing on human connectedness rather than separation and perceiving actors as situated in a web of relationships which they care about and wish to maintain (and which constitute their 'identity' or self). It suggests that women are more prone than men to experience the world this way, which accounts for why it is often considered to be more compatible with a 'woman-centred' perspective. When applied to the issue of reproductive rights for women, the 'ethic of care' approach highlights the physical connection between the woman and the fetus. It implies that a special relationship develops between the mother and the fetus so that she feels her interests to be bound up with those of the fetus.[48] A 'masculinist' perspective, it is suggested, ignores the attachment that a mother comes to have as the result of her biological capacity to bear the child.

Signalling how pervasive the 'ethic of care' language has become when dealing with matters connected to reproductive rights for women, matters which are sure to elicit conflict and controversy, the Report of the Royal Commission on New Reproductive Technologies takes it as its guiding principle. It associates the term 'ethic of care' with a number of themes, among them 'focusing on how our interests are often interdependent' and finding solutions that 'can remove or reduce conflict, rather than simply subordinating one persons's interests to another.'[49] Although the Commission's Report does not address the abortion issue directly, it recommends support for what is at the bottom of it – women's right to govern their own bodies and labour power – in its stance on 'judicial intervention' (the use of legislation to regulate women's behaviour during pregnancy for the sake of the fetus). It poses this right, in liberal terms, as something that women can exercise for any reason they wish: 'women do not give up their right to control their own bodies or to determine the course of their medical treatment just because they are pregnant. A woman has the right to make her own choices, whether they are good or bad, because it is the woman whose body and health are affected.'[50] The Report opposes 'judicial intervention' as imposing on women an obligation to apply their reproductive labour to the care of the fetus: 'If we impose a legal obligation upon a woman to care for her fetus – even it were possible to legislate a caring and nurturing relationship – the potential for curtailing women's choices and behaviour becomes staggering.'[51]

The confirmation of women's right to govern their own bodies is immediately followed with or coupled with the suggestion that we ought to see the interests of the fetus and the pregnant woman as intertwined. To do otherwise, the Report goes on to say, is to open up the call for 'judicial intervention' for the sake of the fetus: 'Considering the interests of the fetus in isolation from those of the woman has the potential to establish adversary relationships that, at their extreme, can lead to efforts to force the pregnant woman to act in the interests of this "separate patient." This may mean that a woman's right not to be subject to unwanted interference with her physical integrity is taken away from her.'[52] This may be the case. But the problem is that invoking the 'ethic of care' approach does not really meet the challenge of overcoming the conflicts and complications that surface in attempting to maintain for women on liberal terms the right to govern their own bodies and labour power. The 'ethic of care' approach does not get us away from what I suggest are the Hobbesian implications of the right to abortion: that it cedes to women the power of life and death over another.

To say that a perspective which separates the interests of the pregnant woman from the interests of the fetus is a 'masculinist' perception and that one which assumes a relationship between the two is a 'woman-centred' one obscures the issue. It does not change this fact: the right to govern her own body and labour power gives the woman an unqualified right to choose to end that relationship by causing the death of the fetus. To put it another way: she can choose to end the relationship by choosing to refrain from using her reproductive labour to 'care' for the fetus, thereby causing its death.

Moreover, by emphasizing the connection between the woman and the fetus and implying there is an attachment there that derives from the woman carrying it in her body, one is also suggesting that a fetus is more than merely a collection of cells or an inanimate entity. To assume that an attachment is possible is to enhance the fetus's status and to imbue it with characteristics that make it resemble a human being. Commenting on a dispute between a separated husband and wife over who should have 'custody' over their cryo-preserved embryos, Overall reports that the woman testified 'that she regarded herself as the mother of the embryos, that she felt an attachment to them, and viewed them as children.'[53] It is difficult to propose that a woman forms an attachment to a fetus without implying that it is something she may care about because she recognizes it as having human qualities and perhaps even interests. One may even be implying that the fetus is closer to 'personhood' than most advocates of the right to abortion would find acceptable or comfortable, and thereby giving stimulus to the position that it requires public protection. In other words, to emphasize the attachment between the mother and the fetus is to make the latter more visible as a human life. This in turn shows up the Hobbesian implications of the right to abortion, which brings us back to square one.

Similar difficulties emerge in emphasizing women's attachment to the fetus as grounds for challenging a 'father's rights.' The new reproductive technologies also bring to the forefront an issue which has become part of the abortion debate – the question of what 'rights' the 'father' may have over the disposition of a 'fetus.'[54] Feminists and pro-choice advocates usually dispute the idea that men may have the same reproductive rights as women. They tend to argue on three grounds, all of which emphasize women's unique (biological) reproductive capacities. First, they argue, since a woman carries a fetus in her own body, the right to govern her own body gives her and no one else, including the 'father,' the right to determine what to do with it: 'Because pregnancy is an event in a woman's body, the moral relationship of the pregnant woman and the man who impregnated her to the foetus cannot be regarded as symmetrical. Provided the pregnant woman is competent, the responsibility for deciding what happens in and to her body rests with her.'[55]

Second, when it comes to deciding the disposition of something that may no longer be housed in her body – such as a cryo-preserved embryo – feminists emphasize women's greater contribution to its generation. Overall, for example, maintains that men's contribution (providing the sperm) does not require as much 'bodily labour' or time and effort as women's contribution (providing the egg). Women's contribution, moreover, may require a greater 'invasion' of her 'bodily integrity' – through repeated attempts to 'harvest' or to 're-implant the eggs,' for example.[56] As a result, according to Overall, the woman, not the man, ought to have the right to control the dispersal of the embryos:

> it cannot be assumed that reproductive freedom for men – the absence of which might mean loss of control over donated or commercially supplied sperm – is comparable to women's reproductive freedom, the absence of which means forced reproductive labour and the loss of bodily integrity. Once their sperm has been used to fertilize a woman's ovum, men do not have a right to determine whether a child will be born.[57]

Third, feminists often accentuate women's potential for attachment to the fetus to contest the notion that a man's reproductive rights are commensurate with a woman's. Shelley Gavigan, for instance, suggests there is a unique potential for attachment between the 'mother' and the fetus that cannot be experienced by the 'father.'[58] As a result, fathers cannot lay claim to commensurate rights with the mother on the grounds that they can just as easily forge an attachment to the fetus as mothers.

All three positions emphasize women's different, biologically based relations to reproduction, as we find them in Hobbes and Locke. And all three bring forth the familiar contradictions of women's place in the liberal scheme. For example, accentuating women's greater contribution to reproduction may summon up with greater force the idea that they have an obligation to employ their reproductive labour in ways that ensure the perpetuation of society. Overall seems to recognize this when she endorses a strong form of the 'right not to reproduce' (which would entail access to abortion) but repudiates a strong form of the 'right to reproduce' (which would entail access to surrogacy contracts and *in vitro* fertilization) because it would 'create an active right of access to women's bodies and in particular to our reproductive labour and products.'[59]

Furthermore, emphasizing the attachment of the pregnant woman to the fetus, drawing on the 'ethic of care' approach, brings up some of the issues I have already mentioned. It seems to imply, or at least makes it more difficult to deny, that the fetus is a human life. It also bolsters the assumption that the woman is its 'natural' care-giver after birth. Similarly, to argue that the woman alone is responsible for the decision whether or not to 'care' for the fetus before birth may make it easier to assert that she alone is responsible for the care of the infant after birth. Fathers may claim that, since they have no legitimate say in determining whether the fetus lives, they are absolved of responsibility for the care of the infant after birth. This points to a deeper problem.

Demanding the right to abortion for women on liberal premises and in a liberal society fosters the idea that reproduction is a private matter, something that concerns the woman alone. Both the pro-choice and the pro-life lobbies contribute to this perspective, the former by posing the decision of whether to 'care' for a fetus before birth as a personal, private matter, the latter by posing the care of the infant after birth as a personal, private matter (by refusing to support state-provided day-care). Yet women's interests seem to require that reproduction – the having and care of children – be deemed to be political. Recognizing it as having political ends encourages society and the larger community to take an interest in and responsibility for the care of children, including providing incentives and assistance to both men and women to engage themselves in reproduction. In this sense, acknowledging the 'personal' or the private as the 'political' seems to enhance the prospects for women's emancipation. The recognition that it is political, however, also means that extending to women the right to govern their own bodies and labour power may be perceived either as threatening to the perpetuation of the political community or as legitimately subject to community standards. In this sense, the recognition that the 'personal' is the 'political' is what places women in such a contradictory situation.

In other words, posing women's right to govern their own bodies as a private matter that concerns the individual woman alone, to be decided by her alone, without any obligation to consider or advance the well-being, interests, or needs of the greater community, may make it more difficult to pose the care of children as something that concerns the community as a whole and therefore as something for which society and the larger political community ought to be responsible. Without an emphasis on the political and communal implications of reproduction, ceding to women the right to abortion may reinforce the assumption that the care of children is a private matter, exempt from community responsibility or state support.[60]

The issues surrounding abortion have become even more complex, Mary Anne Warren observes, with the development and availability of technologies allowing for pre-natal genetic testing for abnormalities, sex selection, and the selective termination of one or more fetuses in a multiple pregnancy.[61] These technologies pose a dilemma for feminists who are troubled by their eugenic implications and their impact on the status of women. To oppose (as many do) the new reproductive technologies such as pre-natal testing for genetic defects or sex selection, which present women with more information on the status of the fetus and have an influence on their decision to abort, is to place limits and conditions on the right to abortion. But this undermines what most feminists and advocates of the right to abortion want to preserve and reaffirm for women – their right to abortion in its unqualified liberal form. To confirm such a right, however, is to confirm that women have the right to govern their own bodies and reproductive labour as they see fit, without any obligation to consider the implications of their actions or to wield them in ways that advance the well-being of the fetus, the father, the disabled, or the larger community of women.

Spallone, for example, supports the right to abortion but opposes the new reproductive technologies aimed at embryo research or isolating genetic fetal defects. She states: 'We can be both *for* women's right to abortion and *against* embryo research because we are concerned with women's reproductive freedom and health.'[62] She does not clarify, however, how she can both be against the idea of eugenic abortion when the fetus is judged to have Downs Syndrome, for example, and still maintain that 'The right to abortion is not dependent on certain circumstances: it is our absolute and essential right to have control over our bodies.'[63] The effect in practice is to make it easy for women to abort a healthy fetus requiring relatively minimal care, but to make it more difficult for her to abort one with genetic defects requiring relatively extensive care.[64]

There is a danger in attributing the demand for sex selection or prenatal genetic testing solely to the influence of a patriarchal society which undervalues women or the disabled. One is then implying either that women cannot be entrusted to make a decision in a society where they can too easily be coerced by the pressure to have perfect children or male children, or that they do not realize the harm their actions may lead to, or that they ought to wield their right in a way that refrains from harming others. These assumptions, however, are incompatible with the core principles that defenders of the right to abortion in its liberal form want to maintain: that women can exercise their right to abortion by having an abortion on any grounds they wish; that they are capable of making these decisions on their own; and that any decision they do make has to be accepted as a legitimate expression of that right.

Debates surrounding such new reproductive technologies as prenatal genetic testing and sex selection indicate that the conflict over reproductive rights for women is not exclusively a matter of a sexual power play between men and women. To suggest that the main problem with the new reproductive technologies is that they are developed by men to appropriate women's reproductive capacities and ensure sexual access to their bodies[65] or that opposition to abortion can simply be understood as a male desire to control women's reproductive labour[66] obscures a deeper dilemma – how to circumvent the predicaments that emerge in extending to women the right to govern their own bodies and reproductive labour capacities, in its unqualified liberal form, against the backdrop of liberal assumptions about parent-child relations. These predicaments are very much connected to women's unique biologically grounded reproductive capacities, which take on political importance because the having and care of children are deemed to have political importance.

It is not clear how a 'woman-centred' approach (usually this means that it draws on 'ethic of care' assumptions)[67] which wants to preserve women's right to govern their own bodies and labour power on liberal grounds would obviate some of the problems I have discussed. We might say, moreover, that it is just as 'masculinist' to draw on 'ethic of care' premises if 'masculinist' simply means that it is a conception articulated by 'male thinkers.'[68] We find the seeds of the 'ethic of care' approach in Mill, where it makes women bearers of the greater share of 'political duties.' In all three thinkers, women's role in reproduction is fundamentally connected to their political status.

WOMEN AND POLITICS

Several themes have emerged in my reading of Hobbes, Locke, and J.S. Mill. One is that women's role in reproduction is a sign not of their *incapacity* but their *capacity* to participate in political life. In the context of the importance placed on securing and accounting for parent-child ties, however, women's role in reproduction is also what places them in the middle of the tension between rights and duties (indeed, introducing the question of reproductive rights for women discloses the friction between rights and duties in the liberal framework) and ultimately prevents them from enjoying equal political status. This holds true whether women are considered to be essentially the same as men (Hobbes and Locke) or different from men in their capacities and predilections (J.S. Mill).

In Hobbes and Locke, women's activity in the realm of reproduction is an indicator that they have the same faculty as men for reason (including self-interested deliberations) and therefore for political life. Yet, their different (biologically grounded) relations to reproduction, coupled with their capacity for reason, also make it problematic for them to achieve the same political status as men. It makes it problematic to extend to them a fundamental political right enjoyed by men – the right to govern their own bodies. In Mill, where women are presented as having different tendencies and predilections from men – being more inclined to the care of others, more prone to subsume their interests in the care of their families, more predisposed to choose domestic life, more competent in household management and more practical-minded – these differences are not deemed to be a liability when it comes to politics. Indeed they seem to make women peculiarly suited for politics, in part because the political realm is depicted as being increasingly an extension of the household one.

This brings me to another theme I find pervasive in the liberal framework: what I call the 'feminization of politics'; that is politics is associated less with 'masculinist' preoccupations and requirements than 'feminine' ones. For example, in Hobbes, citizenship is *not* associated with the 'warrior hero' who is often deemed to embody the 'masculinist' biases of traditional conceptions of politics. The Hobbesian subject is more worried about bodily self-preservation, a concern usually attributed to women. Locke comes close to upholding women's practical everyday reason as a virtue of the good citizen. In Mill we find that the requirements of the political realm are depicted as resembling those of the domestic realm – the administration of everyday matters and financial management – so that women's peculiar talents and predilections – their practical bent, and their experience in the household – would seem to give them an advantage over men.

Paradoxically, however, the 'feminization of politics' does not necessarily benefit women when it comes to achieving equal political status. In Mill, for example, their distinctive predilections, which revolve around the domestic realm, make them as capable as, if not more capable than, men of participating in politics and give rise to different interests that require political representation. Yet their responsibility for the domestic realm is also what prevents most from engaging in politics at a meaningful level (beyond simply voting) to the same degree as men. There are exceptions – women whose domestic duties are over, those few who choose public life over domestic life, or those who have the means to hire paid domestic help may move on to hold political office.

Furthermore, in Mill's account women get the equal opportunity to exercise their political rights. But the result is inequality of outcome. They are expected to undertake the greater share of political duties inside and outside the family. Yet, this does not seem to secure for them much political power, that is much influence in determining the political agenda. Inequality of outcome is exacerbated for working-class women who do not have the means to hire domestic help.

Paying attention to why it is difficult for women to achieve equal status in the conceptual models we find in Hobbes, Locke, and J.S. Mill can inform the debate over why they are under-represented in the political life of modern liberal societies such as Canada. Most of the studies on the issue conclude that women participate to the same extent as men at mass levels of activity such as voting but are relatively (numerically) absent from elite levels of activity such as holding political office, especially leadership positions.[69] Usually we find two kinds of explanations for this situation. The first, the 'structuralist' one, suggests that there are certain structural barriers that impede women's access to the system, such as the rising costs of electoral success, party recruitment practices, the single-member plurality system, or the preference for incumbents built into the party system.[70] In time, and with remedial measures aimed at removing some of these barriers, such as allocating funds for female candidates, implementing affirmative action policies to encourage the recruitment of female candidates, or adding seats based on proportional representation, women will eventually achieve equal representation to men, it is assumed.

A second kind of explanation, the 'masculinist' one, suggests that there is a deeper problem. The political realm, it is argued, is a sphere defined by men, for men.[71] The requirements for politics are 'masculine' ones, which are incompatible with women's different capacities, skills, and needs. This is why we find fewer women than men at elite levels of politics. The masculinist explanation implies that remedial measures may not make much difference. They may simply leave intact the fundamentally masculine nature of politics, but pressure women into becoming 'like men' to achieve success. Until the requirements for political success are changed to reflect female qualities and experience, women will continue to be excluded.[72]

Heeding what we find in Hobbes, Locke, and Mill can alert us to deficiencies in both kinds of explanations. The 'structuralist' explanation seems to suppose the following: women have essentially the same capacities as men for politics and the same motivations for entering it; they already enjoy the same political rights as men, such as the right to vote and hold office; it is just a matter of removing the structural barriers such as party recruitment practices for them to enjoy equal political status to men. These kinds of assumptions may hide what we find in Hobbes – that women's differences, deriving from the biologically grounded relations to reproduction, make the extension of equal rights to them problematic. The right to govern their own bodies is difficult for them to secure for the reasons I have addressed (witness the opposition to abortion, which has not abated since the 1988 Supreme Court ruling and which has taken a violent turn with the recent bombings of abortion clinics and doctors in major Canadian cities).[73] A second problem with the structural explanation is that it does not capture what Mill's model shows to be an important dimension of the issue: by soliciting women to engage in politics one may be asking them to undertake the greater share of the political duties without increasing their power to influence the political agenda (I will return to this point).

The theme we find in liberal thought – the 'feminization of politics' – can alert us to some deficiencies in the 'masculinist' explanation. Ironically, it seems that the requirements for politics are becoming more 'feminine' or 'female' just as it being more forcefully argued, by feminists in particular, that they are based on 'masculine' or 'male' means. For example, Jane S. Jaquette distinguishes among four kinds of power – coercion, authority, manipulation, and persuasion.[74] The problem, according to Jaquette, is that the kinds of power women tend to use and have access to – manipulation and persuasion – are not as easily transferable to the public arena as the kinds of power that men use – coercion and authority.[75] It seems, however, that manipulation and persuasion are precisely the kinds of powers that are amenable to success in modern liberal societies where the naked exercise of force or coercion is for the most part seen as illegitimate, and where those who wield the legitimate authority of the state are perceived to be increasingly powerless and subservient to the interests of pressure groups. Moreover, the most successful of these groups are depicted as relying on manipulation and persuasion in the form of behind-the-scenes negotiations with elected officials and civil servants to influence the political agenda before it is subject to the formal decision-making process.[76] The most powerful groups, those most able to promote their interests, despite obstacles, seem to be those whose activities are most 'hidden.'[77] As Nancy F. Cott observes, women's organizations can be seen as forerunners in the successful use of pressure group tactics.[78]

Assuming that politics is a 'masculinist activity' may obscure the extent to which male politicians are using means traditionally associated with women to achieve success. The assumption may be detrimental to women by prompting them to use and acquire 'masculinist' qualities and means just as the changing nature of politics makes them less amenable to success. For example, increasingly, male politicians are relying on dress, image, and appearance in response to the growing influence of the media on politics; yet female politicians may be encouraged to rebel against the preoccupation with dress and image as detracting from their political competence.[79]

The 'feminization of politics' we find in the liberal framework can alert us to three possibilities:(1)With the changing nature of politics in modern liberal societies such as Canada, the qualities and means associated with women may increasingly be relevant to political success. (2)

But we cannot assume that the 'feminizing of politics' will ensure that women achieve equal political status. (3) There may be something other than the inherently 'masculinist' criteria for political success to account for women's absence from elite-level politics. Mill's model suggests that their domestic responsibilities are the key.

Much in line with Mill's prediction that only older women whose family responsibilities were diminished or those without families would likely go beyond voting to become members of Parliament, Sylvia Bashevkin notes that in Canada, 'as a group, female legislators have tended to be unmarried; either childless or with children older than those of their male counterparts; and older than men upon their first election to public office.'[80] Mill's model suggests a number of things, among them that women's role as the 'caretakers' in society may be incompatible with the exercise of elite levels of politics not because it undermines their capacity for politics but because it gives women a disadvantage in accumulating the economic resources that are integral to successful electoral politics (or interest group lobbying). When Brodie suggests that 'The constraints of motherhood in a society that does not provide much recognition for the need for child care may delay a woman's career in politics but does not in itself explain why so few women choose a full-time political role,'[81] she seems to disregard the advantage which the 'delay' gives to men. She may also be overlooking the extent to which the constraints of motherhood are based on perceived as well as 'real' responsibilities. When she mentions that women candidates consistently cited finances as a more significant barrier to their success than family obligations, she fails to highlight that many cited funding as a problem because of the *costs* of child care and domestic help.[82] This suggests that these women did perceive family obligations to be a constraint in the sense that they felt that they could only engage in politics if their family duties were undertaken by paid help.

Mill can attune us to other dimensions of the problem. First, the degree to which women undertake and carry out the 'duty' aspect of political citizenship, in the form of activity that advances the well-being of others and the community as a whole, may be hidden if one assumes a 'narrow' definition of politics[83] which focuses on the realm in which government office holders are elected and make decisions.[84] It becomes more apparent that women's activity in the domestic realm, including the care of children, contributes to and advances political ends when women fail to do it, when the state is called in to take over. Second, in light of their greater share of the political duties inside the home, asking them to participate outside the home may be perceived as an added burden to their already greater political responsibilities.[85] There is evidence that women have traditionally engaged in electoral politics more out of a sense of duty – advancing the welfare of others – than of 'rights' – pursuing their own interest[86] – and that their motivations may continue to be coloured by such expectations.[87] Third, it may be a question of expecting women to undertake the larger share of duties in the form of 'caring' for others, without necessarily expanding their opportunity to further their own interests or increase their power – to influence the political agenda. It seems incongruous that there is so much emphasis on getting women into party politics and representative institutions just as there is a growing perception that the rewards of political life are diminishing, that political parties have declined as a vehicle for advancing political interests, and that there is not much real power to be had in representative institutions.[88] Some analysts have noted that the increasing numbers of women elected to the Canadian House of Commons in the last few years have not necessarily improved the status of women in society.[89] Others like Bashevkin allude to the limits of electoral politics alone,[90] but affirm that numbers do count when it comes to placing women's (differential) interests on the political agenda:

> Study after study of political elites in Canada, the US and other liberal democratic systems demonstrates that *women's numerical presence does make a substantive difference*. Whether measured with reference to the content of women's speeches in a legislature, their roll call behaviour on legislative bills or their policy preferences for future legislative action, the evidence of a policy differential vis-à-vis men is sustained across a considerable body of empirical literature.[91]

This brings us to another consideration coming out of Mill: it may be important to get women into positions where they can influence the political agenda, whether through representative institutions, interest groups, or the civil service, because women may have 'different' interests which can best be advanced by women themselves. Yet, assumptions about women's difference – if they are assumptions about their 'ethic of care' orientation – may in fact work against their interests.

Mill's model brings us to a final important consideration. The idea that women have a greater predilection for having and caring for children and for the care of others in general is too easily coupled with the idea that the care of children and the 'caretaking duties' in society on the whole are something for which individuals, women in particular, are responsible out of their own means, without state support. In others words, the Millian option of associating women with an ethic of care sits quite comfortably with (Lockean) neo-conservatism, a defining characteristic of which is to call for a less interventionist state. It may make it easier to support and implement state withdrawal from the provision of care (whether for children, the elderly, or the infirm) when it is assumed that women have a predilection for that kind of work. Without state-provided incentives for men to undertake it, women easily end up with the responsibility for the care of children (and others who need it) and the domestic realm, which in turn prevents them from participating in politics at levels where they can influence the political agenda. (In addition, state cut-backs have also been directed at women's groups and organizations, undercutting the economic resources which are essential for successful lobbying efforts.)

It is disconcerting that 'ethic of care' assumptions have pervaded feminist discourse (since the early 1980s) at the same time as 'neo-conservative' principles have gained political force (since the early 1980s). It is disturbing that the Royal Commission on New Reproductive Technologies invokes the 'ethic of care' to profess a commitment to providing a 'supportive and caring environment' for women[92] but also sets out as a guiding principle of the 'ethic of care' 'the appropriate use of resources' in 'difficult economic and political times.'[93] What we cannot be sure of is that women will not end up bearing the 'costs of caring.'

CHAPTER FIVE

Feminist Alternatives?

Does feminist thought overcome, reconcile, or avoid the contradictions that we see arising for women in the liberal framework as articulated by Hobbes, Locke, and J.S. Mill? Does it point us in the direction of alternative models that are inclusive of women, children, and men? It is difficult to begin to answer such questions without becoming engaged in the growing debate over what constitutes a 'feminist' perspective. This debate is spurred by the proliferation of assorted and conflicting viewpoints on what exactly is wrong with women's position or with the feminist theory that tries to describe that position. Some have tried to encompass this growing diversity by defining 'feminism' very loosely,[1] compelling one observer to conclude that 'currently feminism seems to be a term without any clear significance. The "anything goes" approach to the definition of the word has rendered it practically meaningless.'[2]

More typically, analysts have tried to sort out different kinds of feminisms, classifying them according to a range of criteria, such as the position they take on 'women's nature' or the political traditions they assume. Alison Jaggar, for example, distinguishes among liberal, radical, Marxist, and socialist feminists.[3] Liberal feminists (J.S. Mill and Mary Wollstonecraft) assume women have the same capacity as men for reason and advocate that they be given the same rights as men. Radical feminists (who first emerged in the 1960s) emphasize women's subordination by men in a system of domination known as 'patriarchy.' Marxist feminists claim that the abolition of capitalism will do away with the need to oppress women. Finally, socialist feminists attempt to synthesize Marxist and radical feminist precepts.

Jaggar's scheme, although useful in showing how feminists draw on the Western tradition of political thought, needs some refining. Under the category of 'radical' feminists she places writers who have opposing views on the significance of the female body and the role biology plays in women's oppression. Moreover, many of the feminists she labels as 'socialists,' Nancy Chodorow and Dorothy Dinnerstein for example, could more appropriately be labelled 'maternal feminists,' since they emphasize women's maternal function to account for their situation. Jaggar's classification also makes no room for an important feminist thinker – Simone de Beauvoir.[4]

Rosemarie Tong assumes Jaggar's basic framework but expands on it, subdividing 'radical feminists' into those who focus on psychoanalysis, gender, and reproduction and adding existentialist (Simone de Beauvoir) and post-modern feminism.[5] In addition she provides a useful summary of the common criticisms made of each type of feminism from the perspective of alternative feminist standpoints. She thereby illustrates that there is considerable debate within feminist circles over what feminism ought to be; over which feminist positions are more conducive to women's liberation than others; and over whether some feminist perspectives are compatible with 'reactionary' movements. But Tong's list of feminisms does little to sort out the conceptual differences or similarities among them (for example, it does not show the similarity between liberal feminists and Simone de Beauvoir).

It is indeed difficult to determine which kind of feminism is 'radical' or 'reactionary.' As Hester Eisenstein observes, the term 'radical' has been applied to opposing kinds of feminist positions.[6] What may once have been deemed 'radical' may now be considered 'reactionary.' In the 1960s, the 'radical' feminists were those, like Betty Friedan and Simone de Beauvoir, who suggested that women were the same as men, that sex made no difference. By the 1970s, however, these earlier feminists became known as 'liberal feminists' and were perceived to be quite 'conservative.' They spurred a reaction of (real)'radical' feminists who maintained that women's difference from men was the foundation for their liberation. According to Eisenstein, feminism offers three alternatives for women. The first, the 'liberal feminist' one, counsels women to accept male values and to compete in the male world on male terms. The second, a 'reactionary' one espoused by such writers as Mary Daly and Susan Griffin, uses the idea of women's difference to claim female superiority and advises women to withdraw from the male world to a (superior) female one. And the third alternative, the only truly 'radical' one, Eisenstein concludes, proposes that women enter the male world and change it using 'woman-centred' values.

Eisenstein's analysis is valuable for revealing that there may be considerable disagreement over whether an emphasis on women's difference undermines or enhances feminism's radical and liberatory potential. But her distinction between 'radical' and 'reactionary' feminism is not that clear. The feminists she designates as 'radical,' such as Nancy Chodorow and Adrienne Rich, do in fact imply that women are superior to men. As a result, they would have to be deemed as 'reactionary' according to Eisenstein's own criteria.

Josephine Donovan shows how disputes over women's difference/sameness have led to political disagreements.[7] She distinguishes between 'liberal feminists' (rooted in J.S. Mill and Mary Wollstonecraft), who assume women have the same faculties for reason as men, and 'cultural' feminists, who focus on women's difference from men and highlight their maternal function. Representatives of both groups coalesced in the American women's suffrage movement, but the clash between the two re-emerged in the debate over the Equal Rights Amendment. 'Cultural' feminists opposed the Amendment, arguing in favour of protective legislation for women. 'Liberal' feminists supported the Amendment as a way of securing equal opportunity for women. Each side accused the other of working against the best interests of women.[8] Donovan's distinction between 'liberal' and 'cultural' feminists, although valuable in highlighting the conflict over sameness/difference, seems to have no place for the other kinds of feminisms she briefly mentions, such as Marxist, Freudian, and psychoanalytical feminism. Lynne Segal offers a broader definition of 'cultural feminism' – as including all positions which focus on women's difference from men.[9] But this does not tell us which kinds of differences are deemed to be most important.

A number of analysts have emphasized the historical dimension of debates over women's nature and disputes over what strategies might best serve women. Starting from the eighteenth and nineteenth century, Karen Offen finds traces of two divergent ways of thinking about women's emancipation in Anglo-American and European ideas – an 'individualist' and a 'relational' one.[10] The former poses the individual, irrespective of sex or gender, as the basic unit of society and emphasizes women's potential to become such an 'individual.' The latter poses the companionate, male-female couple as the basic unit of society, emphasizing women's distinctive, often her child-bearing, role. Olive Banks finds three 'faces' of feminism emerging in the eighteenth and nineteenth century.[11] 'Welfare feminism,' with its roots in Evangelical Christianity, maintained that women's difference from men consisted in their moral superiority, derived from their maternal capacities. It arose as the predominant strand of feminism in the inter-war years and lobbied for protective legislation for women. The ideals of the Enlightenment brought forth the second strand – 'equal rights' feminism – which maintained that women were essentially the same as men and consequently should be given the same rights. The third strand of feminism, associated with socialism, preached free-love and communitarianism. It re-emerged in the 1960s as radical feminism. But as Banks herself admits, her three faces of feminism may not capture the diversity of ideas that emerged in the 1960s.

Another difficulty that arises in defining feminism, according to Naomi Black, is that women's groups who may declare themselves to be 'anti-feminist' may nevertheless be committed to increasing women's autonomy.[12] Black identifies two kinds of feminisms – 'social' and 'equity' feminism. In the former she places those who focus on values and experiences identified with women, including groups such as the 'maternal feminists' of the nineteenth century and the 'radical' feminists of the twentieth century. In the category of 'equity feminists' she places all those, such as 'liberal,' 'Marxist,' and 'socialist' feminists, who 'extend(s) existing belief systems to include women previously excluded.'[13] Black's study gives us some valuable insights into how women's groups or movements that declare themselves to be 'anti-feminist' may be reacting to a particular definition of feminism. However, her framework pays too little attention to the distinctions among 'equity feminists,' the dissimilarities between liberal and Marxist feminists, for example.[14]

Judith Grant proposes that there are three core concepts at the base of 'feminist theory' shared by all types of feminisms: (1) 'woman' (2) 'experience' (3) 'personal politics.'[15] She then goes on to challenge these concepts, showing how they are imbued with problematic assumptions. In her conclusions she calls for a feminism that challenges the 'ideology of gender,' defines the 'feminist subject' through practice, and aims for 'the creation of new human beings who are self-determining.'[16] The importance of her analysis is that it suggests that there is some coherence to feminist thought, despite its growing diversity. What is needed, however, is a way of classifying how feminists have defined the content of concepts such as 'woman.'

Defining feminism in a way that encompasses the variety of positions espoused by feminist writers, sorts them out conceptually, and makes sense of historical variations is no easy task. Moreover, the legitimacy of such an endeavour is increasingly being thrown into question by the influence of 'post-modern' or 'post-structuralist' assumptions on feminist thought. Defining, labelling, categorizing, and classifying are deemed to be 'masculine' or 'phallocentric' pursuits exemplifying in a particularly insidious way the exclusionary exercise of power, or what Judith Butler refers to as the drive for 'conceptual mastery.'[17] 'Post-structuralist' warnings aside, it is important to provide a conceptual framework for sorting out different kinds of feminist perspectives if one wants to say anything about the potential of feminist thought to lay the groundwork for alternative models of the community (an enterprise which post-structuralist assumptions also challenge, for reasons I will turn to shortly).

Drawing on the strengths of the efforts outlined above and trying to avoid their weaknesses, I define a feminist perspective as including the following propositions: that women's position either in theory or in practice is oppressed (the dictionary usage – to be subject to a burdensome or harsh exercise of authority or power); that a sign of their oppression is their exclusion from or inferior status in any number of realms, whether the social, the political, or the economic; and that their position ought to be changed – their oppression ameliorated or eliminated.

Variations or types of feminisms emerge out of diverse explanations for why it is that women are oppressed and call for diverse strategies for changing that position, whether in theory or in practice. On this basis I distinguish between two broad categories. The first is a 'feminism of sameness,' according to which the main source of women's oppression is that they are *not* treated as if they were the same as men; the second is a 'feminism of difference,' according to which the main source of women's oppression is that their differences are either devalued, unacknowledged, or ignored. 'Feminism of difference' subdivides, depending on what is assumed to be the main source of women's difference: for 'maternal' feminism it is women's role in reproduction; for 'sexual feminism' it is women's sexuality ('post-structuralist' feminism is an outgrowth of this type of feminism); for 'experiential' feminism it is their experiences, very much influenced by their activities in the private realm. These kinds of feminisms add up to different ways of approaching the problem of women's oppression. Of course not all writers who address the issue fit neatly into these categories, but most have a central orientation compatible with these variations.

From the perspective of feminism of sameness, the problem with

Western political thought is this: Women are excluded from and inferior in the social or political realm because of the perception that there are natural differences between men and women that justify treating them differently, or because the obvious biological differences between men and women have been exaggerated to the point where they are deemed to have important social and political implications. The solutions a 'feminism of sameness' approach offers usually take one of two forms. The first is to show that women, having the same capacities as men, can be incorporated into existing models of the community or existing practices, even those hitherto established by men. The second is to show that existing models or practices are tainted by assumptions about women's differences and to come up with new models that treat men and women as being the same, that is which minimize the social and political implications of any biological differences. We find in Simone de Beauvoir a good example of the first alternative and in Susan Moller Okin an example of the second one.

From a 'feminism of difference' perspective, the problem with Western political thought is not that women are considered to be different from men, but that their difference is either overlooked, unacknowledged, or deemed to be a sign of inferiority; as a result it is neither valued nor incorporated into traditional articulations of politics. This makes it difficult if not impossible to assimilate women into the conceptions articulated by these mostly male theorists. What may be needed, 'feminism of difference' implies, are alternative models that draw on women's difference.[18]

Moreover, sometimes tacitly but often explicitly, a 'feminism of difference' approach challenges the viability and desirability of a 'feminism of sameness.' By emphasizing that women are the same as men, it is argued, one may be attributing to women qualities that are inherently masculinist or assuming a male standard by which to judge what women are or ought to be. Thereby one is hiding and inadvertently perpetuating the innate masculinity of Western conceptions. One is also then denying women's difference (or in the case of 'poststructuralist' approaches the principle of difference itself). This is not to say that all who challenge a 'feminism of sameness' approach or who try to demonstrate that the Western tradition is beset by masculinist assumptions take a 'feminism of difference' perspective. But most do, in part because it is difficult to show that something is innately 'masculine' without assuming that there is something 'feminine' which is missing.[19]

I have avoided using the term 'liberal feminism.' Although more awkward, 'feminism of sameness' is a more accurate name for the kind of feminism usually labelled as 'liberal.' Moreover, to use the former is to imply that traditional liberal theorists emphasize women's similarity to men, grounds on which they support the extension of equal rights to them. Yet Mill, who is often cited as a forerunner or example of 'liberal feminism,' in fact presents women as having different predilections from men. It is on this basis, moreover, rather than on the ground that they are the same as men, that he makes a case for extending to them equal rights. If there is an element in the liberal tradition that provides a foundation for liberal feminism, it is to be found in Hobbes and Locke more than in J.S. Mill.

To use the phrase 'liberal feminism' also implies that only those who emphasize the similarities between men and women are beset by liberal assumptions. Yet, we find liberal premises throughout 'feminism of difference,' in particular when it comes to the issue of reproductive rights or parent-child relations. This brings me to how I want to assess these feminist approaches. I ask questions which I think are integral to sketching out alternatives. The difficulties we see in liberal thought can make us mindful of two things. The first is: How does a feminist approach account for the having and care of children? This is a fundamental question. Any theoretical model has to account for how the community can perpetuate itself. The second question is connected to the first: How do various feminist approaches address the issue of reproductive rights or depict women's role in reproduction? In particular, how do they deal with what poses a problem in the liberal framework – women's biologically grounded relations to reproduction?

FEMINISM OF SAMENESS

As Simone de Beauvoir describes it, the main source of women's oppression is that they have been treated as if they were different from men – as if they were not as capable or desirous of engaging in what she depicts as the highest form of active and creative engagement in life – 'transcendence.'[20] The central requirement for their liberation is repudiating what they have been defined as by men – the 'other' and rejecting what they have been confined to for much of their history – 'immanence' or the passive repetition of life. In pre-history, the obvious biological differences between men and women may have had some social and political significance, but in the modern world they need not determine what women are or what they do. De Beauvoir's central assertion is

'One is not born, but rather becomes a woman. No biological, psychological, or economic fate determines the figure that the human female presents in society; it is civilization as a whole that produces this creature intermediate between male and eunuch which is described as feminine.'[21] Women must recognize that what has been ascribed to them – the 'feminine' – is artificial. Their task is to assume and demonstrate that they can as well as men acquire the loftiest attitudes that transcendence (as men have experienced and articulated it) entails – 'heroism, revolt, disinterestedness, imagination, creation.'[22]

De Beauvoir often repudiates, quite adamantly, the idea that women's liberation consists in the setting up of female values in contradiction to male ones. In particular she opposes the notion that women's bodily differences can or ought to be the foundation for the creation of new (female) values: 'But one should not make it a value in itself either; one should not believe that the female body gives one a new vision of the world. That would be ridiculous and absurd.'[23] Neither is their bodily difference a basis for a new form of expression or language: 'I consider it almost antifeminist to say there is a feminine nature which expresses itself differently, that a woman speaks her body more than a man because after all, men also speak their bodies when they write.'[24] Women have accepted male values as human values in the past, de Beauvoir maintains: 'In truth women have never set up female values in opposition to male values; it is man who, desirous of maintaining masculine prerogatives, has invented that divergence.'[25] She speculates that they will likely continue to do so in the future: 'But I do not think women will create new values. If you believe the opposite, then what you are believing in is a feminine nature – which I have always opposed.'[26] The challenge for women is not to contest the 'human' values men have articulated but to show how they apply to women. The 'modern woman,' de Beauvoir writes, 'accepts masculine values: she prides herself on thinking, taking action, working, creating, on the same terms as men; instead of seeking to disparage them, she declares herself their equal.'[27]

In contrast with her assertions about women having the same capacity as men for transcendence and accepting male-articulated values as 'human values,' her depiction of women's situation seems to support a 'feminism of difference' in places. For example, women's relegation to immanence is biologically induced, she implies – the result of their unique biologically grounded reproductive capacities. In one passage, de Beauvoir describes women as being governed by a reproductive cycle which ties them closer than men to nature, to their species being, and to immanence, making 'the female ... the victim of the species.'[28] This seems to be more compatible with a 'maternal feminist' approach. Moreover, she hints that women's eroticism is more diverse, their sexuality more complex than men's and less governed by the desire to dominate, a perspective that is compatible with sexual feminism and with post-structuralism's emphasis on 'multiplicity.'[29] Furthermore, de Beauvoir intimates at times that, since women have had different experiences or life situations (such as not having had as much power as men), they might bring a different perspective to bear on public life. By entering society they might transform it: 'In my view, the real task of feminism can only be the transformation of society along with the transformation of women's place in it.'[30] She also hints in places that women's distinctive experience of life may make it problematic to apply 'male' norms to them, an attitude that is compatible with experiential feminism.[31]

While maintaining a self-professed 'feminism of sameness' stance, de Beauvoir often provides evidence in support of a 'feminism of difference' position, which is perhaps one of the reasons her rich and complex work has been extensively criticized and analysed from a 'feminism of difference' perspective. De Beauvoir's approach, it is argued, illustrates the costs of sustaining a feminism of sameness – whatever is associated with women, such as their unique role in reproduction, is devalued and ultimately rejected. The main problem with de Beauvoir is that as well as accepting a male definition of humanity, she also accepts male assumptions about what reproduction is, including the supposition that it is 'natural' and that the giving of life is less important than the risking or taking of life. According to Virginia Held, for example:

> That even de Beauvoir, so perceptive of the domination of women by men in so many ways, should share the mistaken construction of birth and child care as inherently 'natural' reminds us of how gendered are the underlying assumptions with which we must begin and from which we can of course not break free all at once.[32]

It is clear that de Beauvoir deems motherhood to be incompatible with women's liberation. She writes in *The Second Sex*: 'There is one feminine function that it is actually almost impossible to perform in complete liberty. It is maternity.'[33] In an interview, she says: 'And I think that motherhood is the most dangerous snare for all those women who want to be free and independent, for those who want to earn their living, for those who want to think for themselves, and for those women who want to have a life of their own.'[34]

It is also evident, as Held and others point out, that de Beauvoir considers mothering as something that confines women to nature, to the passive repetition of life and as a result to immanence: 'But in any case giving birth and suckling are not activities, they are natural functions; no project is involved; and that is why woman found in them no reason for a lofty affirmation of her existence – she submitted passively to her biologic fate.'[35] Furthermore, according to de Beauvoir, 'The worst curse that was laid upon woman was that she should be excluded from these warlike forays. For it is not in giving life but in risking life that man is raised above the animal; that is why superiority has been accorded in humanity not to the sex that brings forth but to that which kills.'[36]

Is de Beauvoir's rejection of motherhood proof of her masculinist moorings as Held claims it is? Is it proof that she accepts what Held regards as pervasive in Western (including liberal) thought – a distinctively male construct which associates reproduction, mothering in particular, with nature? Held's analysis does not quite apprehend what is at work in de Beauvoir. As I have argued, 'mothering' is more rational than natural in Hobbes and Locke. Moreover, in Hobbes' depiction it is an engagement in transcendence – choosing whether to give or take life – rather than a confinement to immanence – the passive repetition of life.[37] I want to suggest, however, that what de Beauvoir may be accepting are liberal assumptions about parent-child relations (found mainly in Hobbes and Locke), in which 'mothering' easily becomes irrational. It becomes irrational not because women are considered to be incapable of reason or tied to nature, but precisely because they are considered to be capable of rational deliberations about what is in their interest. Such deliberations, if one does not recognize, accept, or have at one's disposal what liberal thought offers – state-provided incentives (Hobbes), a belief in one's (God-given) duty to procreate (Locke), and the assumption that women have a predilection for mothering (J.S. Mill) – are likely to lead to the conclusion that there are no good reasons for becoming a parent. De Beauvoir's own account of why she and Sartre decided against having children may serve as an illustration. The conclusion they arrived at a result of their deliberations was that they could see no benefits to the undertaking.[38] We might say that de Beauvoir rejects mothering for herself and for women in general not only for the obvious reasons she gives (that it confines them to nature) but also because she assumes a liberal framework in which it is difficult to show that mothering or fathering is in the parents' interests.

De Beauvoir supports giving women the right to abortion as a prerequisite for their liberation from 'natural necessity,' as a way of securing for them, we might say, a more rational control over reproduction.[39] Yet, as we see in Hobbes and Locke, the problem is not that women are subject to 'natural necessity.' The problem is that their reproductive capacities make them subject to political and social necessity – or what is considered to be integral to the social and political well-being of society.[40]

We might say that de Beauvoir is advocating that women be given what Hobbes attributes to them in the state of nature. Yet once mothering becomes an opportunity for transcendence, in de Beauvoir's terms a project that can be freely chosen, it easily becomes irrational to actively choose to engage in it. We are then back to the problem of the Hobbesian state of nature. What incentives does civil society have to offer women (or men) for undertaking what is necessary to its perpetuation?

Feminism of sameness has been extensively criticized for recommending that women do what men have traditionally done – enter the public sphere – and forego what women have traditionally done – care for children. The problem, as critics have noted, is that it leaves a gap: Who does cares for the children? Susan Moller Okin tries to address this issue.

According to Okin, the problem with modern and traditional notions of the just society is that they are founded on the assumption that there are natural differences between men and women which make women the 'natural' caretakers of the family or private realm.[41] Embedded in the very structural arrangements of liberal societies and liberal thought, these assumptions make it difficult if not impossible for women to achieve equal status in the public realm. Okin proposes an alternative model. Its chief condition is that women and men would be treated as if they were the same. In particular, one would find no assumptions about a natural basis for women's role in the care of children inherent in its structures or practices:

> A just future would be one without gender. In its social structure and practises, one's sex would have no more relevance than one's eye colour or the length of one's toes. No assumptions would be made about 'male' and 'female' roles: childbearing would be conceptually separated from child rearing and other family responsibilities.[42]

In repudiating the idea that there are differences between men and women that have social and political implications, Okin also repudiates the notion that women have a natural predilection to care for children. In addition, the way she recommends support for laws which establish paternity at birth and oblige fathers to contribute to child support implies that there is no natural paternal instinct to care for children.[43]

The central requirement of Okin's sketch for a society in which justice would be achieved for women in both the private and public realms is that responsibility for the care of children be shared by both parents: 'First, public policies and laws should generally assume no social differentiation of the sexes. Shared parental responsibility for child care would be both assumed and facilitated.'[44] What I find wanting, however, is a consideration of why women or men would have and care for children, if parenting is not influenced by natural maternal or paternal predilections. Without such considerations, it becomes difficult to envision how a just society could perpetuate itself. I think what Okin and others critical of the liberal tradition consistently tend to overlook or underplay is that the liberal difficulty in accounting for community is a problem more of explaining relations between the generations (mothers and fathers and children) than of explaining relations among adult men and women. This brings me to a second point.

Okin wants to eliminate any reason for treating men and women as if they were different. This is evident in the way that she approaches pregnancy. She recommends that we treat it as a temporarily disabling condition.[45] Employers would be mandated to provide a leave for it which might vary among women, depending on the degree to which the pregnancy disabled them. Okin does not seem to consider what came up earlier in my discussion of abortion: the fact that a woman carries a new life may not give her a natural instinct to care for it, but it does give her first access to it. Moreover, it may be the case that in the just society Okin envisions both men and women can share the care of an infant after birth, yet it remains necessary for the woman to 'care' for the fetus before birth. Okin does, of course, criticize the liberal framework. Interestingly, she reproaches Robert Nozick for neglecting to consider the impact on women of his theory of entitlement and the ownership of one's body.[46] She also notes that women's right to control their own bodies raises a dilemma because it involves the potential lives of others.[47] Yet, she gives no indication that she would spurn the liberal legacy when it comes to women's right to govern their own bodies, nor does she affirm outright that a just society would include for women such a right. In her eagerness to treat men and women as if they were the same, as if their biological reproductive capacities had few social and political implications, Okin puts aside the ramifications women's bodily reproductive differences might have when it comes to the question of enjoying the same reproductive rights as men.

This preliminary exploration indicates that the difficulties of the liberal legacy are not overcome in the 'feminism of sameness' approach. We find (de Beauvoir) liberal assumptions about parent-child relations. Coupled with the desire to extend to women the right to govern their own bodies (the right to abortion) and without a consideration of the incentives that might have to put into place to prevent mothering from becoming irrational, feminism of sameness points to a model of liberation in which women would refuse to have and care for children. Moreover, (Okin) we see that the attempt to treat women as the same runs into obstacles when it comes to the issue of reproductive rights, which inevitably bring up the matter of women having different bodies – different reproductive capacities. Furthermore, if neither men nor women have a natural predilection to care for children, then one must consider why they would do it, if one wants to come up with a model that ensures generational continuity. Although a 'maternal feminism' approach emphasizes the importance and value of child-rearing, it too seems to be wanting when it comes to explaining why men would 'mother.'

FEMINISM OF DIFFERENCE: MATERNAL FEMINISM

In various ways, Dorothy Dinnerstein, Nancy Chodorow, Mary O'Brien, and Nancy Hartsock consider women's engagement in having and caring for children to be a source of difference which ought to be valued. They also account for women's oppression both in society and in Western theoretical constructions by referring to their role in reproduction. Each makes recommendations for changing women's situation either by incorporating into the larger society qualities associated with women's maternal function or by constructing alternative theories founded on women's distinctive reproductive consciousness.

According to Dorothy Dinnerstein, women's subjugation by men can be attributed to two factors: (1) that humans are born helpless and develop independence slowly compared to other animals and (2) that women are almost universally in charge of child care.[48] She goes on to propose that the psychodynamics of the infant's early relationship with the mother, different for boys and girls, can help to explain the differences that men and women exhibit as adults. Most important, it can help to explain why men may feel the need to oppress women. Although both men and women probably have an ambiguous attitude towards women (based on their memory of the power their mothers had over them as infants), this ambiguity is amplified in men. Because they are of the opposite sex, it is more difficult for men than women to undergo and to complete the process of differentiation from the mother that is part of moving away from infancy. This may manifest itself in the search for the 'lost mother' in adult heterosexual relationships and the need to dominate women both as a way of conquering (repressed) fears of the power that women as mothers once had over them and as a way of carrying out the difficult and uncompleted process of separation and differentiation.

Our ambivalence towards women, according to Dinnerstein, derives from women's engagement in the care of children after birth; it does not necessarily rest on the fact that they bear them.[49] If their role in caring for both sexes has been responsible, to a large degree, for women's oppression, then the solution, according to Dinnerstein, is to engage men in the care of children. Once men 'mother,' they too will be attributed the powerful and ambiguous associations at present assigned to women alone.[50] What Dinnerstein does not adequately explain, however, is how and why this solution would come about, given that she explains why women 'mother' by referring to the natural biological instincts and urges they share with other animals. The milk let-down response to an infant's cry, Dinnerstein suggests, shows that mothers have a natural instinct to care for children.[51] If this is the case, then it seems difficult to account for why men would do the 'mothering.'

A similar difficulty emerges in Nancy Chodorow's analysis.[52] According to it, women become mothers not because they have a natural maternal instinct but because the experience of being mothered by a woman reproduces in them the desire and the need to have children as well as the capacity to care for them. Chodorow uses object relations theory to describe the dynamics of the early infant-mother relationship. As adults, both sexes may try to recapture the emotional intensity of the pre-Oedipal relationship with the mother. Men can seek to recapture it in their heterosexual relationships with women. But since homosexual relationships for women are generally taboo, women have a more difficult time reviving the emotional dynamic of the pre-Oedipal relationship with the mother (a woman) in adult sexual relations. As a result, Chodorow implies, they often seek it by having children themselves.

Like Dinnerstein, Chodorow suggests that women's exclusive responsibility for the care of children also facilitates the oppression of women by reproducing in men the psychological propensity to dominate women.[53] Like Dinnerstein, she concludes that equal parenting is a prerequisite for doing away with it. Like Dinnerstein, however, it seems that she provides an incomplete or deficient account of how this might come about. What would induce men to 'mother' if the desire and capacity to do so is passed on to women and not to men? For that matter, what would induce women to 'mother' once they were no longer themselves mothered by other women?

One of the effects of women having almost exclusive responsibility for the care of children, acccording to Chodorow, is that it makes them more other-oriented in general. Because separation from a parent of the same sex is more difficult, the pre-Oedipal phase or phase of identity is longer in girls than in boys. As a result, according to Chodorow, 'women, more than men, will be more open to and preoccupied with those very relational issues that go into mothering – feelings of primary identification, lack of separateness or differentiation, ego and body-ego boundary issues and primary love not under the sway of the reality principle.'[54] The daughter's closer and longer identification with the mother leads to feelings of connectedness to individuals in later life. Because they are of a different sex from the mother, differentiation is the key dynamic for sons. As a result, they are prone to feel more detached from others in later life. The difference between men and women as adults is that 'Feminine identification processes are relational, whereas masculine identification processes tend to deny relationships.'[55]

Women's 'relational predilections' make them more open to parenting. Chodorow suggests that women undertake to have and care for children as a result of their greater sense of connectedness to, and disposition to care for, others in general, which in turn stems from their experience of being mothered by a woman. If this is the case, then the main impetus women have for mothering, as well as the main source of what is distinctive about their outlook, presumably would disappear once men undertook the care for children (as Chodorow proposes they do). Moreover, it is not clear why men would undertake it either.

It seems necessary to explain why they would, since Chodorow depicts the care of children as requiring considerable labour and effort. At the infant stage, it demands that the mother give all for nothing. The infant's ultimate aim is to 'be loved and satisfied, without being under any obligation to give anything in return,' so that 'good maternal behaviour requires both a constant delicate assessment of infantile needs and wants and an extreme selflessness.'[56] But why would that selflessness be forthcoming? How does one explain why anyone would provide that kind of care? Chodorow provides a partial answer by suggesting that women might assume it in the hope of fulfilling their own emotional needs and longings. She makes use of the extensive literature tracing the psychological dynamic of infant-mother relations, which suggests that women may care for the infant because they see it as an extension of themselves: 'Women get gratification from caring for an infant, analysts generally suggest, because they experience either oneness with their infant or because they experience it as an extension of themselves.'[57] Chodorow's analysis reveals the degree to which the psychoanalytical literature on infant-mother relations, as well as her own theory, mirrors liberal assumptions (evident in Hobbes and Locke) which explain the mother's care of the child by either showing how it is compatible with her own interests or well-being or suggesting that the child is an extension of the mother and that the mother in essence therefore is caring for herself.

At the same time as she advances them, Chodorow herself points to the inadequacies of these explanations. First, it cannot easily be shown that having children does in fact benefit the mother: to try to meet one's emotional needs by having children is likely to lead to emotional frustration. Second, it may not benefit the child itself to have its care undertaken in the hope that it will benefit the parent: the perception that the infant is part of oneself can make it difficult to acknowledge and encourage the child's independence, which is instrumental to its well-being.

If the capacity and desire to care for children derives from a sense of connectedness to others and a general disposition to be more caring of others, which in turn arises out of women's experience of being mothered by a woman, then, in a society of equal parenting, would women no longer have those distinctive dispositions which we value and want to disperse throughout society and which induce them to 'mother'? Furthermore, by suggesting that women 'mother' because it is unacceptable for them to seek to recapture the emotional intensity of pre-Oedipal relationship with a woman (mother) in intense or sexual relations with other women, Chodorow implies that in societies where such relations are not taboo or where women are less isolated from other women, they might not want to have children.[58] And what of men? How does one get them to 'mother' in the first place so that they too might acquire the other-oriented outlook that comes from having been engaged in the care of children? The reluctance of men to take over responsibility for the care of children is well documented. It seems that what is missing in Chodorow's account is a comprehensive consideration of such questions. Without such considerations, her proposals for equal parenting as a means of doing away with women's oppression seem unfeasible and unconvincing.

The key to women's liberation, according to Mary O'Brien, is rational control over reproduction: 'The consolidation of rational control over the reproductive processes is the precondition of liberation, and it is urgent.'[59] This conclusion, however, does not seem to fit with what she tells us will happen once women achieve such control: they will construct models of the political community very different from the ones hitherto established by men and which constitute the Western tradition. The models we find in the Western tradition, O'Brien suggests, are a reflection of male reproductive consciousness. The models that women will construct when given the opportunity would be a reflection of female reproductive consciousness. What is the difference between the two? It has to do with men's and women's different biological capacities and experiences:

> There is such a thing as reproductive consciousness, and it differs between men and women. Male consciousness is alienated from the process of reproduction. Man is related to his child only by thought, by knowledge in general, rather than by experience in particular – whereas motherhood is a unity of consciousness and knowing on the one hand, and action (reproductive labour) on the other.[60]

More closely tied to all aspects of the reproductive cycle, women experience a sense of continuity and oneness with nature, reflecting their participation in a process that moves cyclically and by natural necessity through ovulation, copulation, conception, gestation, birth, and care for the infant. The reproductive consciousness this engenders in women is culturally transmitted: 'Women do not need to bear children to know themselves as women, for women's reproductive consciousness is culturally transmitted.'[61] More removed from the whole reproductive cycle and faced with uncertainty over paternity, men's reproductive consciousness, however, is pervaded by a sense of discontinuity. The repercussions of this consciousness, moreover, make themselves felt in the way that Western theory is constructed. The theorizing itself, O'Brien suggests, is spurred by and discloses an attempt to overcome this unsettling sense of discontinuity – and to achieve continuity artificially through the creation of models that are concerned with political perpetuity. The dualism we find in Western theory between nature/nurture, body/mind, private/public, woman/man, however, is a reflection of the failure to overcome the sense of discontinuity. Furthermore, we find evidence of a male desire to appropriate women's reproductive powers in the superiority accorded to the side of the dualism associated with man: nurture, mind, and public life.

Why is it that women have not engaged in the construction of political theory as men have, O'Brien asks? She suggests that it is their consignment to biological or natural necessity. But once freed from it, by having wrested control over new technological innovations from men,[62] women will embark on what men have done for years – elaborate on their 'second nature' and construct models of the political community that try to establish continuity artificially. Most important, they will bring to bear on these constructions their own reproductive consciousness, which O'Brien associates with an outlook that is more caring, emotional, practical, and involved with everyday life than men's.[63]

There is a fundamental contradiction in O'Brien's recommendations. On the one hand, she proposes that women's difference – their reproductive consciousness and the qualities it is compatible with – rests on their embeddedness in natural necessity and that these are the grounds on which they would offer something new in the theories they might construct. Yet, on the other hand, she proposes that the means for women's liberation is rational control over technology which would allow them to overcome natural necessity, by severing the link between sex and procreation.[64] To remove this link might free women to theorize, as O'Brien suggests, but would it not also remove an important element in women's reproductive experience, change their reproductive consciousness, and thereby eradicate the very differences women are supposed to bring to theory? Freed from natural necessity and the unique reproductive consciousness it engenders, why would women create models that are any different from the ones men have created? The new feminist philosophy will be a philosophy of birth, O'Brien speculates. But why would it be?

We might say that O'Brien partially addresses this conundrum by indicating that women can have the best of both worlds, so to speak. Through control over their own reproduction they will be able to experience the kind of separation between sex and procreation and the sense of discontinuity hitherto exclusively reserved for men. Unlike men, they will also be able to experience the sense of continuity that comes from choosing to participate in the whole reproductive cycle of conceiving, gestating, bearing, and caring for children; the qualities this experience engenders will be expressed in the theories they articulate. But having the rational choice of whether to subject oneself to natural necessity is not quite the same as having no choice but to be governed by natural necessity. It seems that the latter is more fundamental to women's distinctive reproductive consciousness as O'Brien describes it.

Moreover, if one assumes that women would continue to maintain the reproductive consciousness that comes from taking part in the whole reproductive cycle of ovulation, conception, birth, and care (even after they had secured 'rational' control over reproduction), then one must also be supposing that women would indeed overwhelmingly continue to *choose* to participate in this whole cycle even when faced with the opportunity to choose not to. But why? Because they have a natural maternal instinct seems to be O'Brien's answer. She explains examples of women abandoning their children as the outcome of men's having appropriated women's natural affinity for motherhood.[65]

O'Brien's proposals hinge on the existence of a natural maternal instinct which it is assumed would remain a constant in the face of historical, technological, and social changes granting women greater command over their reproductive capacities. This instinct would continue to propel women to take part in the whole reproductive cycle (including caring for children after birth) and thereby continue to perpetuate in them a distinctive reproductive consciousness. Paradoxically, O'Brien's analysis hinges on what she thinks is also wrong with the Western tradition: it defines mothering as natural at the cost of ignoring its historical, material, and potentially rational basis.[66]

I think O'Brien is correct to say that extending to women control over their reproductive capacities would have radical implications. But she is off the mark in supposing that it has such radical implications because Western (male) theory has always perceived reproduction, in particular women's role in it, to be natural. As I have argued, this is not the case when it comes to Hobbes and Locke. (Ironically, it is O'Brien's model, not Hobbes' and Locke's, which assumes that mothering is propelled by a natural maternal instinct.) By misinterpreting what is wrong with some of the Western tradition, O'Brien is in danger of replicating the difficulties it places women in. Of course she does not envision women achieving technologically facilitated control over their mothering capacities in a 'liberal society' founded on market relations. But by inviting feminists to work towards securing for women 'rational' control over their reproductive activities as a condition for their liberation, she may in fact be uncritically appropriating a 'liberal' notion of the right to govern one's own body and labour power and along with it some of the complications and contradictions the liberal legacy generates for women.

The final maternal theorist I consider, Nancy Hartsock, extracts from the ideas of the three analysts I have already discussed.[67] Like Dinnerstein and Chodorow, she attributes differences between men and women to the dynamics of the pre-Oedipal infant-mother relation. The outcome of this dynamic is that women have a greater sense of attachment to others, men a sense of detachment. The need for men to separate themselves from their mothers leads to a type of 'masculinity' which defines itself by rejecting whatever is associated with the female world.[68] Hartsock proposes that the male obsession with death and domination, including the domination of women, is a form of expression of the desire to dispel whatever is identified with the experience of being mothered by a woman: 'The key structuring experience can be seen to be fear of ceasing to exist as a separate being, ceasing to exist because of the threat posed by a woman.'[69]

Hartsock also draws on Mary O'Brien's idea that men's consciousness of being removed from reproduction generates in them a sense of discontinuity. Male reproductive consciousness lends itself to a world-view characterized by duality and hostility towards others. In contrast, women's experience of reproduction lends itself to a world-view characterized by a sense of unity with nature, continuity, and closeness to others.[70] Women's engagement in reproduction, Hartsock emphasizes, includes a wide range of activities that contribute to the production and reproduction of material existence. But it is women's experience in mothering, in caring for a dependent being (and having been cared for by a woman), that is at the root of their distinctive outlook on power. In this outlook, power is not about domination or wielding the power of life and death over another being. It is about using one's power to encourage and facilitate the growth and independence of another being:

> The female experience not simply of mother (but more broadly the general education of girls for mothering, and the experience of being mothered by a person of one's own gender) is one in which power over another is gradually transformed by both the power holder and the being over whom

power is exercised into autonomy and (ideally) mutual respect. The power of the mother over the child, and the sensual and erotic relations with the child, issue (in healthy relations) in the creation of an independent and autonomous being. Thus, the point of having power over another is to liberate the other rather than dominate or even kill her.[71]

Hartsock proposes that what is wrong with the Western tradition, starting with the Greeks, is that whatever is associated with women is denied, repressed, or repudiated. She attributes women's inferior status, their exclusion from the political realm, to the inherent masculinity of Western articulations which makes the warrior the ultimate public hero and defines 'masculine' as excluding what is associated with the female: nature, the body, and generation.[72] Although Hartsock's analysis examines these themes in the classic Greek origins of Western thought, she also suggests that they pervade the whole tradition. I have argued that when it comes to Hobbes, Locke and J.S. Mill, however, such explanations are insufficient. They fail to apprehend what is at work in these liberal thinkers.

Most interesting, however, is that the idea of power of life and death over another being which Hartsock deems to be a 'masculine' construct is the kind of power that Hobbes attributes to women as mothers in the state of nature. In contrast, the kind of power that Hartsock attributes to women as mothers is described as a 'life-affirming' and 'non-coercive' one which is exercised for the well-being of the child. It both reflects and facilitates a conception of power which sees it as the capacity to do things rather than the capacity to dominate others.[73] To simply conclude that Hobbes' conception is a 'masculinist' one which he wrongly applies to women and that Hartsock's is a 'feminine' one which actually describes women's experience is to obscure this: Hobbes' depiction of maternal power does capture the radical implications of extending to women the right to govern their own bodies and labour power, especially in the modern context where the line between the 'fetus' and the 'new-born' becomes increasingly blurred. Hartsock does not consider whether alternative models of the community would include extending to women such rights. It weakens her discussion of the implications of women's reproductive capacities. Trying to secure for women the right to govern their own bodies in its liberal form raises difficulties. But it is just as problematic to ignore these difficulties. Part of the liberal legacy for women that feminists must grapple with is that the issue of reproductive rights has been placed on both the political and the theoretical agenda.

178 Women, Politics, and Reproduction

A second issue Hartsock does not confront is whether models based on women's mothering capacities and attitudes to power would retain a division of labour. It seems that women have the qualities needed for the care of children and men do not. Underlying Hartsock's analysis of both the Western tradition and her proposal for an alternative model is the image of the mother as benign and benevolent. It is an image which seems to recall what Heather Maroney finds widespread in maternal feminism – references to an idyllic, pre-patriarchal, matriarchal state:

> Matriarchal society and motherhood are thought to be cooperative, natural, sex positive and permissive, peaceful and able to integrate males on a basis of equal exchange. In contrast, patriarchy is hierarchial, ultimately technologically rational, sexually repressive and violent for women, associated with militarism and the state and based on the oppressive exploitation of female productive and reproductive powers.[74]

As Maroney and others have pointed out, the importance and usefulness of the idea of such a female state of nature does not rest on its historical accuracy but on the alternative (to patriarchal) vision of society and motherhood it presents.[75] But this image of motherhood becomes less useful once we introduce the (Hobbesian) notion of women's right to govern their own bodies. And it seems to leave us with this: women are the most natural caretakers of children in any society, whether patriarchal or not.

This preliminary exploration of a 'maternal feminism' approach shows that a number of issues are left unresolved. How does one get men to undertake the care of children so that they can acquire the desirable qualities that 'mothering' engenders and leave behind the emotional dynamic that makes them want to dominate women (Dinnerstein and Chodorow)? How does one account for why women would bring to bear on society a different reproductive consciousness once they have rational control over reproduction (O'Brien)? And what happens to the image of benevolent 'maternal empowerment' once we insert for women the right to govern their own bodies and labour power (Hartsock)?

FEMINISM OF DIFFERENCE: EXPERIENTIAL FEMINISM

An 'experiential feminism' approach suggests that women's difference is engendered by the way they have responded to and digested their environment, rather than by their maternal function *per se*. Women's environment, it is pointed out, has been historically quite different from men's. Its parameters have been the private realm, whereas men's activity has extended to the public one. This division is not necessarily based on any natural predilections. But it has shaped women's experience in a way that has given them a distinctive outlook. The problem is that this experience and the outlook it generates have been overlooked, undervalued, and excluded from the standards by which men and women are judged. As a result, women often fall short by these standards.

Carol Gilligan's *In a Different Voice* has been central in the debate over whether women's experiences lead to a distinctive perspective.[76] Her work is spurred by the concern that traditional models of moral development may be deficient. When they are used to account for women's moral reasoning, the result is often that women seem to be lacking in their capacity for moral development. Gilligan suggests that the problem may rest in the models themselves, not in women's inadequacies.

In her investigations Gilligan finds what she calls 'a different voice.' She describes it as expressing more of a concern with an 'ethic of care' than an 'ethic of justice': 'This conception of morality as concerned with the activity of care centers moral development around the understanding of responsibility and relationships, just as the conception of morality as fairness ties moral development to the understanding of rights and rules.'[77] Although Gilligan warns at the beginning of her book that she is making no claims about this being a 'woman's voice,'[78] she does end up presenting it as such. It is a voice that men may exhibit but it is found more often in women than in men: 'although not characteristic of all women, [an emphasis on care in moral reasoning] is characteristically a female phenomenon in the advantaged populations that have been studied.'[79] Related to women's experience in the private realm, the 'ethic of care' emphasizes personal relationships and connections among people. Men's experience of the public realm is compatible with an 'ethic of justice,' which is more a 'morality of rights' emphasizing individuation and detachment from others.[80] Gilligan cites studies showing 'men seeing danger more often in close personal affiliation than in achievement and construing danger to arise from intimacy, women perceiving danger in impersonal achievement situations and construing danger to result from competitive success.'[81]

Gilligan's description of women's thinking about the abortion dilemma highlights what I have suggested earlier – that women are wedged between rights (self-interest) and duty (care for others) in liberal theory and practice and that the conflict between the two comes to the forefront when it is a matter of women exercising their right to govern their own bodies and labour power. Gilligan notes it is the element of choice that now comes with reproduction that makes it amenable to moral deliberations.[82] She also observes that the women she interviewed knew that they had the right to abortion, but this did not solve the dilemma of choice for them. The problem is that women are still very much influenced by the idea that for them moral virtue is self-sacrifice:

> However, while society may affirm publicly the woman's right to choose for herself, the exercise of such choice brings her privately into conflict with the conventions of femininity, particularly the moral equation of goodness with sacrifice. Although independent assertion in judgement and action is considered to be the hall-mark of adulthood, it is rather in their care and concern for others that women have both judged themselves and been judged.[83]

Gilligan emphasizes that the 'ethic of care' is distinct from the traditional notion of self-sacrifice. The former is 'a critical ethical perspective that calls into question the traditional equation of care with self-sacrifice.'[84] The distinction between the two, according to Gilligan, is this. First, the ethic of care entails women using their reason to think about the options open to them and *choosing* to care, whereas the traditional morality of self-sacrifice entails a passive acquiescence to what is considered to be morally virtuous. Second, the 'ethic of care' is informed by women recognizing they have rights which allow them to acknowledge that their own self is equal to others. This changes the responsibility of care to include care for their own self as well as others. But a third element in the ethic of care – the key that links the other two – is the recognition that self and others are connected. The sense of this connection informs the decision to care both for oneself and for others. The ethic of care then, according to Gilligan, does not show women being passive and selfless. It shows them actively choosing to care for themselves and others as the result of a rational deliberation, informed by a sense of the connection between self and other. In expressing the ethic of care, women exhibit a developed sense of self which is capable of reacting to and against the notion of self-sacrifice.

The reasoning that women undergo in the dilemma over abortion, according to Gilligan, illustrates this sequence. First, the focus on caring for the self is censured as being selfish. Then, a new understanding of the connection between self and others, articulated by the notion of responsibility, is fused with a 'maternal morality' that is concerned with the care for the dependent and the unequal. The good at this stage is equated with caring for others. Traditionally for women, this has meant self-sacrifice or passive self-abnegation.[85] But the 'ethic of care' involves a third state where the tension between selfishness and responsibility is dissipated with a new understanding of the interconnection between self and others.[86] This stage revolves around a central insight – that self and others are related and that care for others must be coupled with care for oneself. The insight arises from the capacity to assert that there is a moral equality between the self and other and 'to include both in the compass of care.' Care then becomes something that is chosen and which, 'freed from its conventional interpretation, leads to a recasting of the dilemma in a way that allows the assumption of responsibility for choice.'[87]

Is Gilligan revealing a voice in which women are able to overcome or move beyond the liberal tension between rights (self-interest) and duties (care for others)? The ethic of care seems to resolve the tension in a Millian fashion – with women ending up being expected to undertake the greater share of caretaking duties in society, especially when it comes to generation. That the traditional morality of self-sacrifice entails passive acquiescence whereas the 'ethic of care' entails choosing to care for others may be important for Gilligan's purpose – which is to show that the 'ethic of care' is a sophisticated form of moral reasoning precisely because it entails deliberation and choice – but it does not make much difference to the Millian implications of that choice. The presence of the 'ethic of care' as Gilligan describes it may reflect women having incorporated in a new form the expectation that they subsume their interests in the well-being of others, most importantly their families. To suggest that the conflict between self-interest and the duty to care for others is overcome when women recognize the connection between self and others seems to hide the following when it comes to the care of children – it cannot always be shown to benefit the mother and there may indeed be a conflict between the well-being of the two which is resolved in favour of one or the other. As the abortion dilemma shows, although the ethic of care incorporates both care for others and care for self (informed by the connection between the two), it does not resolve the conflict between self and other:

> Once obligation extends to include the self as well as others, the disparity

between selfishness and responsibility dissolves. Although the conflict between self and other remains, the moral problem is reconstructed in light of the realization that the occurrence of the dilemma itself precludes non-violent resolution.[88]

The conflict is heightened by what Gilligan's findings support – that women recognize that they are wielding a power to take a life: 'The abortion decision comes to be seen as a "serious" choice affecting both self and others: "This is a life that I have taken, a conscious decision to terminate, and that is just very heavy, a very heavy thing".'[89]

Ethic of care assumptions drawn from Gilligan's work have permeated feminist discussions of reproductive rights. In a study of the attitudes and behaviour of women faced with the choice of aborting an 'abnormal' fetus, Dorothy Wertz finds that women do make decisions in which their own interest is paramount, but that they are also very much concerned about being 'selfish' (and being regarded as 'selfish'): 'Usually they [women] mention their own quality of life first, closely followed by considerations about the potential child, the marriage, and the rest of the family. Women often use the word "selfish" to describe what they wish to avoid or to condemn.'[90] The way feminist theorists often account for women's behaviour, however, simply reinforces the idea that it is unacceptable for women to be 'selfish' or 'self-interested.' For example, in a discussion on the selective termination of fetuses in a multiple pregnancy, Christine Overall writes: 'Uncritical use of the claim that certain women "demand" selective termination implies that they [women] are just selfish, unable to extend their caring to more than one or two infants, particularly if one has a disability.'[91] Instead of questioning why women ought to be expected to undertake the extensive care that is entailed in not terminating some of the fetuses, or why deeming women to be 'selfish' is indeed a reproach, Overall goes on to insist that participants in an *in vitro* fertilization program are very eager for a child, and that they are even encouraged to be self-sacrificing by being asked to submit their body to numerous manipulations. She adds: 'There is no evidence that most are not willing to assume the challenges of multiple pregnancy.'[92] In her eagerness to show that women are not behaving 'self-interestedly,' Overall implies that 'selfishness' for women is indeed a sin.

Gilligan does not make any particular recommendations on how her findings could serve as the basis for an alternative model of the political community that would incorporate both women and men. Her main goal is to point out the deficiencies of standard frameworks of moral development, to elucidate the 'different voice' that may help us make sense of women's experience, and perhaps to look for things in men's experience that traditional notions of moral development may not be able to describe. But the 'ethic of care' approach that has emerged from her findings points us in the direction of the Millian alternative where women are increasingly expected to care for the public as well as the private realm.

It seems difficult to get away from the liberal legacy even if one deliberately sets out to do so. This is evident in the next theorist I consider. Virginia Held also suggests that women's experiences in the private realm, in particular their experience of mothering, may provide the groundwork for a moral perspective which challenges the more traditional ones. (Her emphasis on mothering also makes her resemble a maternal feminist.) Held sets out to criticize and challenge the liberal contractual model of parent-child relations and to pose an alternative model based on women's experience of mothering. Yet she also misinterprets the liberal legacy to a degree. Perhaps this is why she often ends up either resuscitating it or failing to move beyond it.

The problem with traditional male theory, Held argues, is that it has neither valued nor incorporated women's experience of mothering in its formulations. There are two reasons for this, according to Held. The first is that mothering has been deemed to be a 'natural' activity (rather than one influenced by rational deliberation):

> Birth is spoken of as a natural, biological process. That women give birth is said to make them 'essentially' close to nature, resembling other mammals in this important and possibly dominant aspect of their lives. Human mothering is seen as a kind of extension of the 'natural,' biological event of childbirth. It is thought that women engage in the activity of mothering because they have given birth and that mothering should be incorporated into the framework of the 'natural.'[93]

A second related reason, according to Held, is that the contractual model has rarely been applied to women's role in reproduction. As a result, 'it has been supposed that while contracting is a specifically human activity, women are engaged in an activity which is not specifically human. Women have accordingly been thought to be closer to nature than men.'[94]

But Held is wrong on both accounts. Hobbes and Locke do depict mothering as involving rational deliberation and they do attempt to apply contractual assumptions to the relations between parents (mothers and fathers) and children. What is distinctive about Held's attempt, however, is that she wants to present mothering as being 'rational' without the kind of self-interested assumptions we find in liberal contract models, in Hobbes particularly. She emphasizes the rational element in mothering to show that women's experience of it can be used as the basis for a moral theory. But she also wants to leave behind the notion of self-interested contractual exchanges to show that a moral theory based on women's experience would pose an alternative to the contractual (male) models of market relations so prevalent in liberal thought and society.[95]

The contractual model, according to Held, is unsuitable as a way of thinking about parent-child relations for a number of reasons.[96] First, children are not capable of contracting with their parents. (I have argued that Hobbes recognizes this but tries to show how, through contracts cemented by the state, parents can be given an incentive to care for their children.) Second, the contract cannot be voluntary on the child's part; children cannot choose their parents. (This is certainly true in most cases although recently the courts have granted a child's right to choose to stay with its adoptive parents or return to its biological ones.)

Third, market relations are inapplicable to relations between parents and children because children are not replaceable commodities. The tie beween parents and children is permanent. What Held means is that the ties need to be permanent (in fact they are not in many cases – parents do give up their children and children as adults do break with their parents). That is, the child's well-being requires that parents do not one day simply decide they no longer wish to care for it. For the sake of the child, parenting ought to be a permanent commitment. The question this leads to is why anyone would undertake something requiring such a lengthy commitment. This leads us to the crux of Held's criticism of the market analogy. It is inappropriate as a model for parent-child relations, Held argues, because mothers do not expect a return when they care for children:

> [The] emotional satisfaction of a mothering person is a satisfaction in the well-being and happiness of another human being, and a satisfaction in the health of the relation between the two persons, not the gain that results from an egoistic bargain. The motive behind the activity of mothering is thus entirely different from that behind a market transaction.[97]

Held is describing what is necessary to the well-being of the child. Yet the problem that Hobbes points us to remains: how to explain why the extensive care and commitment the child's well-being demands is forthcoming.

At one point Held suggests that mothering may be a form of artistic self-expression: 'Giving birth may be closer to artistic expression than it is to the production of material objects; both can involve very hard work but the desire to express oneself in the activity may be paramount, and certainly the activity of mothering can be more expressive than productive.'[98] Here Held comes close to saying that a mother is putting part of herself into the child and in effect caring for it as an expression of herself: '*In both giving birth and mothering the woman expresses the kind of woman she chooses to be.*'[99] Held is trying to argue against de Beauvoir, to show that mothering is a creative activity, not simply a repetitive one: 'in bringing up children, those who mother create new human *persons*.'[100] But in using the analogy of artistic creation, her account begins to resemble the liberal one which explains that parents will care for their children because they see them as extensions of themselves.

A fourth reason that the contract model is not amenable to parent-child relations, according to Held, is that the liberal idea of obligation directs individuals to leave others alone. This is inadequate when it comes to caring for children, which requires an active engagement and considerable effort: 'To be a mothering person is to be subjected to the continual demands and needs of others.'[101] In another context Held refers to the 'burdens of work and anxiety normally expended in bringing up a child.'[102] This kind of emphasis now exacerbates the difficulty we have – how to explain why adults will undertake the considerable effort, time, and commitment that parenting requires?

At the same time as she warns us about the deficiencies of the liberal contract model of obligations and rights when it comes to parent-child relations, Held also invokes it in places. She recommends that parents make detailed calculations of exactly how much effort each parent is expending on the children. The reason she gives is that without such contract-like agreements, it is the mother who will end up doing most of the work. She anticipates the objection that 'such counting of hours and calculation of who is doing how much will spoil the harmonious relations between parents and with children, or will turn family affection into the pursuit of selfishness and turn children into products.'[103] She replies that similar charges have in the past been levelled at other disadvantaged groups (such as factory workers) to prevent them from changing their subordinate position. Here she seems to say that since women live in a liberal society they can only change their disadvantaged position within its terms.

A fifth reason contract theory is not amenable to articulating a model of parent-child relations, according to Held, is that the idea of power it presupposes is inapplicable to the mother-child experience: 'The mothering person seeks to *empower* the child to act responsibly, she neither wants to "wield" power nor to defend herself against the power "wielded" by the child.'[104] This is, of course, what ought to happen as the mother cares for the growing infant, but at the very beginning of such a potential relationship, at the point at which the mother may be deciding whether or not to 'care' for the being within the womb, it seems hard to deny that the exercise of the mother's power is indeed the power of life and death over it. It is difficult to get away from the Hobbesian aspect of maternal power as the line between caring for a life within the womb and without becomes increasingly blurred.

Held admits that she is presenting an idealized form of the relation between mothering person and child to challenge the liberal contractual model (whose assumptions she proposes are no less idealized). She also notes that she is looking at 'what the characteristic features of this practise [mothering] would be without patriarchal domination.'[105] Her description of what mothering might be like in a non-patriarchal society begins to resemble the idyllic, cooperative, caring, pre-patriarchal, matriarchal state that maternal feminism often refers to. For example, Held speculates that society as a whole would be organized 'to nurture creativity, cooperation, and imagination, with the point of view of those who give birth and nurture taken as primary,' rather than, as it is now, 'in terms of expected male tendencies toward aggression, competition, and efforts to overpower, and in terms of institutions to contain male aggression by balancing and equalizing the power to bend others to one's will.'[106]

It also seems that women would be the nurturers in such a society. Held declares that she does not want to deal with the disputed question of whether 'human mothers do or do not have a strong natural tendency to love their children.'[107] She suggests that it is not necessary to do so. We can use women's experiences of being mothers to inform our theories of morality. Whether these experiences are based on nature is irrelevant. Yet, Held places herself in the maternal feminist camp in the way she recounts the reasons women might be more inclined than men to care for children. For example, she speculates that the biological differences in women's reproductive capacities, such as the ability to bear children and experience the pain of childbirth, might account for women having a greater attachment to their children than men. She considers that women might be more attached to a child because they contribute more 'energy and effort toward the production of this particular child.'[108] Held also draw on the 'ethic of care' approach both to describe women's experience of mothering and to point the way for a moral theory of parent-child relations.

The experience of mothering, Held suggests, would lead one to recognize the importance and value of care. It would also lead one to realize that the self and other are connected and related. Another reason that the contractual model is inappropriate both for describing the mothering experience and as the foundation for an alternative theory of relations between mothering person and child, Held proposes, is that it assumes and emphasizes a 'separated self.' Held seems to say that women's unique capacity to carry the child (and therefore to literally experience a greater physical connection between self and other) may make them more aware of the deficiency of an account, like the contractual one, which accentuates detachment over connectedness.

But Held also proposes that both men and women can acquire the ethic-of-care-like outlook because it is generated by the actual experience of caring for a child and because both men and women can 'mother.' Yet, just as we saw in other theorists who want to encourage men to care for children, women are presented as having the advantage (or disadvantage) right from the start. Held cannot seem to tell us why or how men would 'mother' in the first place in order to acquire the ethic-of-care-like outlook that would predispose them to value mothering. Taken together, Held's references to a cooperative and caring matriarchal state, her recounting of the biological factors that might make mothers more attached than fathers to their children, and her suggestion that women might be more prone to value and acknowledge an ethic of care outlook add up to a picture of women as being more predisposed to parenting than men from the start.

The problem of getting men to mother is intensified in Held's account for two reasons. First, she emphasizes that mothering is rational. It entails deliberation and choice. One asks oneself whether one indeed wants to undertake it. Second, she accentuates that it involves extensive commitment and effort. It seems that women, who already have a greater disposition to value the activity, would be much more likely than men to *choose* to mother.

The other effect of presenting women as more predisposed to caring is that it tones down the radical Hobbesian implications of depicting mothering as contingent on rational deliberation and choice. Held wants to present mothering as 'rational' but without the assumptions about maternal self-interest that underscore this idea in the liberal framework, in Hobbes particularly. In trying to eliminate the Hobbesian side of the equation, however, she comes close to invoking both the Lockean idea of women using their reason to act out of duty and commitment to the larger community and the Millian idea that women, being predisposed to caring for others, will make choices that are beneficial all around. For example, to challenge de Beauvoir's claim about mothering, Held notes that women can choose to give birth for similar reasons that men have chosen to die – reasons that may involve a sense of commitment to a larger good.[109]

Held acknowledges that if mothering is based on deliberation and choice, then it also entails the choice of not caring for another being, before or after birth: 'for one person to be in a position of caretaker means that person has the power to withhold care, to leave the other without it.'[110] Yet her depiction of women as more caring at the start suggests that when confronted with the choice of caring or not caring either for a fetus before birth or for an infant after birth, they will be predisposed to undertake the care and commitment that the perpetuation of the political community requires.

The decision of whether to care for a new life before birth is the woman's alone because she carries it in her body, Held affirms. She warns us that we cannot assume that as a result she ought to be exclusively responsible for the care of the infant after birth.[111] Yet Held recognizes that if the decision is the woman's alone, then it may be more difficult to argue that the father or the community ought to take responsibility for the child after birth. Held very cautiously intimates that, if men are expected to share the parenting, they might also have some say in the decision a woman makes while it is in the womb: 'And there may be very good reasons why child care should be fully shared by men, and reasons for men to be able in nonsexist society to participate in decisions concerning the creating of new persons.'[112] This suggestion is unusual in feminist thought. It does not sit well with the idea of women having the right to govern their own bodies and labour power in the form that most feminists, including Held, want to maintain it for women in liberal society.

Held's analysis shows that even when feminism wants to challenge or move beyond the liberal framework, it is very difficult to let go of women's right to govern their own bodies. Women need this right, Held insists, at least as things stand. She opens up the possibility that women might leave it behind in a non-patriarchal society: 'the power to give birth remains the mother's, and the right to use or refrain from using this power ought to be hers, at least until patriarchy has been safely overcome.'[113] Held's analysis also shows that trying to retain the notion of mothering as rational but leaving behind the element of rational self-interest that characterizes it in its Hobbesian format leaves a space too easily filled with the expectation that women act in ways that benefit the larger community.

FEMINISM OF DIFFERENCE: SEXUAL FEMINISM

A sexual feminist approach emphasizes the differences between male and female sexuality. We find two variations here – the one which spotlights male sexuality and associates it with the desire to dominate and the other which accentuates female sexuality and associates it with what challenges (patriarchal) order. For the former the main source of women's oppression is the institutionalization of the male desire to dominate, conquer, and have sexual access to women. Catharine MacKinnon is an example of a theorist who takes this approach.

According to MacKinnon, feminism must recognize sexuality 'as a social construct of male power: defined by men, forced on women, and constitutive of the meaning of gender,' and identify 'sex – that is, the sexuality of dominance and submission – as crucial, as a fundamental, as on some level definitive, in that process.'[114] Much of her work is devoted to elaborating the ways in which the state embodies a male standpoint and male values and to showing how, as a result, it systematically and unrelentingly oppresses women in all its endeavours. Male power is evident even in those state laws and policies that supposedly benefit women – laws on abortion, rape, and sex discrimination, for example. 'Male power is systemic. Coercive, legitimated, and epistemic, it *is* the regime,' MacKinnon writes.[115]

This kind of approach describes women's oppression as an institutionalized sexual power play between men and women. Perhaps as a result it pays little attention to parent-child relations. Although MacKinnon is right to point out that the laws granting reproductive rights to women may have implications that work against their interests or that the context in which these rights are granted ought to be questioned, her approach misses a lot. By explaining the matter of reproductive rights almost exclusively as a matter of the systemic male domination of women, it directs our attention away from other important considerations such as the premises about parent-child relations within which these rights are framed, the radical implications of extending to women the right to govern their own bodies, and the political implications of having and caring for children. MacKinnon, like many others, ends up advocating that women be give reproductive rights as a necessary step to controlling their own bodies.[116] Yet there is little consideration that this may bring with it difficulties which cannot be accounted for as being exclusively the result of a systemic, coercive, distinctively 'male' desire to oppress women.

MacKinnon's framework of sexual domination, moreover, implies that there is no way out. She claims to be using the term 'male' as a 'social and political concept, not a biological attribute.'[117] Yet her frequent references to rape as the emblem and the reality of institutionalized relations between the sexes implies that the pervasiveness of male power and the control over women it aspires to is sexually grounded in male biology. If male power is so pervasive, all-encompassing, and unrelenting and if it aims at sexual access to women, then it becomes difficult to imagine any kind of alternative structural arrangements where men, as men, would not continue to strive to oppress women. The solution then would seem to be a model which exludes men and the strategy for achieving it would seem to be the separation of men and women. MacKinnon's kind of approach points feminism in this direction.

In the other variation of sexual feminism, female sexuality is the important side of the equation. It is associated with qualities that threaten not only the social (patriarchal) order but all order. Variations on this theme are expressed in the writings of Luce Irigaray, Hélène Cixous, and Julia Kristeva. For Luce Irigaray, women's sexuality is oppressed by the patriarchal structures of language itself, which is dualistic, phallic, and two-dimensional. Liberation entails countering male phallic sexuality with the exploration of the multifaceted dimension of female sexuality. She refers to the possibility of creating a women's space and language, situated in the female body and resting on the revival of the repressed and lost memory of the pre-Oedipal mother-daughter bond. By releasing what is repressed by the phallic symbolic order (which is embedded in language), women's sexuality illuminates the possibility of reviving the mother-daughter bond in close woman-to-woman relations.[118]

In Hélène Cixous's work we find a similar idea: the feminine libido expresses sexual difference, multiplicity, and plurality, as opposed to the unity and duality of patriarchal phallic constructions. Women's liberation starts with their anatomy, the liberation of their sexuality through the expression of sexual pleasure or 'jouissance.' This may include attempting to create a (new) language which expresses women's bodies and thereby enables them to recover their sexuality: 'By writing her self, woman will return to the body which has been more than confiscated from her.'[119]

In Julia Kristeva, the 'feminine' is associated with multiplicity, irrationality, sexuality, and 'otherness.' As a representation of the negative, the void, and the marginal, the 'Other' is something to exalt not reject.[120] But women's difference – their sexuality, their otherness – is difficult to define or express because the vehicle for doing so – language – is itself a product of the masculine, patriarchal symbolic order. This order defines itself by repressing the feminine energy of the 'semiotic.' The 'feminine' in Kristeva becomes what is untranslatable, unspeakable, and therefore not amenable to rational articulation. Kristeva calls on women to destroy, challenge, and negate male language and the male symbolic order that it embodies: 'If women have a role to play in this on-going process, it is only in assuming a negative function: rejecting everything finite, definite, structured, loaded with meaning, in the existing state of society.'[121] But she repudiates, as part of the other side of the same coin, the feminist enterprise of setting up alternative communities reflective of women's sexuality and difference. As countersocieties they are beset by the same logic (which defines and excludes) as the patriarchal society they purport to reject: 'As with any society, the countersociety is based on the expulsion of an excluded element, a scapegoat charged with the evil of which the community duly constituted can then purge itself; a purge which will finally exonerate that community of any future criticism.'[122]

Although all three writers accentuate the importance of the pre-Oedipal phase as one in which the 'maternal' and the 'feminine' dominate, they do not necessarily equate the actual experience of childbirth with liberation for women.[123] Kristeva refers to the 'maternal' as what is associated with the realm of the body, with the unknowable, with non-language, with a pre-patriarchal 'semiotic' state, not necessarily the actual biological experience of bearing and caring for children:

> By 'maternal' I mean the ambivalent principle that derives on the one hand

from the species and on the other hand from a catastrophe of identity which plunges the proper Name into that 'unnameable' that somehow involves our imaginary representations of femininity, non-language, or the body.[124]

Furthermore, she implies that the desire to experience difference through pregnancy may be simply another version of the feminist desire to build a maternal utopia, a project of which Kristeva is critical.[125] In the way they challenge and protest the patriarchal symbolic order, feminist ideologies with affinities to matriarchal beliefs simply become part of that order. They are 'no less exposed to the risks of violence and terrorism.'[126]

All three writers point to the difficulty of expressing the 'feminine' or women's difference in the context of male culture and language: 'To claim that the feminine can be expressed in the form of a concept is to allow oneself to be caught up again in a system of "masculine" representations, in which women are trapped in a system of meaning which serves the auto-affection of the (masculine) subject.'[127] If women's difference cannot be mediated by patriarchal language, then women must create an alternative language with which to express it (Cixous) or it becomes the inexpressible (Kristeva): 'in speaking of a *woman*, it is impossible to say what she *is* – for to do so would risk abolishing her difference.'[128] In Cixous and Irigary the 'feminine' is more closely associated with women; in Kristeva it is not necessarily more easily expressed by women. It may not even be associated with women themselves. Indeed, to attempt to define the concept of 'woman' or to attribute any essential characteristics to it is to submit to the patriarchal urge to construct dualisms and to the masculinist preoccupation with order – to liberate women's disorderly sexuality is to challenge the notion of order itself.[129]

The writings of Cixous, Irigaray, and Kristeva are often associated with a post-structural or post-modern feminism. We might say that post-modern or post-structuralist feminism is an outgrowth of the kind of sexual feminist approach we find in these three thinkers. There is an ongoing and extensive debate over whether the tenets of 'post-modernism' or 'post-structuralism' are compatible with feminist endeavours, whether a 'post-modern feminism' is possible (or whether it even exists) and whether the prevailing influence of post-structuralist assumptions signals an end to feminist theorizing.[130]

In a number of ways, the project I am proposing for feminist thought – to lay the groundwork for alternative formulations of politics that incorporate women, children, and men – is incompatible with post-structuralist feminist warnings. First, the idea of laying foundations is suspect. Foundations are deemed to be shifting, contingent, and exclusionary.[131] Second, to use such terms as 'woman' or 'man' and to assume they have a recognizable shared meaning is problematic, it is argued. It suggests that there is something distinctive and essential about a 'woman' or a 'man' that is not artificially or socially constructed, when in fact there is no necessary correlation between having a certain set of physical characteristics and being masculine, feminine, man, woman, or even male and female. These constructs are mediated by and ultimately ascribed by language.[132] Moreover, to decide that a particular combination of biological components does add up to male or female or man or woman is to exercise a form of power.

A third theme in post-structural feminism is that to engage in the activity of theorizing itself – to delineate, generalize, take a stance, or argue against one – is to place oneself in the position of superior agent or subject who decides what is to be embraced and what is to be barred. To define woman, for example, brings up the question of whom one places in this category and whom one excludes and thereby silences, marginalizes, and oppresses. Or to generalize about women is to ignore differences of race, class, and age and in the end to deny the specificity of each individual woman. Even to do what I am doing here – to define post-structuralism, to attribute to it certain characteristics, to criticize its tenets, to designate certain writers as post-structuralist ones – is to do exactly what post-structural feminism cautions against: 'Poststructuralism is not, strictly speaking, a position but rather a critical interrogation of the exclusionary operations by which 'positions' are established.'[133] As a result, 'there is some question whether one can debate for or against this postmodernism.'[134]

The post-structuralist feminist approach has generated a lot of theorizing about the problems of theorizing. But it leads to a self-consciousness and a reluctance to define, delineate, classify, and generalize which hinders the construction of alternatives to the beleaguered Western tradition. Its effect overall has been to discourage feminist thought from taking on the building of new paradigms. By emphasizing disorder, it may also turn feminist attention away from the importance of generational continuity.

THE FEMINIST LEGACY

Feminist thought has a difficult time moving beyond the liberal framework. In some cases feminist theorists misinterpret the liberal legacy –

in particular what is wrong with it when it comes to women – and unwittingly revive its dilemmas for women. They draw on liberal notions of self-interest, obligation, and maternal predilection to account for the care of children. And they draw on liberal notions of women's right to govern their own bodies and labour power in wanting to secure for women greater rational control over reproduction. As I have described it, feminist thought is caught between two equally troublesome poles. At the one end, when it takes on liberal assumptions about parent-child relations and wants to achieve for women the same right as men to govern their own bodies, it takes on the kinds of contradictions we find for women in liberal thought and practice. At the other end, when it ignores the question of parent-child relations or the issue of reproductive rights for women, its capacity to explain generational continuity or why men or women would 'mother' is limited. In addition, it then fails to address the political implications of women's unique reproductive capacities.

Is the task of feminist thought to purge itself of its liberal assumptions and start afresh? This is one option, but it is a difficult one. First, feminist theorizing is undertaken in liberal societies where it directly or indirectly leads to prescriptions that will have an impact on women's position. Second, there are things in the liberal legacy – the idea of the right to govern one's own body – that are difficult to leave behind.[135] (Now it seems that women need and want the rights initially slated for men more than men need or want them.)

If feminism finds it difficult to extricate itself from the liberal legacy, what can be salvaged from the legacy? I think what is radical in it for women can be found in Hobbes and Locke (particularly Hobbes) more than in Mill. But how does one respond to the charge that Hobbes, especially, 'masculinizes' women? By attributing to them qualities such as rational self-interest, by depicting women's role in reproduction as being rational in the way I have described – uninfluenced by a natural maternal instinct or a predilection for caring, and entailing the power of life and death over another being – Hobbes is attributing to women (so the argument goes) qualities that are male in origin, the male experience of parenting and a male outlook obsessed with power as domination. Most often this kind of criticism is made from a perspective of what women's real qualities and experience of mothering are like or would be like if allowed to flourish in a non-patriarchal society, and most often these are benign qualities.[136]

The problem with this kind of deliberation is that one becomes embroiled in a debate about a 'feminine' state of nature or a speculation about what woman is if she is removed from patriarchal oppression. It is not only difficult, if not impossible, to distinguish those qualities that are the result of male oppression from those that are the result of a non-patriarchal or potentially unoppressed state, it may not even be that helpful to women to discover them. A more fruitful line of inquiry is to address what is probably at bottom of the 'masculinist' rebuke – a concern that attributing to women 'masculine' qualities is detrimental to them because it leads to prescriptions that work against their interests and are incompatible with their needs or to theoretical formulations that bar women from achieving equal status. If we ask whether a quality, practice, or theory is beneficial to women, we find that whether it is 'masculine' or 'feminine' may become less important.

In fact, I have suggested that in Mill's model, where women are endowed with 'feminine' qualities of caring and concern (increasingly being imputed to women in a similar form by ethic of care feminism), the results are not necessarily propitious for women. In Hobbes' model we find the grounds for extending to women radical rights over all stages of the reproductive process. They would be extended on the assumption that women are rational, self-interested, and without a natural predilection for caring or a natural maternal instinct. To prevent the chaos of a return to a state of nature, the state would have to provide the support and inducements for women (and men as well) to have and care for children in appropriate ways. Since women have first access to a new life and no natural predilection for caring, the need for positive inducements is amplified if women are to wield their reproductive powers to care for children and perpetuate the community. In contrast, the notion of the caring and benevolent woman as mother we find in Mill and which pervades maternal and experiential ethic of care feminism may be detrimental to the interests of women. It easily leads to a disregard for the extent to which women (and men) need societal support and incentives to 'mother.' Without an adequate account of what might induce men to do it, ethic of care and maternalist assumptions support a division of labour where women are almost exclusively responsible for the care of children and the dependent.

Hobbes' model is also useful in clarifying the implications of greater rational control over reproduction in modern liberal society. As the distinction between the fetus and the newborn clouds, the image of the woman as mother exercising the power of life and death becomes more a real description of the power women potentially exercise over a new life than a mythological one (produced by male fantasy).[137] The challenge for feminism is not to shy away from maternal power, either by denying that it is a power over another life or by invoking the image of the caring maternal woman. Both are harmful to women. To say that an abortion is taking a life is *not* to say that women do not have a right to abortion. To deny that it is taking a life is to diminish the responsibility and the power that accrue to women in wielding the right to govern their own bodies and to trivialize the decision to abort. When women are deemed to be naturally benevolent and caring, extending to them rational control over reproduction as a prerequisite for liberation appears less threatening. It insinuates that women will exercise their power in ways that are beneficial to others, their families, and the larger community. Yet this also makes it easier to assume that women are the natural caretakers of society and that they need little state support to do what is already natural to them.

To suggest that Hobbes is the best bet for feminism is not to obscure the limitations of the liberal framework which I have explored throughout. It cannot always be shown, even with state incentives, that the care of children directly benefits the parents. Parental duties and obligations may have to fill the gap. But these fall more heavily on women. Men may care for the infant once born but in order for it to be born women have to apply more of their care to it than men.

Nevertheless, it may be possible to take a synthetic approach which draws from feminist theory certain valuable precepts, which amends them in light of the limitations and possibilities of the liberal legacy, and which is informed by what is essential to any model – a concern with accounting for how the community perpetuates itself. What is valuable about feminism of sameness is the idea that women are the same as men in terms of their capacities (for reason and politics) and desires (for freedom and control over their bodies). We can amend it by emphasizing that women may have the same capacities but that they have different bodies, in particular different biologically grounded reproductive capacities. Maternal feminism draws our attention to the dynamics of parent-child relations – an important concern if one wants to explain how a community perpetuates itself. Experiential feminism leads us to consider that someone has to do the caring in society. We can correct maternal and experiential feminism by proposing that the differences in women's reproductive capacities do not mean that they have a greater natural instinct to have and care for children or a greater predilection for caring on the whole. An emphasis on parent-child relations can modify sexual feminism's exclusive focus on sexual relations between adult men and women. Against post-structuralist warnings, feminism can take as a fundamental characteristic of the human condition that infants are born helpless requiring the care of adults and as a starting point for its theorizing an acccount of how that care is forthcoming.

Notes

INTRODUCTION

1 For example, see Lorenne Clark and Lynda Lange, *The Sexism of Social and Political Theory* (Toronto: University of Toronto Press, 1979); Susan Moller Okin, *Women in Western Political Thought* (Princeton: Princeton University Press, 1979); and Diana Coole, *Women in Political Theory: From Ancient Misogyny to Contemporary Feminism*, 2nd edition (Boulder: Lynne Rienner, 1993).
2 Kathryn Pauly Morgan, 'Women and Moral Madness,' in *Feminist Perspectives*, ed. Lorraine Code, Sheila Mullett, and Christine Overall (Toronto: University of Toronto Press, 1988).
3 Ibid., 160.
4 Zillah Eisenstein, *The Radical Future of Liberal Feminism* (New York: Longman, 1981).
5 Ibid., 16.
6 Jean Bethke Elshtain, 'Moral Woman and Immoral Man: A Consideration of the Public-Private Split and Its Political Ramifications,' *Politics and Society* 4 (1974): 453–73, and *Public Man, Private Woman* (Princeton: Princeton University Press, 1981).
7 Carole Pateman, *The Sexual Contract* (Stanford: Stanford University Press, 1988).
8 Ibid., 225.
9 Christine Di Stefano, 'Masculinity as Ideology in Political Theory: Hobbesian Man Considered,' *Women's Studies International Forum* 6 (1983): 633–44, and *Configurations of Masculinity* (Ithaca: Cornell University Press, 1991).
10 Janine Brodie, for example, contends that we can look to the origins of liberalism in the writings of such classic theorists as Thomas Hobbes to inform our understanding of women's under-representation in Canadian politics.

Janine Brodie with the assistance of Celia Chandler, 'Women and the Electoral Process in Canada,' in *Women in Canadian Politics: Towards Equity in Representation*. ed. Kathy Megyery (Toronto: Dundurn Press, 1991), 10–16.

11 They are also principal exponents of 'liberalism,' which Roger Scruton defines as 'a loose term used to mean a body of modern political doctrine, some parts of which have been given systematic exposition, and other parts of which have been left inchoate or tacit by its adherents.' *A Dictionary of Political Thought* (London: Pan Books, 1983), 268–70.

12 In contemporary discussions of political participation, the 'political' is defined quite narrowly as the sphere in which government office-holders are elected and make decisions. For example, see William Mishler and Harold D. Clarke, 'Political Participation in Canada,' in *Canadian Politics in the 1990s*, 3rd edition, ed. Michael S. Whittington and Glen Williams (Scarborough: Nelson, 1990), chapter 9.

13 Carole Pateman, *Participation and Democratic Theory* (New York: Cambridge University Press, 1970), 69–70. Whether this definition is compatible with a feminist-inspired emphasis on 'empowerment' will be addressed in chapter 5.

14 See Geraint Parry's discussion of the difference between instrumental and developmental accounts of why individuals participate in politics. 'The Idea of Political Participation,' in *Participation in Politics*, ed. Geraint Parry (Manchester: Manchester University Press, 1972).

15 What constitutes 'politics' and hence 'political participation' or 'political citizenship' in contemporary discussions of modern liberal politics cannot be conflated with what constitutes them in Hobbes, Locke, and J.S. Mill. But there is some continuity here. Contemporary articulations of these dimensions of political life in liberal polities are largely drawn from traditional liberal thought.

16 Rather than emphasizing the historical context in which they wrote or the legal status of women in their time, I accentuate the logical and conceptual requirements of Hobbes,' Locke's, and J.S. Mill's formulations. My approach is influenced by my concern with responding to feminist interpretations which maintain that Western frameworks cannot logically sustain the inclusion of women. I assume that these are thinkers whose works we continue to read, reflect on, and worry about defects in, such as the placement of women, because we recognize them as influencing modern thinking about politics.

17 In chapter 5 I define feminism and distinguish several strands of feminist thought.

18 Mary O'Brien, *The Politics of Reproduction* (London: Routledge and Kegan

Paul, 1981) and *Reproducing the World: Essays in Feminist Theory* (Boulder: Westview Press, 1989).
19 Virginia Held, 'Birth and Death,' in *Feminism and Political Theory*, ed. Cass R. Sunstein (Chicago: University of Chicago Press, 1990), 89.
20 Virginia Held, 'Feminism and Moral Theory,' in *Women and Moral Theory*, ed. Eva Feder Kittay and Diana T. Meyers (Totowa: Rowman and Littlefield, 1987), 114–15.

CHAPTER 1: Thomas Hobbes

1 For example, see Laurence Berns, 'Thomas Hobbes,' in *History of Political Philosophy*, ed. Leo Strauss and Joseph Cropsey (Chicago: Rand McNally, 1963), 354–78; William E. Connolly, *Political Theory and Modernity* (New York: Basil Blackwell, 1988), chapter 2; John Plamenatz, *Man and Society*, vol. 1 (New York: McGraw-Hill, 1963), chapter 4; George H. Sabine, *A History of Political Theory*, 3rd edition (New York: Holt, Rinehart and Winston, 1961), chapter 23; *History of Political Thought*, 2nd edition, ed. Raymond G. Gettell and Lawrence C. Wanlass (New York: Appleton-Century-Crofts, 1953), chapter 14; and Sheldon S. Wolin, *Politics and Vision* (Boston: Little, Brown and Co., 1960), chapter 8.
2 Carole Pateman, *The Disorder of Women* (Cambridge: Polity Press, 1989).
3 Ibid., 33.
4 Nevertheless, there are shortcomings in Pateman's account of Locke which I address in chapter 2.
5 Pateman, *The Disorder of Women*, 5.
6 Teresa Brennan and Carole Pateman, '"Mere Auxiliaries to the Commonwealth": Women and the Origin of Liberalism,' *Political Studies* 22 (June 1979): 183–200.
7 Carole Pateman, *The Sexual Contract* (Stanford: Stanford University Press, 1988), 48; and '"God Hath Ordained to Man a Helper": Hobbes, Patriarchy and Conjugal Right,' in *Feminist Interpretations and Political Theory*, ed. Mary Lyndon Shanley and Carole Pateman (Pennsylvania: Pennsylvania State University Press, 1991), 65.
8 Jane Flax, 'Mother-Daughter Relationships: Psychodynamics, Politics and Philosophy,' in *The Future of Difference*, ed. Hester Eisenstein and Alice Jardine (Boston: G.K. Hall, 1980).
9 Christine Di Stefano, 'Masculinity as Ideology in Political Theory: Hobbesian Man Considered,' *Women's Studies International Form* 6 (1983): 633–44; and *Configurations of Masculinity* (Ithaca: Cornell University Press, 1991), chapter 2.

10 Di Stefano, *Configurations of Masculinity*, 13.
11 Ibid., 54.
12 Ibid., 24.
13 Ibid., xii.
14 Ibid., 4.
15 Ibid., 64.
16 Di Stefano, 'Masculinity as Ideology in Political Theory,' 643.
17 Di Stefano, *Configurations of Masculinity*, 74, 85.
18 Ibid., 72.
19 Ibid., 89.
20 The passage in Hobbes reads: 'Let us return again to the state of nature, and consider men as if but even now sprung out of the earth, and suddenly (like mushrooms) come to full maturity, without all kind of engagement to each other.' Thomas Hobbes, *De Cive or The Citizen*, ed. and intro. Sterling P. Lamprecht (New York: Appleton-Century-Crofts), VIII:1, 100.
21 Di Stefano writes: 'The fantasized mother is the mother of huge proportions – terrifying in her power and wrath, overwhelmingly seductive in her promise of a recaptured "oceanic" environment.' *Configurations of Masculinity*, 14.
22 I return to this point in chapter 5.
23 She refers to the notion of a 'space-off' to describe her vantage point. *Configurations of Masculinity*, 190.
24 Ibid., 103.
25 Ibid., 43–55.
26 Jane Flax, 'The Family in Contemporary Feminist Thought: A Critical Review,' in *The Family in Political Thought*, ed. Jean Bethke Elshtain (Amherst: University of Massachusetts Press, 1982).
27 Di Stefano also suggests that Hobbes' 'mushroom' analogy deals a blow to parenthood. *Configurations of Masculinity*, 87, 89.
28 Pateman, *The Disorder of Women*, 73.
29 Ibid., 38.
30 Pateman, *The Sexual Contract*, 49.
31 Ibid., 183.
32 Thomas Hobbes, *Leviathan*, ed. and intro. C.B. Macpherson (Middlesex: Penguin Books, 1968), XX, 253–5.
33 It becomes apparent, however, that, in order to perpetuate themselves, all forms of civil society rest on the dominion of parents over children.
34 Hobbes writes: 'Besides, since dominion, that is, supreme power is indivisible, insomuch as no man can serve two masters, but two persons, male and female, must concur in the act of generation; it is impossible that dominion should at all be acquired by generation only.' *De Cive*, IX:1, 105.

35 Hobbes, *Leviathan*, XX, 253.
36 Hobbes, *De Cive*, IX:3, 106.
37 Hobbes writes: 'Add also that in the state of nature it cannot be known who is the father, but by the testimony of the mother; the child therefore is his whose the mother will have it, and therefore hers. Wherefore original dominion over children belongs to the mother: and among men no less than other creatures, the birth follows the belly.' Ibid., IX:3, 106–7.
38 Hobbes, *Leviathan*, XX, 254.
39 Ibid., XX, 254.
40 Hobbes, *De Cive*, IX:2, 106.
41 Hobbes, *Leviathan*, XX, 254.
42 Hobbes writes, 'and of the voluntary acts of every man, the object is some *Good to himselfe*.' Ibid., XIV, 192.
43 In this passage Hobbes does not rule out the possibility of individuals conferring on others something that may not benefit them immediately, in the form of a 'gift' or a 'free donation.' *De Cive*, II:8, 35.
44 Ibid., 106.
45 Simone de Beauvoir, *The Second Sex*, ed. and trans. H.M. Parshley (New York: Vintage Books, 1952), 72.
46 De Beauvoir writes: 'The worst curse that was laid upon woman was that she should be excluded from these warlike forays. For it is not in giving life but in risking life that man is raised above the animal; that is why superiority has been accorded in humanity not to the sex that brings forth but to that which kills.' Ibid., 72.
47 According to Lynda Lange, in her comments on an earlier version of this chapter, the sense in which motherhood is an engagement in transcendence in de Beauvoir's terms is that the mother risks her own life in giving birth. A more detailed discussion of de Beauvoir's thought will follow in chapter 5.
48 Maternal dominion is more 'natural' than paternal dominion in the sense that it is more likely in the state of nature and more compatible with women's peculiar biological make-up. At the same time, mothering is not 'natural' in the sense that it rests on a natural maternal instinct to care for children or in the sense that caring for children is an involuntary response to giving birth to them.
49 Hobbes writes: 'But if she [the mother] expose it [the infant], and another find, and nourish it, the Dominion is in him that nourisheth it.' *Leviathan*, XX, 254.
50 Ibid., XX, 253.
51 Ibid., XIX, 250.
52 Hobbes, *De Cive*, IX:15, 112.

53 Ibid., IX:18, 113.
54 Hobbes, *Leviathan*, XIX, 250.
55 Ibid., XIX, 250.
56 John Zvesper notes that 'Hobbes' portrait of children's relations with their parents is if anything even more harsh and calculating than his view of the war of male and female.' 'Hobbes' Individualistic Analysis of the Family,' *Politics* 5 (October 1985): 31.
57 Hobbes, *De Cive*, 12.
58 Hobbes, *Leviathan*, XIII, 187.
59 The Laws of Nature may exist in people's minds in the state of nature but they are not acted upon consistently. Not only may individuals differ in their interpretation of what constitutes the means for 'peaceable, sociable, and comfortable living' (*Leviathan*, XV, 216), they may also be unable to see any benefit in abiding by these Laws: 'most men, by reason of their perverse desire of present profit, are very unapt to observe these laws, although acknowledged by them.' *De Cive*, III:27, 55. Consequently, the Laws of Nature do not act as laws until there is a common authority to enforce them. As such, they 'onely concern the doctrine of civill society.' *Leviathan*, XV, 214.
60 In the state of nature, only contracts which involve the simultaneous giving up or exchanging of rights are plausible, since both parties instantly perform their side of the bargain. But covenants, which rest on the promise of 'after-performance,' are improbable if not impossible, since there is no common authority to induce individuals to hold to their promise of after-performance. Hobbes, *De Cive*, II:2, 36.
61 Hobbes writes: 'For it [the child] ought to obey him by whom it is preserved; because preservation of life being the end, for which one man becomes subject to another, every man is supposed to promise obedience, to him, in whose power it is to save, or destroy him.' *Leviathan*, XX, 254.
62 Ibid., V, 116.
63 Hobbes, *De Cive*, II:12, 37.
64 According to Gordon J. Schochet, *Patriarchalism in Political Thought* (Oxford: Basil Blackwell, 1975), chapter 12, Hobbes attempts to derive paternal dominion from the consent of the child because he wants to show that all power relations, even among obvious unequals such as a parent and a child, are based on consent rather than nature and are therefore legitimate. I argue that what is more important about the child's consent in Hobbes is that it provides parents with an incentive to raise their children.
65 Hobbes, *Leviathan*, XXVI, 317.
66 There is no 'Dominion of Persons' in the state of nature, Hobbes emphasizes, because to have dominion over another is to have the right to their obedi-

ence, in return for having saved their life. But this obedience can be guaranteed only where civil laws ensure that obedience is forthcoming. Ibid., XVI, 219–20.
67 The state of nature, as Carole Pateman suggests, is a childless state in which the human species is unable to perpetuate itself. *The Sexual Contract*, 49.
68 For example, vain-glory or pride, a major cause of dissent in the state of nature, remains a major cause of crime in civil society. *Leviathan*, XXVII, 341.
69 Ibid., XV, 209.
70 Given the secular nature of Hobbesian civil society, the biblical injunction to honour one's parents is related to the civil law, specifically the Law of Gratitude.
71 Hobbes, *De Cive*, IX:8, 109.
72 Schochet, *Patriarchalism in Political Thought*, 241–2.
73 For a discussion of the problem that Hobbes has in accounting for how children, as children, would be able to consent to their parents, see Jeffrey Blustein, *Parents and Children* (New York: Oxford University Press, 1982), 67–74.
74 Hobbes writes: 'For honour (as hath been said in the section above) is nothing else but the estimation of another's power' (*De Cive*, IX:8, 109); and 'Honour consisteth onely in the opinion of Power' (*Leviathan*, X, 156). To be considered powerful enhances one's ability to exert power over others.
75 Hobbes, *De Cive*, IX:4–9, 107–9.
76 Pateman, *The Sexual Contract*, 49.
77 We can read Hobbes as indicating that differences in physical strength, whether between women, and men, men and men, or women and women, are not in and of themselves indicators of weakness in the state of nature. Those who have less physical strength can use cunning to exert power over another. *Leviathan*, XIII, 183. Hobbes writes: 'For ... we look on men full-grown, and consider how brittle the frame of our human body is, (which perishing, all its strength, vigour, and wisdom itself perisheth with it) and how easy a matter it is, even for the weakest man to kill the strongest.' *De Cive*, I:3, 25.
78 Indeed, Carole Pateman notes that there is little reason why any woman or man would 'contract to become a lord over an infant.' *The Sexual Contract*, 49.
79 Hobbes, *De Cive*, IX:5, 107.
80 Ibid., IX:5, 107.
81 Ibid., IX:5, 107.
82 Hobbes writes: 'And universally, if the society of the male and female be such an union, as the one have subjected himself to the other, the children belong to him or her that commands.' Ibid., IX:5, 108.

83 It is a civil contract regulated by the civil laws, rather than a religious sacrament falling under the jurisdiction of the Church. Ibid., VI:16, 82.
84 Ibid., IX:6, 108.
85 Ibid., IX:6,108.
86 For Mary Lyndon Shanley, the marriage contract, including the Hobbesian one, exemplifies the power that men exercise over women in civil society. See 'Marriage Contract and Social Contract in Seventeenth Century English Political Thought,' in *The Family in Political Thought*, ed. Jean Bethke Elshtain (Amherst: University of Massachusetts Press, 1982). Teresa Brennan and Carole Pateman conclude that married women in particular pose a problem for Hobbes (and Locke). '"Mere Auxiliaries to the Commonwealth,"' 183–4.
87 Pateman, '"God Hath Ordained to Man a Helper,"' 64–5.
88 Gordon Schochet agrees that the Hobbesian state of nature consists of families headed by the father, who then contracts the whole family out of that state into civil society. *Patriarchalism in Political Thought*, 238–9.
89 At the end of *Leviathan*, 725, Hobbes says that governing a Commonwealth is like governing a family because it requires knowledge of the 'natural' inclinations of mankind and the laws of nature. In *De Cive*, VI:15, 80, when arguing that property ownership is established by common authority in civil society rather than in the state of nature, Hobbes notes that 'a family is a little city.' In a third passage, Hobbes compares the family to a kingdom on the basis that, in both, one has dominion over the many: 'Where such a right is gotten, there is a kind of a little kingdom; for to be a king, is nothing else but to have dominion over many persons; and thus a great family is a kingdom, and a little kingdom a family.' *De Cive*, VIII:1, 100.
90 According to Sheldon Wolin, for Hobbes 'the state of nature stood as a timeless model built on the causes and consequences of political breakdown. Its meaning remained eternally contemporary and urgent.' *Politics and Vision*, 264.
91 For example: 'And as small Familyes did then; so now do Cities and Kingdomes which are but greater Families (for their own security) enlarge their Dominions, upon all pretences of danger, and fear of Invasion, or assistance that may be given to Invaders, endeavour as much as they can, to subdue, or weaken their neighbours, by open force, and secret arts, for want of other Caution, justly; and are remembered for it in after ages with honour.' *Leviathan*, XVII, 224.
92 Hobbes, *De Cive*, IX:3, 106.
93 Civil society for Hobbes is not coterminous with the existence of government, nor is the state of nature coterminous with pre-civil arrangements in

which there is no form of government. As a theoretical construct, the state of nature is one in which there is no common sovereign authority powerful enough to prevent some individual interest, whether that 'individual interest' is a family, a city, a faction, or an individual, from challenging the authority of the sovereign power. Once that happens, the sovereign authority can longer guarantee security. If civil society is defined as a condition where peace exists, the state of nature is defined as a condition where there is no assurance of peace, or a state of war. The latter can occur even in states which are characterized by a very sophisticated form of government. Not all forms of government or Commonwealths fit Hobbes' definition of civil society, in this sense, since not all forms of government are able to provide security to their members. Similarly, some families may act as Commonwealths or forms of civil society if they have a common authority (a head) with enough power to provide security and protection for all members. *Leviathan*, XVII, 224.
94 Ibid., XX, 253.
95 Ibid., XVII, 228.
96 For example: 'A father, with his sons and servants, grown into a civil person by virtue of his paternal jurisdiction, is called a family. This family, if through multiplying of children and acquisition of servants it becomes numerous, insomuch as without casting the uncertain die of war it cannot be subdued, will be termed an hereditary kingdom; which though it differ from an institutive monarchy, being acquired by force, in the original and manner of its constitution; yet being constituted, it hath all the same properties, and the right of authority is everywhere the same, insomuch as it is not needful to speak anything of them apart' (*De Cive*, IX:10, 110–11); and: 'By this it appears, that a great Family if it be not part of some Common-wealth, is of it self, as to the Rights of Soveraignty, a little Monarchy; whether that Family consist of a man and his children; or of a man and his servants; or of a man, and his children, and servants together: wherein the Father or Master is the Soveraign' (*Leviathan*, XX, 257). The exception (in *Leviathan* and *De Cive*) is a passage in which Hobbes implies that wives, along with children and cattle, are a man's possessions, which are fought over by those motivated by competition: 'The first use Violence, to make themselves Masters of other mens persons, wives, children, and cattell.' *Leviathan*, XXII, 185.
97 In *The Sexual Contract*, 48, Pateman argues that Hobbes means to subsume women under 'servants.'
98 Hobbes, *Leviathan*, XXII, 275.
99 Hobbes writes: 'As for other Lyberties, they depend on the silence of the Law. In cases where the Soveraign has prescribed no rule, there the Subject

hath the liberty to do, or forbeare, according to his own discretion.' Ibid., XXI, 271. The amount of 'harmless liberty' given to the subject is determined by the sovereign. There is nothing which the sovereign authority cannot legitimately legislate. This is not the same thing as saying that it would be wise for the sovereign to legislate in all areas. The one realm in which the sovereign authority does not intrude is the realm of the inner conscience or mind. Hobbes is unconcerned if the inner thoughts of subjects are subversive, as long as their actions are not. Liberty of conscience does not preclude the sovereign from censoring the expression of potentially subversive ideas and opinions. *De Cive*, VI:11, 76. For example, Hobbes advocates that the worship of a subversive religious creed be permitted, as long as it is done in secret.' *De Cive*, XV:12, 182. The purpose of civil society is not to transform human nature or change people's inner thoughts; it is to regulate their outward actions.
100 Hobbes, *Leviathan*, XXII, 285.
101 Ibid., XXII, 287.
102 Ibid., XXI, 264.
103 Hobbes warns that subjects need to be given some 'harmless liberty'; if exposed to too many laws and restrictions they will become unsettled. *De Cive*, XIII:6, 144. Good laws are those that are conducive to peace and what is conducive to peace is allowing subjects some room for voluntary actions, in keeping with their 'natural' love of liberty. *Leviathan*, X, 152. Laws should not limit or confine all voluntary actions, only as much as is necessary to keep individuals directed. Ibid., XXX, 388.
104 Ibid., XXIX, 365.
105 Hobbes, *De Cive*, XIV:9, 161.
106 As Sheldon Wolin suggests, politics loses its primacy in Hobbes because all relations, political, social, and familial, are based on the same principles. *Politics and Vision*, chapter 8.
107 Hobbes, *Leviathan*, XXVII, 352.
108 Hobbes, *De Cive*, I:10, 28.
109 For example, it has become custom for male children, as 'fitter for the administration of greater matters, but specially of wars,' to inherit political power before female children. Ibid., IX:16, 112.
110 Hobbes, *Leviathan*, XIX, 244.
111 Ibid., XX, 255.
112 Hobbes, *De Cive*, XX:3, 116.
113 Schochet, *Patriarchalism in Political Thought*, 241–2.
114 Hobbes, *De Cive*, I:2, 24.
115 Edward Andrew suggests that there can be no self-interest in the Hobbesian

state of nature because there can be no sense of self. *Shylock's Rights: A Grammar of Lockian Claims* (Toronto: University of Toronto Press, 1988), 75. William Connolly maintains: 'The self-interested self is an artifice, an artifice celebrated by Hobbes as the one most conducive to a well-ordered society ... For the self-interested individual is a highly organized self. It is a self that must regulate its utterances by the effects they might have on others, must convert its desires and impulses into interests, must govern its passions by reference to dangers or disadvantages they might generate. The paradox of the self-interested individual is that in its very individuality it must be oriented closely to the attitudes of others and the prospects of the future; it must internalize a set of social norms while pretending only to think of itself in doing so; and it must regulate its most individual impulses to regularize its external appearance.' *Political Theory and Modernity*, 29.
116 Promises based on the fear of the power of God, therefore, have little meaning.
117 According to Berns, the central task of the Leviathan is to ensure that the terror of punishment is greater than any benefit that could accrue from breaking the covenant.' 'Thomas Hobbes,' 361.
118 Some, says Hobbes, may never acquire the reason necessary to see that peace must be sought. *De Cive*, I:2, 22.
119 Hobbes writes: 'Thirdly, because the major part hath by consenting voices declared a Soveraigne; he that dissented must now consent with the rest; that is, be contented to avow all the actions he shall do, or else justly be destroyed by the rest. For if he voluntarily entered into the Congregation of them that were assembled, he sufficiently declared thereby his will (and therefore tacitely covenanted) to stand to what the major part should ordayne: and therefore if he refuse to stand thereto, or make Protestation against any of their Decrees, he does contrary to his Covenant, and therfore unjustly. And whether he be of the Congregation, or not; and whether his consent be asked, or not, he must either submit to their decrees, or be left in the condition of warre he was in before; wherein he might without injustice be destroyed by any man whatsoever.' *Leviathan*, XVIII, 231–2.
120 Hobbes, *De Cive*, 13.
121 Ibid., I:2, 22.
122 Hobbes, *Leviathan*, XX, 254.
123 Ibid., XXIX, 369.
124 Ibid., XXX, 380.
125 Ibid., XV, 209.
126 Hobbes, *De Cive*, I:2, 21–2.
127 Ibid., I:2, 21–2.

128 Ibid., VIII:1, 100.
129 This teaching in itself does not guarantee that children will in fact honour their parents; it must be backed by a civil law incorporating the Law of Gratitude.
130 Hobbes, *Leviathan*, XXX, 382.
131 Berns, 'Thomas Hobbes,' 357.
132 Pateman, *The Disorder of Women*, 45.
133 Mary O'Brien, *The Politics of Reproduction* (London: Routledge and Kegan Paul, 1981), Introduction.
134 Hobbesian man, says Plamenatz, 'always remains a passionate creature. His actions are determined primarily by his desires and emotions and only secondarily by reason.' *Man and Society*, 121. Berns says of Hobbes: 'He attempted to deduce the natural law from what is most powerful in most men most of the time: not reason, but passion.' 'Thomas Hobbes,' 355.
135 Hobbes, *Leviathan*, XIX, 241.
136 As Carole Pateman argues in *The Problem of Political Obligation* (Berkeley: University of California Press, 1985), 44, consent in Hobbes does not entail much choice for the individual.
137 This includes the power to interpret the Divine Laws, making the sovereign authority the final appeal in civil society. *Leviathan*, XV, 217 and XXXIII, 415.
138 Ibid., X, 150.
139 Hobbes writes: 'For if we look on men full-grown, and consider how brittle the frame of our human body is, (which perishing, all its strength, vigour, and wisdom itself perisheth with it) and how easy a matter it is, even for the weakest man to kill the strongest, there is no reason why any man trusting to his own strength should conceive himself made by nature above others: they are equals who can do equal things one against the other; but they who can do the greatest things, (namely, kill) can do equal things.' *De Cive*, I:3, 25.
140 Hobbes, *Leviathan*, XX, 253.
141 Power entails the ability to convince others that one has something which is valuable or desirable. Ibid., XX, 150–152.
142 Ibid., XIX, 250.
143 Ibid., XIX, 250.
144 Hobbes, *De Cive*, IX:16, 112.
145 Ibid., X:16, 126.
146 Hobbes, *Leviathan*, XXXI, 401.
147 Ibid., X, 152.
148 For example, see Nancy C.M. Hartsock, *Money, Sex, and Power* (Boston: Northeastern University Press, 1985), chapter 8.

149 Hobbes, *Leviathan*, VI, 125.
150 Ibid., VI, 125.
151 Ibid., XXI, 270.
152 Ibid., XXI, 269.
153 Hobbes writes: 'Nature hath made men so equall, in the faculties of body, and mind; as that though there bee found one man sometimes manifestly stronger in body, or of quicker mind then another; yet when all is reckoned together, the difference between man, and man, is not so considerable, as that one man can thereupon claim to himselfe any benefit, to which another may not pretend, as well as he. For as to the strength of body, the weakest has strength enough to kill the strongest, either by secret machination, or by confederacy with others, that are in the same danger with himselfe.' Ibid., XIII, 183.
154 Ibid., XX, 253.
155 Ibid., XV, 211.
156 Ibid., XXVIII, 362.
157 The rights of the sovereign authority include the right to determine the law and to wield absolute power. Ibid., XXI, 269 and XXX, 376.
158 Civil laws ought to be compatible with the Laws of Nature, which are guidelines conducive to peaceful living. They are not hard and fast. It is up to the sovereign authority to determine what is most conducive to peace and therefore to determine the extent of the political rights granted to subjects.
159 Providing subjects with a certain quality of life is desirable, Hobbes advises, because it is more conducive to peace. Citizens who have some of the 'good things belonging to life' are less likely to disobey. *De Cive*, XIII:4, 143.
160 Hobbes, *Leviathan*, XV, 212.
161 Hobbes refers to it in the following passage: 'As it is necessary for all men that seek peace, to lay down certain Rights of Nature; that is to say, not to have libertie to do all they list: so is it necessarie for mans life, to retaine some; as right to governe their owne bodies.' Ibid., XV, 212.
162 Thomas Hobbes, 'De Corpore Politico, or the Elements of Law,' in *The English Works of Thomas Hobbes*, vol. 4, ed. Sir William Molesworth (London: Scientia Aalen, 1962), IV:1, 154.
163 According to Hobbes: 'And they may alienate them, that is, assign his or her dominion, by selling, or giving them, in adoption or servitude to others; or may pawn them for hostages, kill them for rebellion, or sacrifice them for peace, by the law of nature, when he or she, in his or her conscience, think it to be necessary.' 'Ibid., IV:8, 157.
164 Hobbes, *De Cive*, II:18, 40.

165 Hobbes writes: 'In like manner, not every killing of a man is murder, but only that which the civil law forbids.' Ibid., VI:16, 81.
166 Pateman, '"God Hath Ordained to Man a Helper",' 68.
167 Hobbes tries to base the political activity of ruling, of wielding the power of the sovereign authority, on self-interest as well, by claiming that the sovereign's self-interest is really the interest of all.
168 Hobbes, *Leviathan*, XXVI, 318.
169 Andrew, *Shylock's Rights*, 55.
170 Hobbes, 'De Corpore Politico,' IX:3, 214.

CHAPTER 2: John Locke

1 Zillah R. Eisenstein, *The Radical Future of Liberal Feminism* (New York: Longman, 1981), chapter 3.
2 Ibid., 41.
3 Ibid., 43.
4 Melissa A. Butler, 'Early Liberal Roots of Feminism: John Locke and the Attack on Patriarchy,' *American Political Science Review* 72 (March 1978): 135–50.
5 Ibid., 143.
6 Ibid., 149, 150.
7 Carole Pateman, *The Sexual Contract* (Stanford: Stanford University Press, 1988), 21.
8 Ibid., 52.
9 Ibid., 94.
10 Ibid., 96.
11 Carole Pateman, *The Disorder of Women* (Cambridge: Polity Press, 1989), 38.
12 Ibid., 52.
13 Pateman, *The Sexual Contract*, 187.
14 The modern form of prostitution, according to Pateman, can be understood as a male demand for public access to women's bodies. Ibid., 194, 199.
15 Ibid., 85.
16 Ibid., 91.
17 Ibid., 92.
18 Lorenne M.G. Clark, 'Women and Locke: Who Owns the Apples in the Garden of Eden?,' in *The Sexism of Social and Political Theory*, ed. Lorenne M.G. Clark and Lynda Lange (Toronto: University of Toronto Press, 1979).
19 Ibid., 32.
20 Locke writes: 'And the great Principle and Foundation of all Vertue and

Worth, is placed in this, That a Man is able to *deny himself* of his own Desires, cross his own Inclinations, and purely follow what Reason directs as best, tho' the Appetite lean the other way.' John Locke, 'Some Thoughts Concerning Education,' in *The Educational Writings of John Locke*, ed. James L. Axtell (New York: Cambridge University Press, 1968), sec. 33, 138. And, 'It seems plain to me, that the Principle of all Vertue and Excellency lies in a Power of denying our selves the Satisfaction of our own Desires, where Reason does not authorize them,' Sec. 38, 143.
21 Locke uses the analogy of wax to depict the way in which children can be moulded. Ibid., sec. 216, 325.
22 Ibid., sec. 103, 207.
23 Ibid., sec. 103, 207 and sec. 116, 225.
24 Ibid., sec. 105, 207 and sec. 110, 213.
25 I agree with C.B. Macpherson, *The Political Theory of Possessive Individualism* (London: Oxford University Press, 1962), 236–7, that Locke's warning against covetousness is an indictment of laziness rather than an indictment of the desire to accumulate possessions or property beyond what one needs.
26 Locke, 'Some Thoughts Concerning Education,' sec. 126, 234.
27 Ibid., sec. 78, 177.
28 John Locke, *Two Treatises of Government*, ed. and intro. Peter Laslett (New York: Cambridge University Press, 1963), II:232, 467 and II:242–3, 476–7. For a discussion of Locke's defence of a right to resistance, see Edward Andrew, *Shylock's Rights: A Grammar of Lockian Claims* (Toronto: University of Toronto Press, 1988), chapter 5.
29 Locke writes: '*Esteem* and *disgrace* are, of all others, the most powerful Incentives to the Mind, when once it is brought to relish them. If you can once get into Children a Love of Credit, and an Apprehension of Shame and Disgrace, you have put into them the true Principle, which will constantly work, and incline them to the right.' 'Some Thoughts Concerning Education,' sec. 56, 152–3.
30 Locke, *Two Treatises of Government*, II:57, 347, and II:59, 349.
31 This is the kind of reason that Locke refers to when he states that, for the purpose of education, children must be considered as rational creatures: 'For I advise their Parents and Governors always to carry this in their Minds, that Children are to be treated as rational Creatures.' They are 'rational creatures' in the sense that they too are motivated by the hope of reward and the fear of punishment, which are 'the Spur and Reins, whereby all Mankind are set on work, and guided.' 'Some Thoughts Concerning Education,' sec. 54, 152.
32 Ibid., sec. 58, 154.
33 Locke distinguishes the divine laws from the civil laws and the laws of opin-

ion or reputation. *An Essay Concerning Human Understanding*, vol. 1, ed. John W. Yolton (London: J.M. Dent and Sons, 1961), bk. 2, ch. 27, 296–7. Yet he also suggests that they are connected. In 'Some Thoughts Concerning Education,' sec. 61, 155–6, he advises that the true measure of virtue can only be the knowledge that each individual has of following the God-given laws of nature, which ought to be the foundation for the civil laws, but that the judgment of others comes closest to that knowledge.
34 Locke writes: '*Wisdom* I take in the popular acceptation, for a Man's managing his Business ablely, and with fore-sight in this world.' 'Some Thoughts Concerning Education,' sec. 140, 244.
35 Ibid., sec. 198, 312.
36 Ibid., sec. 93, 190.
37 Locke writes: 'Breeding is that, which sets a Gloss upon all his other good qualities, and renders them useful to him, in procuring him the Esteem and Good Will of all that he comes near.' Ibid., sec. 93, 190.
38 Ibid.,' sec. 93, 192.
39 Ibid., sec. 6.3, 117.
40 Ibid., sec. 9, 122.
41 Ibid., sec. 9, 122.
42 Ibid., sec. 11, 123.
43 This happened, Locke tells us, when the little girl first came home from the wet nurse. Ibid., sec. 78, 178.
44 Ibid., sec. 34, 138.
45 Ibid., sec. 70, 165–167.
46 Ibid., sec. 70, 166.
47 If 'too much shamefacedness better becomes a girl than too much confidence,' in a similar fashion, forwardness is not necessarily a desirable trait in boys. See, respectively, 'Locke's Letter to Edward Clarke on Education, 1684–91,' in *The Educational Writings of John Locke*, ed. James L. Axtell (Cambridge: Cambridge University Press, 1968), 345, and Locke, 'Some Thoughts Concerning Education,' sec. 70, 165–7.
48 Locke, 'Some Thoughts Concerning Education,' sec. 178, 289.
49 Ibid., sec. 189, 300.
50 Ibid., sec. 168, 277.
51 Boys like girls, should be kept at home in order to delay their exposure to the vices of the outside world. Children exposed to the temptations of the world before they have been taught to control their desires and their love of liberty might be tempted to act on rather than control their desires.
52 According to Carole Pateman, the attempt to show that women have the same capacities as men obscures the fact that 'there is no need to try to show

that women are (have the capacities of) free beings. Modern contractual patriarchy both denies and *presupposes women's freedom* and could not operate without this presupposition.' *The Sexual Contract*, 231–2. But Pateman does not apply these conclusions to her analysis of Locke, since she contends that Locke views women as being natural inferiors to men.

53 In Pateman's words: 'If women have been forcibly subjugated by men, or if they naturally lack the capacities of "individuals," they also lack the standing and capacities necessary to enter into the original contract. Yet the social contract theorists insist that women are capable of entering, indeed, must enter, into one contract, namely the marriage contract. Contract theorists simultaneously deny and presuppose that women can make contracts. Nor does Locke, for example, explain why the marriage contract is necessary when women are declared to be naturally subject to men.' Ibid., 54.
54 Locke, *Two Treatises of Government*, I:44–9, 207–12.
55 Ibid., I:47, 209.
56 Ibid., I:47, 210.
57 Ibid., II:82, 364.
58 Locke, *An Essay Concerning Human Understanding*, vol. 2, bk. 4, ch. 17, 262–80.
59 Ibid., 265.
60 Locke, *Two Treatises of Government*, I:48, 210; In another passage, Locke writes: 'God gave not any Political Power to *Adam* over his Wife and Children, but only subjected *Eve* to *Adam*, as a punishment, or foretold the Subjection of the weaker Sex, in the ordering the common concernments of their Families.' Ibid., I:67, 226.
61 Ibid., II:182, 364.
62 Perhaps Locke's main concern here is to demonstrate that there is a limit to the spoils that a conqueror may legitimately appropriate; nevertheless, in doing so, he also acknowledges that a wife may own property in her own right and that she can be assumed to have laboured for her property. Ibid., II:183, 438.
63 Ibid., II:82, 364.
64 Ibid., I:92, 247.
65 Ibid., II:82, 364.
66 Ibid., II:82, 364.
67 Ibid., II:78, 362.
68 Ibid., II:81, 364.
69 Ibid., I:59, 220.
70 Ibid., I:54, 215.
71 Ibid., I:54, 216.
72 Ibid., I:55, 216.

73 Ibid., I:55, 216.
74 Ibid., I:57–9, 218–20. See also Locke, *An Essay Concerning Human Understanding*, vol. 1, bk. 1, ch. 3, 30–3.
75 Locke, *Two Treatises of Government*, I:52–3, 214–15.
76 Ibid., I:56, 217–18.
77 Ibid., I:58, 219.
78 Locke observes, 'nor need we seek so far as *Mingrelia* or *Peru* to find instances of such as neglect, abuse, nay and destroy their children, or look on it only as the more than brutality of some savage and barbarous nations, when we remember that it was a familiar and uncondemned practice amongst the *Greeks* and *Romans* to expose without pity or remorse their innocent infants.' *An Essay Concerning Human Understanding*, vol. 1, bk. 1, ch. 3, 33.
79 Locke, *Two Treatises of Government*, I:56, 217.
80 '*It is the duty of parents to preserve their children.*' But 'what duty is cannot be understood without a law.' Locke, *An Essay Concerning Human Understanding*, vol. 1, bk. 1, ch. 3, 33.
81 Locke, *Two Treatises of Government*, II:79, 362.
82 Ibid., II:79, 362–3.
83 Ibid., II:80, 363.
84 I am indebted to Edward Andrew for pointing out the extent to which the art of governing for Locke is associated with the imperative to 'be fruitful and multiply.'
85 Locke, *Two Treatises of Government*, II:42, 339–40.
86 Ibid., I:33, 200.
87 Ibid., I:59, 220.
88 A child has 'no Right to demand Rule or Dominion' from his parents, Locke writes. Ibid., I:93, 248.
89 As much as Locke wants to demonstrate that children have a right to inherit property from their parents, he wants to demonstrate that this right is separate from and excludes the right to inherit either political power or political allegiance from them. To separate political power from property, Locke emphasizes that they serve different ends. Property is acquired for the benefit of the proprietor, legitimate political power or the right to govern is acquired to serve the interests of the many. Ibid., I:92, 247.
90 Ibid., II:118, 391–392.
91 Ibid., II:117, 391.
92 'And this is the Power Men generally have to *bestow their Estates* on those, who please them best. The Possession of the Father being the Expectation and Inheritance of the Children ordinarily in certain proportions, according

to the Law and Custom of each Country; yet it is commonly in the Father's Power to bestow it with a more sparing or liberal hand, according as the Behaviour of this or that Child hath comported with his Will and Humour.' Ibid., II:72, 357.

93 Ibid., II:73, 358.
94 Locke therefore advocates that parents ensure that their adult children view them as friends and consequently fear the breaking of a friendship in not following their parents' wishes. 'Some Thoughts Concerning Education,' sec. 9, 202.
95 Ibid., sec. 42, 146.
96 Locke writes: 'And thus we see, that *Foreigners*, by living all their lives under another Government, and enjoying the Priviledges and Protection of it, though they are bound, even in Conscience, to submit to its Administration, as far forth as any Denison; yet do not thereby come to be *Subjects* or *Members of that Commonwealth.*' *Two Treatises of Government*, II:122, 394.
97 Ibid., II:121, 393–4.
98 'Nothing can make any Man so, [Subjects or Members of that Commonwealth] but his actually entering into it by positive Engagement, and express Promise and Compact.' Ibid., II:122, 394.
99 Ibid., II:96–7, 375–6.
100 Ibid., II:154, 416 and II:158, 420.
101 Ibid., II:138, 406 and II:142, 409.
102 Ibid., II:62, 351–2.
103 Ibid., II:57, 348.
104 Ibid., II:59, 349.
105 The capacity to become free and equal is based on the capacity to become rational enough to understand the laws of civil society and of nature: 'Thus we are *born Free*, as we are born Rational; not that we have actually the Exercise of either.' Ibid., II:61, 350.
106 Ibid., II:63, 352.
107 Ibid., II:56, 347. Locke is careful to state that this responsibility does not rest on the notion that parents give their children life by begetting them. God creates the new life by means of the parent.
108 The children's lifelong obligation to honour their parents may include esteeming them, refraining from injuring or endangering them, and providing them with assistance if required. Ibid., II:66, 354.
109 Ibid., II:70, 356–7.
110 Ibid., II:67, 354. It is the parents' responsibility to ensure that their children receive a proper education, whether the child is educated at home by the

parents themselves or whether the task is transferred to another person in the form of a tutor. Ibid., II:69, 356.
111 Ibid., II:67, 354.
112 Ibid., II:71, 357.
113 Locke writes: 'And thus, 'tis true, the *Paternal* is a natural *Government*, but not at all extending it self to the Ends, and Jurisdictions of that which is Political.' Ibid., II:170, 428.
114 Ibid., II:65, 353.
115 Locke, 'Some Thoughts Concerning Education,' sec. 41, 145.
116 Locke, *Two Treatises of Government*, II:67, 355.
117 Locke, 'Some Thoughts Concerning Education,' sec. 34, 138.
118 Locke warns that anyone who has not yet developed enough reason to know the limits of his freedom should never be 'let loose to the disposure his own Will (because he knows no bounds to it, has not Understanding, its proper Guide) but is continued under the Tuition and Government of others all the time his own Understanding is uncapable of that Charge.' *Two Treatises of Government*, II:60, 350.
119 Ibid., II:55, 346–7.
120 This does not entail children pledging political allegiance to the parents themselves, which according to Locke may historically have been the basis for hereditary or elective kingdoms. Ibid., II: 75, 360–1. It entails children pledging allegiance to the non-parental political authorities.
121 With the spoilage principle in effect, hoarding more than one could use was a 'foolish thing, as well as dishonest.' Ibid., II:46, 342.
122 Ibid., II:48, 343. I agree with C.B. Macpherson, *The Political Theory of Possessive Individualism*, 208, that Locke's discussion of the spoilage principle was not intended to show that it is morally wrong to appropriate more than one can use, but to show that the effect of the spoilage principle was to provide less incentive for men to be industrious.
123 God gave the Earth to be made use of by the 'Industrious and Rational.' *Two Treaties of Government*, II:34, 333. To be industrious, it seems, is to cultivate more of the earth or accumulate more money than one can make use of for oneself.
124 Ibid., II:86, 242–3 and II:25, 327 and II:28, 329–30.
125 Ibid., I:29, 247.
126 John Plamenatz has pointed out that Locke's theory of the origin of private property, which stipulates that anything an individual has not put his labour into reverts to the common lot, is incompatible with the principle of a child's right to inherit property, which essentially stipulates that one has a

right to own what one did not labour for. *Man and Society*, vol. 1 (New York: McGraw-Hill, 1963), 226–7.
127 Locke, *Two Treatises of Government*, I:87, 243.
128 Ibid., I:88, 244.
129 The child might become an other to its parents, according to Locke's speculations in the following passage: 'Thus any part of our bodies, vitally united to that which is conscious in us, makes a part of our *selves*; but upon separation from the vital union, by which that consciousness is communicated, that which a moment since was part of our *selves* is now no more so than a part of another man's *self* is a part of me; and it is not impossible but in a little time may become a real part of another person.' *An Essay Concerning Human Understanding*, vol. 1, bk. 2, ch. 27, 291.
130 Locke, *Two Treatises of Government*, II:190, 441.
131 Similarly, owning property in one's person, Locke insists, does not mean one can legitimately take one's own life; it belongs to God. Ibid., II:6, 311.
132 See Carole Pateman, *The Sexual Contract*, chapter 5, for a discussion on the extent to which Locke's concept of selling one's labour power justifies slave labour.
133 Locke, *Two Treatises of Government*, II:170, 428.
134 Ibid., II:65, 353.
135 Ibid., II:173, 430.
136 Ibid., II:64, 352.
137 Ibid., I:89, 245.
138 Ibid., I:88, 244–5.
139 At the same time, Locke wants to indicate that parents do benefit from caring for their children and accumulating property for them. He stipulates that children have an obligation to provide 'Support and Subsistence' to their parents, if required. But this does not mean that children should repay their parents before they would pass on property to their own children. Ibid., I:90, 245.
140 Ibid., II:80, 363.
141 Although Locke does not refer explicitly to men's experience of uncertainty over paternity, he refers to it implicitly when he says that a man may not know that a child has been conceived. Ibid., I:54–5, 216.
142 Clark, 'Women and Locke,' 38.
143 He begins his discussion of paternal power by pointing out that it should more accurately be called 'parental power,' since it includes the mother as well as the father. Locke, *Two Treatises of Government*, II:52, 345.
144 Locke's intention may be to demonstrate that the father's power over the

child is limited to what the mother may exercise as well, but he also indicates that women are capable of exercising parental power and that mothers have a legitimate right to such power. Ibid., I:61, 221 and I:65, 225.
145 Ibid., II:82, 364.
146 Ibid., II:77. 362.
147 Eisenstein, *The Radical Future of Liberal Feminism*, 41.
148 Pateman, *The Sexual Contract*, 185.
149 Pateman also maintains that the idea that one can contract out one's labour power in general is a myth. Ibid., 231.
150 Locke, *Two Treatises of Government*, II:78, 362.
151 Pateman, *The Sexual Contract*, chapter 6.
152 Locke, *Two Treatises of Government*, II:77, 362.
153 Ibid., II:56, 347.
154 Ibid., II:27, 328–329.
155 Ibid., I:55, 216.
156 C.B. Macpherson, *The Political Theory of Possessive Individualism*, 231.
157 Locke, *Two Treatises of Government*, II:4, 309.
158 Ibid., II:6, 311.
159 Ibid., I:42, 206.
160 Ibid., I:93, 248.
161 Locke describes life in the womb in several passages. In *An Essay Concerning Human Understanding*, vol. 1, bk. 2, ch. 1, 88, he describes the fetus' sensate life in the following terms: 'He, I say, who considers this will perhaps find reason to imagine that a *foetus in the mother's womb differs not much from the state of a vegetable*, but passes the greatest part of its time without perception or thought, doing very little but sleep in a place where it needs not seek for food, and is surrounded with liquor, always equally soft, and near of the same temper, where the eyes have no light and the ears, so shut up, are not very susceptible of sounds, and where there is little or no variety or change of objects to move the senses.' And in another passage: 'For, bating perhaps some faint *ideas* of hunger, and thirst, and warmth, and some pains which they may *have* felt in the womb, there is *not* the least appearance of any settled *ideas* at all in them.' Ibid., vol. 1, bk. 1, ch. 4, 44.
162 Ibid., vol. 1, bk. 2, ch. 2, 38 (my emphasis).
163 John Locke, *A Letter on Toleration*, ed. Raymond Klibansky and J.W. Gough (Oxford: Clarendon Press, 1968), 91.
164 This includes the power of bequeathing property to the children. *Two Treatises of Government*, II:72, 357.
165 Locke, *An Essay Concerning Human Understanding*, vol. 1, bk. 2, ch. 21, 200.
166 Locke, *Two Treatises of Government*, II:190, 441.

167 Differences in natural or aquired merit, Locke implies, do not detract from that '*equal* Right that every Man hath, *to his Natural Freedom*, without being subjected to the Will or Authority of any other Man.' Ibid., II:54, 346.
168 Ibid., II:4, 309 and II:57, 348.
169 Ibid., II:6, 311.
170 Pateman, *The Disorder of Women*, 74.
171 Locke, *Two Treatises of Government*, II:171–2, 429.
172 Ibid., II:11, 314.
173 Ibid., II:3, 308.
174 Ibid., I:47, 209–10.
175 Ibid., II:192, 442.
176 Locke emphasizes that the aim of civil society is the preservation of property: 'For the preservation of Property being the end of Government, and that for which Men enter into Society, it necessarily supposes and requires, that the People should *have Property*, without which they must be suppos'd to lose that by entring into Society, which was the end for which they entered into it, too gross an absurdity for any Man to own.' Ibid., II:138, 406.
177 Yet, given their unique reproductive capacities, women may have more at stake than men in the enjoyment of property in their own person. They may require, more so than men, state protection of such 'property rights.' The contradiction this engenders will be addressed in chapters 4 and 5.
178 The government, in wielding its legislative power, Locke writes, must not '*raise Taxes* on the Property of the People, *without the Consent of the People*, given by themselves, or their Deputies.' Ibid., II:142, 409.
179 Ibid., II:154, 416.
180 He writes: 'But still it must be with his own Consent, *i.e.* the Consent of the Majority, giving it either by themselves, or their Representatives chosen by them. For if any one shall claim a *Power to lay* and levy *Taxes* on the People, by his own Authority, and without such consent of the People, he thereby invades the *Fundamental Law of Property* and subverts the end of Government.' Ibid., II:140, 407.
181 For example, see Antonia Fraser, *The Weaker Vessel: Woman's Lot in Seventeenth-Century England* (London: Methuen, 1985), chapter 12.
182 Richard Ashcraft too notes that there were debates in Locke's time over whether women should be given the right to vote for parliamentary representatives. Although Ashcraft attempts to present Locke's *Two Treatises of Government* as advocating a radical stance that would support the extension of suffrage to a much wider group than was prevalent in Locke's time, he does not directly speculate on whether or not Locke would have supported the extension of suffrage to women. *Revolutionary Politics and*

Locke's Two Treatises of Government (Princeton: Princeton University Press, 1986), 236.
183 Locke, Two Treatises of Government, II:232, 467.
184 Ibid., II:20, 22.
185 Ibid., II:242, 476–7.
186 Ibid., II:242, 477.
187 Ibid., II:209, 453.
188 Ibid., II:225, 463.
189 Ibid., II:183, 437.
190 Ibid., II:147–8, 412.

CHAPTER 3 John Stuart Mill

1 For example, see *Sexual Equality: Writings by John Stuart Mill, Harriet Taylor Mill, and Helen Taylor*, ed. Ann P. Robson and John M. Robson (Toronto: University of Toronto Press, 1994). For a discussion of Harriet Taylor's influence on Mill, see Alice S. Rossi, 'Sentiment and Intellect: The Story of John Stuart Mill and Harriet Taylor Mill,' in *Essays on Sex Equality*, ed. Alice S. Rossi (Chicago: University of Chicago Press, 1970).
2 John Stuart Mill, *The Subjection of Women*, in *The Collected Works of John Stuart Mill*, vol. 21, ed. John M. Robson (Toronto: University of Toronto Press, 1963–84), 259–340.
3 Robson and Robson note that John Stuart Mill, Harriet Taylor Mill, and Helen Taylor thought 'far too much was being made of apparent differences between female and male "natures"' (*Sexual Equality*, x), but that there are also passages where Mill suggests that, on the average, women may have different but complementary tendencies from men. Implicitly, one might see in Mill 'an attempt to unite "economic" man and "moral" woman, competition and caring.' Ibid., xxxiii.
4 Julia Annas, 'Mill and the Subjection of Women,' *Philosophy* 52 (April 1977): 179–94.
5 Moira Gatens, *Feminism and Philosophy* (Bloomington: Indiana University Press, 1991), 33.
6 Christine Di Stefano, *Configurations of Masculinity* (Ithaca: Cornell University Press, 1991), chapter 4.
7 Ibid., 175–6.
8 Diana Coole, *Women in Political Theory: From Ancient Misogyny to Contemporary Feminism*, 2nd edition (Boulder: Lynne Rienner, 1993), 117.
9 Zillah Eisenstein, *The Radical Future of Liberal Feminism* (New York: Longman, 1981), 118, 127.

10 Coole, *Women in Political Theory*, 118.
11 Nadia Urbinati, 'J.S. Mill on Androgyny and Marriage,' *Political Theory* 19 (November 1991): 626–48.
12 Robson and Robson make a similar point in *Sexual Equality*, xviii–xix.
13 Carole Pateman, *The Sexual Contract* (Stanford: Stanford University Press, 1988), 162–3.
14 Susan Moller Okin, *Justice, Gender and the Family* (New York: Basic Books, 1989), 20, 37.
15 Susan Moller Okin, *Women in Western Political Thought* (Princeton: Princeton University Press, 1979), chapter 9.
16 Eisenstein, *The Radical Future of Liberal Feminism*, 137–9.
17 Barbara Cameron, 'Mill's Treatment of Women Workers and Private Property,' *Canadian Journal of Political Science* 13 (December 1980): 775–83.
18 Mary Lyndon Shanley, 'Marital Slavery and Friendship: John Stuart Mill's "The Subjection of Women,"' *Political Theory* 9 (May 1981): 229–47.
19 Susan J. Hekman, 'John Stuart Mill's *The Subjection of Women*: The Foundations of Liberal Feminism,' *History of European Ideas* 15 (1992): 681–6.
20 Coole, *Women in Political Theory*, 117.
21 Mill, *The Subjection of Women*, 277.
22 Ibid., 276.
23 According to Robson and Robson, the younger Mill subscribed to his father's psychological theory that the mind was at birth a 'blank sheet on which experience wrote all knowledge and ideas, and consequently promoted the view that all, female and male alike, were born equal in ability.' *Sexual Equality*, xiii.
24 Mill, *The Subjection of Women*, 277–8.
25 Ibid., 269–70.
26 J.S. Mill, 'Speech on Women's Suffrage 4,' in Robson and Robson, *Sexual Equality*, 289–90.
27 Jennifer Ring, *Modern Political Theory and Contemporary Feminism* (Albany: State University of New York Press, 1991), 62–3.
28 Mill, *The Subjection of Women*, 274. And: 'Under complete freedom of choice, wherever there are real diversities of aptitude, the great number will apply themselves to the things for which they are on the average fittest, and the exceptional course will only be taken by the exceptions.' *Considerations on Representative Government*, in *Collected Works*, vol. 19, 479.
29 Mill, *The Subjection of Women*, 280–1.
30 Ibid., 327, 335.
31 Ibid., 311.
32 Ibid., 305.

33 They may have achieved second-best but they have not yet achieved the best, as men have done, according to Mill. Ibid., 300.
34 Ibid., 320.
35 Ibid., 306.
36 Ibid., 316.
37 Ibid., 320.
38 'It cannot be inferred to be impossible that a woman should be a Homer, or an Aristotle, or a Michael Angelo, or a Beethoven, because no woman has yet actually produced works comparable to theirs in any of those lines of excellence.' Ibid., 302.
39 Ibid., 281, 338–9.
40 Ibid., 326.
41 Ibid., 298.
42 Ibid., 326.
43 Ibid., 338.
44 Ibid., 281.
45 Ibid., 300.
46 Ibid., 328–30.
47 Having traditionally wielded less power than men, women have had less opportunity to be corrupted by it. As a result they may appear to be morally superior to men. Ibid., 320–1.
48 Ibid., 328.
49 Ibid., 327.
50 Ibid., 330.
51 Ibid., 330.
52 Ibid., 330.
53 The consequence of this bias, according to Mill, is that ' women's influence is often anything but favourable to public virtue.' Ibid., 329.
54 Ibid., 339.
55 Both J.S. Mill and Harriet Taylor Mill often refer to women's 'family selfishness.' For example: 'The wife is the incarnate spirit of family selfishness unless she has accustomed herself to cultivate feelings of a larger and more generous kind: while, when she has, her (in general) greater susceptibility of emotion and more delicate conscience makes her the great inspirer of those nobler feelings in the men with whom she habitually associates.' Harriet Taylor Mill and J.S. Mill, 'Papers on Women's Rights (1847–50?),' in *Collected Works*, vol. 21, 384.
56 Mill, *Utilitarianism*, in *Collected Works*, vol. 10, 217.
57 Mill, *The Subjection of Women*, 293.
58 This statement is in Helen Taylor's handwriting, but the additions to the

piece in Mill's handwriting suggest that he agrees with the portions written by Helen Taylor, before 1873, 'Nursing,' in Robson and Robson, *Sexual Equality*, 145.
59 This portion of Helen Taylor, before 1873, 'Nursing,' is in Mill's handwriting. Ibid., 146.
60 Mill, *The Subjection of Women*, 344.
61 Women's differences would be perceived as an asset to society rather than a sign of their inferiority 'if their education and cultivation were adapted to correcting instead of aggravating the infirmities incident to their temperament,' Mill writes in ibid., 310.
62 Harriet Taylor and J.S. Mill, 'Papers on Women's Rights (1847–50?),' in *Collected Works*, vol. 21, 388.
63 Mill, *Utilitarianism*, 232.
64 In his discussion of the merits of plural voting, Mill suggests that one's occupation or socio-economic position can serve as an indicator of one's mental abilities (in the absence of standardized tests). An employer can be assumed to be mentally superior to an employee, for example. *Considerations on Representative Government*, 475.
65 John Stuart Mill, *On Liberty*, in *Collected Works*, vol. 18, 213–310.
66 Mill, *The Subjection of Women*, 295.
67 For example, see his discussion in *Principles of Political Economy*, bk. 1, ch. 13, sec. 2 in *Collected Works*, vol. 2, 188.
68 Mill, *On Liberty*, 304.
69 Ibid., 304.
70 Mill, *The Subjection of Women*, 324.
71 Ibid., 325.
72 Mill, *On Liberty*, 301.
73 'The equality of married persons before the law, is not only the sole mode in which that particular relation can be made consistent with justice to both sides, and conducive to the happiness of both, but it is the only means of rendering the daily life of mankind, in any high sense, a school of moral cultivation.' Mill, *The Subjection of Women*, 293.
74 Ibid., 295.
75 Mill, *On Liberty*, 301–2.
76 Ibid., 302.
77 Ibid., 302.
78 Ibid., 304.
79 He refers to liberty of combination in ibid., 226: 'Thirdly, from this liberty of each individual, follows the liberty, within the same limits, of combination among individuals; freedom to unite, for any purpose not involving harm to

others: the persons combining being supposed to be of full age, and not forced or deceived.'
80 Mill describes parental rights as 'those rights over the child's person and conduct, which have no legitimate ground of existence save as a means to the fulfilment of those obligations, or a reward and encouragement for fulfilling them conscientiously.' 'The Suicide of Sarah Brown,' in Robson and Robson, *Sexual Equality*, 55.
81 Mill, *The Subjection of Women*, 295.
82 Robson and Robson, 'Domestic Cruelty and Injustice,' *Sexual Equality*, draw our attention to how appalled and indignant J.S. Mill and Harriet Taylor Mill were at reports of children and women beaten and abused by family members, most often fathers and husbands.
83 Mill, *On Liberty*, 301.
84 Mill, 'The Case of Anne Bird,' in Robson and Robson, *Sexual Equality*, 70.
85 Ibid., 66–7.
86 Mill criticizes laws that cede almost exclusive rights over the children to the father. *The Subjection of Women*, 285.
87 Mill, 'The Case of the North Family,' in Robson and Robson, *Sexual Equality*, 62.
88 Mill, *The Subjection of Women*, 285.
89 By remarking that it is more degrading for women than for men to have their bodies examined – 'men are not lowered in their own eyes as much by exposure of their persons' – Mill implies both that women are more modest and that bodily integrity is more important to them than to men. 'The Contagious Diseases Acts,' in *Collected Works*, vol. 21, 356.
90 Mill, 'Married Women's Property' and 'The Californian Constitution,' in Robson and Robson, *Sexual Equality*, 38–9, 46.
91 Mill, *Principles of Political Economy*, bk. 5, ch. 11, sec. 9, in *Collected Works*, vol. 3, 953.
92 Mill, 'Equality in Education,' in Robson and Robson, *Sexual Equality*, 157.
93 Mill, 'On Marriage,' in *Collected Works*, vol. 21, 44.
94 Mill writes: 'It is by devoting one-half of the human species to that exclusive function, by making it fill the entire life of one sex, and interweave itself with almost all the objects of the other, that the animal instinct in question is nursed into the disproportionate preponderance which it has hitherto exercised in human life.' *Principles of Political Economy*, bk. 4, ch. 7, sec. 3, in *Collected Works*, vol. 3, 766.
95 Mill, *The Subjection of Women*, 291.
96 Mill, *Considerations on Representative Government*, 479–81.
97 Ibid., 479.

98 Mill, *The Subjection of Women*, 308.
99 Mill, 'Women's Suffrage 1,' in Robson and Robson, *Sexual Equality*, 269.
100 Mill, *The Subjection of Women*, 339. And further: 'If we are to meet the demand of the age for a government at once cheap and efficient, which shall cost little, but shall give us all we ought to have for the money, the most vigilant and capable agents for making the money to go as far as it can will generally be found among women.' Mill, 'Women's Suffrage 1,' in Robson and Robson, *Sexual Equality*, 269.
101 Mill says: 'Women, on the average, have more contriving minds than men; in things they are really interested in, they are readier in finding means for the attainment of an end; especially in undertakings the success of which greatly depends on the details of the execution.' 'Women's Suffrage 2,' in ibid., 275.
102 Mill writes: 'When we consider that these princesses have never been seen in public, have never conversed with any man not of their own family except from behind a curtain, that they do not read, and if they did, there is no book in their languages which can give them the smallest instruction on political affairs; the example they afford of the natural capacity of women for government is very striking.' *The Subjection of Women*, 303.
103 Ibid., 302.
104 Ibid., 301.
105 J.S. Mill and Helen Taylor, 'Propagandizing for the Cause,' in Robson and Robson, *Sexual Equality*, 249.
106 Mill, 'Speech on Women's Suffrage 4,' in ibid., 285.
107 Helen Taylor supports this idea when she proposes that women can better feel sympathy for the plight of women than even the best of men: 'Not the noblest and most generous of men can feel, as a woman must, for the misery of an ill-used wife, the horror of a woman's lowest degradation, the anguish of a mother deprived of her children, the helplessness of a poor and solitary girl in the state of society in which we live.' 'Women's Suffrage 3,' in ibid., 283.
108 Mill, *The Subjection of Women*, 339.
109 Ibid., 301. One of the criteria of 'good government' for Mill is the degree to which it is able to make most efficient use of the talents of its community members by recruiting the most capable into government. *Considerations on Representative Government*, 392.
110 Even with the vote, Mill assures us, 'the ordinary occupations of most women are, and are likely to remain, principally domestic.' 'The Admission of Women to the Electoral Franchise,' in Robson and Robson, *Sexual Equality*, 237.

228   Notes to pages 117–20

111 According to Mill, 'When we call anything a person's right, we mean that he has a valid claim on society to protect him in the possession of it, either by the force of law, or by that of education and opinion. If he has what we consider a sufficient claim, on whatever account, to have something guaranteed to him by society, we say that he has a right to it.' *Utilitarianism*, 250.
112 Ibid., 250–1.
113 Mill, *Considerations on Representative Government*, 470–2.
114 Ibid., 475.
115 Creative ability for Mill is a sign of superior mental ability, which is invaluable to the progress of civilization: 'To see the futurity of the species has always been the privilege of the intellectual elite, or of those who have learnt from them; to have the feelings of that futurity has been the distinction, and usually the martyrdom, of a still rarer elite.' *The Subjection of Women*, 294.
116 'If women's literature is destined to have a different collective character from that of men, depending on any difference of natural tendencies, much longer time is necessary than has yet elapsed, before it can emancipate itself from the influence of accepted models, and guide itself by its own impulses.' Ibid., 316.
117 This is the context in which we can understand Mill saying: 'But if, as I believe, there will not prove to be any natural tendencies common to women, and distinguishing their genius from that of men, yet every individual writer among them has her individual tendencies, which at present are still subdued by the influence of precedent and example: and it will require generations more, before their individuality is sufficiently developed to make head against that influence.' Ibid., 316–17.
118 Mill writes: 'If women lived in a different country from men, and had never read any of their writings, they would have had a literature of their own. As it is, they have not created one, because they found a highly advanced literature already created.' Ibid., 316.
119 Ibid., 298.
120 Ibid., 297.
121 Ibid., 297–8.
122 Ibid., 298.
123 Ibid., 297.
124 Ibid., 298.
125 Mill, 'On Marriage,' in *Collected Works*, vol. 21, 43.
126 Knowing that they would be able to support themselves if separated, women would not feel compelled to work while married, Mill seems to say here: 'if she would then find all honourable employments as freely open to

her as to men; it would not be necessary for her protection, that during marriage she should make this particular use of her faculties.' *The Subjection of Women*, 298.
127 He writes: 'There is, first, the superintendence of the family and the domestic expenditure, which occupies at least one woman in every family, generally the one of mature years and acquired experience; unless the family is so rich as to admit of delegating that task to hired agency, and submitting to all the waste and malversation inseparable from that mode of conducting it.' Ibid., 318.
128 Ibid., 318.
129 Ibid., 300.
130 Mill, 'The Suicide of Sarah Brown,' in Robson and Robson, *Sexual Equality*, 54.
131 Mill refers to women's physical subjection 'in the most naturally brutal and morally uneducated part of the lower classes' (*The Subjection of Women*, 296); Harriet Taylor Mill and J.S. Mill remark that 'At present it is the universal belief of the labouring class, that the law permits them to beat their wives – and the wives themselves share the general error' ('The Law of Assault,' in Robson and Robson, *Sexual Equality*, 84). And Helen Taylor comments: 'All the world acknowledges, for example, that the British husband of the lower class is given to brutally ill-treating his wife.' 'Women's Suffrage 3,' in ibid., 282.
132 Harriet Taylor Mill and J.S. Mill call for public flogging as a deterrent for men found beating their wives. Fines, imprisonment, and hard labour are not enough to deter men of the lower ranks, they suggest; these forms of punishment too closely replicate the conditions of their everyday life. Harriet Taylor Mill and J.S. Mill, 'Remarks on Mr. Fitzroy's Bill,' in ibid., 94–5.
133 Harriet Taylor Mill and J.S. Mill, 'The Suicide of Sarah Brown,' in ibid., 56.
134 Harriet Taylor Mill and J.S. Mill, 'The Case of Susan Moir,' in ibid., 81.
135 Mill, *On Liberty*, 225.
136 Mill, *The Subjection of Women*, 270.
137 Ibid., 270.
138 Ibid., 265.
139 Mill writes: 'There is no natural inequality between the sexes; except perhaps in bodily strength; even *that* admits of doubt: and if bodily strength is to be the measure of superiority, mankind are no better than savages. Every step in the progress of civilization has tended to diminish the deference paid to bodily strength, until now when that quality confers scarcely any advantages except its natural ones: the strong man has little or no power to employ his strength as a means of acquiring any other advantage over the weaker in body.' 'On Marriage,' in *Collected Works*, vol. 21, 42.

140 Mill, *The Subjection of Women*, 289–90.
141 Mill, *Considerations on Representative Government*, 481.
142 Mill, *The Subjection of Women*, 327, 335.
143 According to Mill, 'A person is not expected to consult exclusively the public benefit in the use he makes of his house, or his three per cent. stock, or anything "else" to which he really has a right. The suffrage is indeed due to him, among other reasons, as a means to his own protection, but only against treatment from which he is equally bound, so far as depends on his vote, to protect every one of his fellow-citizens. His vote is not a thing in which he has an option; it has no more to do with his personal wishes than the verdict of a juryman. It is strictly a matter of duty; he is bound to give it according to his best and most conscientious opinion of the public good.' *Considerations on Representative Government*, 489.
144 J.S. Mill, 'Speech on Women's Suffrage 4,' in Robson and Robson, *Sexual Equality*, 288.
145 Mill, *The Subjection of Women*, 271, 272, 282.
146 Mill, 'Women's Suffrage 2,' in Robson and Robson, *Sexual Equality*, 274.
147 Helen Taylor, 'The Ladies Petition,' in ibid., 232–3 and Mill, 'The Admission of Women to the Electoral Franchise,' in ibid., 241.
148 According to Michael St. John Packe, 'Of anything Mill ever wrote, *The Subjection of Women* aroused the most antagonism. Those who were always hostile became more hostile still.' *The Life of John Stuart Mill* (New York: Macmillan, 1954), 495.
149 Mill, *The Subjection of Women*, 261.
150 Urbinati, 'J.S. Mill on Androgyny and Marriage,' 640.
151 Ring, *Modern Political Theory and Contemporary Feminism*, 70.

CHAPTER 4: Reproduction and Politics

1 Locke insists that religious tolerance does not include acceptance of those who are atheists: 'Lastly, those who deny the existence of the Deity are not to be tolerated at all. Promises, covenants, and oaths, which are the bonds of human society, can have no hold upon or sanctity for an atheist; for the taking away of God, even only in thought, dissolves all.' *A Letter on Toleration*, ed. Raymond Klibansky and J.W. Gough (Oxford: Clarendon Press, 1968), 135.
2 Angus McLaren and Arlene Tigar McLaren, *The Bedroom and the State: The Changing Practices and Politics of Contraception and Abortion in Canada 1880–1980*, (Toronto: McClelland and Stewart, 1986).
3 For a sense of the immediate public reaction to such initiatives, see Ruth Teichrob, 'Spanking Statute Flayed,' *Winnipeg Free Press*, 7 November 1993.

4 For a brief overview of this phenomenon, see Michael Gillespie and Michael Lienesch, 'Religion and the Resurgence of Conservatism,' in *The Resurgence of Conservatism in Anglo-American Democracies*, ed. Barry Cooper, Allan Kornberg, and William Mishler (Durham: Duke University Press, 1988).
5 For a discussion of the grounds on which the abortion debate has taken place in Canada, see Janine Brodie, Shelley A.M. Gavigan, and Jane Jenson, *The Politics of Abortion* (Toronto: Oxford University Press, 1992); Robert M. Campbell and Leslie A. Pal, *The Real Worlds of Canadian Politics*, 2nd edition (Peterborough: Broadview Press, 1991), chapter 1; and F.L. Morton, *Morgentaler v. Borowski: Abortion, the Charter, and the Courts* (Toronto: McClelland and Stewart, 1992).
6 Brodie, Gavigan, and Jenson, *The Politics of Abortion*, 72.
7 The 1973 Roe versus Wade decision in the United States was based on similar principles – a woman's 'security of person,' tied to her 'right to privacy.'
8 Campbell and Pal, *The Real Worlds of Canadian Politics*, 198.
9 Christine Overall, *Human Reproduction: Principles, Practices and Policies* (Toronto: Oxford University Press, 1993), 37.
10 Ibid., 40.
11 Martha Brandt Bolton, 'Responsible Women and Abortion Decisions,' in *Having Children*, ed. Onora O'Neill and William Ruddick (New York: Oxford University Press, 1979), 42.
12 Overall, *Human Reproduction*, 21.
13 Ibid., 20.
14 Campbell and Pal, *The Real Worlds of Canadian Politics*, 205.
15 Ibid., 20.
16 For an excellent overview of the arguments surrounding this question, see chapter 4 – 'Biological Mothers and the Disposition of Foetuses after Abortion' – of Christine Overall's *Human Reproduction*.
17 David S. Levin, 'Thomson and the Current State of the Abortion Controversy,' *Journal of Applied Ethics* 2: 1 (1985): 125, cited in Overall, *Human Reproduction*, 66. Overall does not endorse this position. She is clearly uncomfortable with it, but has difficulty coming up with an alternative.
18 Brodie, Gavigan, and Jenson, *The Politics of Abortion*, 83.
19 A recent Statistics Canada Report shows that the rate of abortion continues to rise. In 1993, 26.9 abortions were performed for every 100 live births, compared with 25.6 in 1992 and 3 in 1970. In the United States, in 1992 the rate was 37 abortions for every 100 live births. Alanna Mitchell, 'Abortion Numbers Continue to Climb,' *Globe and Mail*, 13 July 1995 and 'Abortion Rate Increase Linked to Recession,' *Globe and Mail*, 4 October 1994.
20 Fabrice Taylor, 'More Choosing to be Childless,' *Globe and Mail*, 8 July 1995.
21 Susan A. McDaniel, 'The Changing Canadian Family: Women's Roles and

the Impact of Feminism,' in *Changing Patterns: Women in Canada*, ed. Sandra Burt, Lorraine Code, and Lindsay Dorney (Toronto: McClelland and Stewart, 1988), 107.
22 Germaine Greer, *Sex and Destiny* (Toronto: Stoddart, 1984), 389.
23 Brodie, Gavigan, and Jenson, *The Politics of Abortion*, 84.
24 Laurie Shrage, 'Fetal Ideologies and Maternal Desires: A Post-Enlightenment Account of Abortion,' in *Moral Dilemmas of Feminism* (New York: Routledge, 1994), 62.
25 For example: 'In general, there is a very close correspondence between the interests of pregnant women and fetuses, and it seems reasonable to expect that in most cases pregnant women are supportive of anything that can be done to improve prospects for their babies.' Ruth Faden, 'Autonomy, Choice, and the New Reproductive Technologies: The Role of Informed Consent in Prenatal Genetic Diagnosis,' in *Women and New Reproductive Technologies: Medical, Psychosocial, Legal, and Ethical Dilemmas*, ed. Judith Rodin and Aila Collins (Hillsdale, New Jersey: Lawrence Erlbaum Associates, 1991), 45.
26 For a description, see Rona Achilles, 'Artificial Reproduction: Hope Chest or Pandora's Box?' in *Changing Patterns: Women in Canada*, ed. Sandra Burt, Lorraine Code, and Lindsay Dorney (Toronto: McClelland and Stewart, 1988); 'Desperately Seeking Babies: New Technologies of Hope and Despair,' in *Delivering Motherhood: Maternal Ideologies and Practises in the Nineteenth and Twentieth Centuries*, ed. Katherine Arnup, Andrée Lévesque, and Ruth Roach Pierson, with the assistance of Margaret Brennan (New York: Routledge, 1990), and 'Assisted Reproduction: The Social Issues,' in *Changing Patterns: Women in Canada*, 2nd edition, ed. Sandra Burt, Lorraine Code, and Lindsay Dorney (Toronto: McClelland and Stewart, 1993).
27 Kenneth D. Alpern, 'Genetic Puzzles and Stork Stories: On the Meaning and Significance of Having Children,' in *The Ethics of Reproductive Technology*, ed. Kenneth D. Alpern (New York: Oxford University Press, 1992).
28 Ibid., 151.
29 Ibid., 151.
30 The list includes such things as: it gives significance to marriage; it is an expression of personal renewal; it contributes to the perpetuation and advancement of society; and it is a way of continuing oneself. At the top of the list is a Lockean directive: 'it may even be felt to by a duty or fulfilment of God's command.' Ibid., 151.
31 Ibid., 158.
32 The desire for genetically linked children may of course be due to other factors as well, such as the growing number of reports on the importance of heredity in determining health. But for a discussion of why a desire for

genetically linked children ought not to be wholeheartedly endorsed, see Susan Sherwin, 'Feminist Ethics and In Vitro Fertilization,' in *Science, Morality and Feminist Theory*, Supplement to *Canadian Journal of Philosophy* 13, ed. Marsha Hanen and Kai Nielson (Calgary: University of Calgary Press, 1987).
33 Achilles, 'Artificial Reproduction: Hope Chest or Pandora's Box?,' 307.
34 Ibid., 302.
35 Linda S. Williams, 'Biology or Society? Parenthood Motivation in a Sample of Canadian Women Seeking In Vitro Fertilization,' in *Issues in Reproductive Technology I: An Anthology*, ed. Helen Bequaert Holmes (New York: Garland, 1992), 264–5.
36 *Proceed with Care: Final Report of the Royal Commission on New Reproductive Technologies*, vol. 1 (Ottawa: Minister of Supply and Services Canada, 1993), 264. In addition, the most common reason for referring women to pre-natal diagnostic services in Canada in 1990 was advanced maternal age (the result of delayed childbearing), which increases the risk of genetic abnormality. Ibid., vol. 2, 757.
37 As Thomas C. Shevory notes, 'The woman's contribution to generating the embryos [is] greater than the man's.' 'Through a Glass Darkly: Law, Politics, and Frozen Human Embryos,' in *Issues in Reproductive Technology I*, ed. Holmes 244.
38 Overall, *Human Reproduction*, 73–4.
39 Initially, there was considerable debate over whether the new technologies could contribute to women's liberation or further their oppression; see Anne Donchin, 'The Future of Mothering: Reproductive Technology and Feminist Theory,' *Hypatia* 1 (Fall 1986): 121–37 and Jean Bethke Elshtain, *Power Trips and Other Journeys* (Madison: University of Wisconsin Press, 1990), chapter 7. Now, it seems, most feminist thinkers and activists oppose them and very few support them wholeheartedly. This is evident in the position taken by the numerous submissions to the Royal Commission on New Reproductive Technologies, established by the Canadian government in 1989, and the controversies that surrounded its activities (several members resigned and were fired). Many felt, feminists in particular, that the chairperson, Patricia Baird – a geneticist – was too receptive to such technologies, from the start. Released in November of 1993, the Commission's report responds to feminist concerns. It takes a middle ground, recommending banning some technologies such as surrogacy arrangement and pre-natal sex selection, offering qualified access to others, such as *in vitro* fertilization, and ensuring that technologies such as pre-natal genetic testing are carefully monitored by a central regulatory agency. See *The Research Studies of the Royal Commission on Reproductive Technologies* (Ottawa: Minister of Supply and Services, 1993) and *Proceed with*

Care, vols. 1 and 2. For a critical review of some aspects of the Commission's activities and recommendations, see Thelma McCormack, 'Reproductive Technologies: Rights, Choice, and Coercion,' in *Women and Canadian Public Policy*, ed. Janine Brodie (Toronto: Harcourt Brace, 1996).
40 Judy Rebick, 'Is the Issue Choice?' in *Misconceptions: The Social Construction of Choice and the New Reproductive and Genetic Technologies*, vol. 1, ed. Gwynne Basen, Margrit Eichler, and Abby Lippman (Hull: Voyageur, 1993), 89. The articles in this volume were spurred by opposition to the tactics and orientation of the Royal Commission on Reproductive Technologies. They include interviews with former and dissenting members of the Commission.
41 'Fetal rights activists' like Joe Borowski have called for court protection for fetuses in Canada on the basis of such claims. See Christine Overall, *Human Reproduction*, 23–4 and Morton, *Morgentaler v. Borowski*, chapters 20, 21.
42 Overall, *Human Reproduction*, 42.
43 Patricia Spallone, *Beyond Conception: The New Politics of Reproduction* (Massachusetts: Bergin and Garvey, 1989).
44 Ellen Wright Clayton observes that the new reproductive technologies bring the interests of the unborn into focus, and as a result, 'There is great pressure to force women to act on behalf of their fetuses.' 'Women and Advances in Medical Technologies: The Legal Issues' in *Women and New Reproductive Technologies*, ed. Rodin and Collins, 104.
45 Spallone, *Beyond Conception*, 39. Overall takes a similar position – proposing that we 're-evaluate the adversarial and individualistic perspective that pits the foetus against the pregnant woman.' *Human Reproduction*, 42.
46 Spallone, *Beyond Conception*, 34. A 'woman-centred' approach opposes both the new reproductive technologies and the anti-abortion position as being 'fetal-centred' and as assuming and encouraging a separation between the fetus and the mother.
47 Carol Gilligan, *In a Different Voice: Psychological Theory and Women's Development* (Cambridge: Harvard University Press, 1982). I examine this work in greater detail in chapter 5.
48 Mary Lyndon Shanley criticizes surrogacy arrangements from this perspective, arguing that they deny the embodied relationship of the biological woman carrying the fetus. Moreover, she acknowledges that underlying this sort of criticism is the premise that there is a greater predilection for women to care for and establish a relationship with others – whether fetuses, infants, or other adults. 'Surrogate Mothering and Women's Freedom: A Critique of Contracts for Human Reproduction,' *Signs* 18 (1993): 618–39.
49 *Proceed with Care*, vol. 1, 52.

50 Ibid., 955–6.
51 Ibid., 958.
52 Ibid., 951.
53 Overall, *Human Reproduction*, 94.
54 This question came up in the Dodd and Daigle cases in Canada, where fathers requested court injunctions to prevent their ex-partners from having abortions. In both cases the injunctions were eventually overturned by the courts. This was deemed to be a victory for the pro-choice lobby, clarifying that women have the right to govern their own bodies and that 'fathers' have no right to encroach on women's security of person. See Brodie, Gavigan and Jenson, *The Politics of Abortion*, 91–6, and Morton, *Morgentaler v. Borowski*, 273–89.
55 Overall, *Human Reproduction*, 41.
56 Ibid., 96–7.
57 Ibid., 86.
58 She writes: 'I remain unconvinced that a man can "forge" a relationship with a foetus, or that he can have his own "experience" of abortion.' Brodie, Gavigan, and Jenson, *The Politics of Abortion*, 140.
59 Overall, *Human Reproduction*, 29.
60 Sylvia Hewlett observes that this assumption is indeed pervasive: 'In America children tend to be defined as a private consumption good. If working women choose to have them it is up to them to cope as best they can, on their own.' Sylvia Ann Hewlett, *A Lesser Life* (New York: William Morrow, 1986), 28.
61 Mary Anne Warren, 'Abortion: New Complexities,' in *Issues in Reproductive Technology I*, ed. Holmes, 120.
62 Spallone, *Beyond Conception*, 35.
63 Ibid., 35.
64 A similar issue arises over the selective termination of fetuses, a practice that is often engendered by the use of fertility drugs. As Overall puts it, 'if abortion is legally permitted in cases where the fetus is seriously handicapped, it is inconsistent to refuse to permit the termination of one handicapped fetus in a multiple pregnancy.' Christine Overall, 'Selective Termination in Pregnancy and Women's Reproductive Autonomy,' in *Issues in Reproductive Technology*, ed. Holmes, 155.
65 This is the line of argument Carole Pateman takes; for example, *The Sexual Contract* (Stanford: Stanford University Press, 1988), 209–18.
66 Laurie Shrage suggests that what is often obscured is that the abortion debate 'is primarily a debate between women.' 'Fetal Ideologies and Maternal Desires,' 59.

67 For example, see Susan Sherwin, 'Feminist Ethics and In Vitro Fertilization,' in *Science, Morality and Feminist Theory*, ed. Hanen and Nielson.
68 I return to this issue in chapter 5.
69 Janine Brodie, *Women and Politics in Canada* (Toronto: McGraw-Hill Ryerson, 1985); Sylvia B. Bashevkin, *Toeing the Lines: Women and Party Politics in English Canada* (Toronto: University of Toronto Press, 1985); Barry J. Kay, Ronald D. Lambert, Steven D. Brown, and James E. Curtis, 'Gender and Political Activity in Canada, 1965–1984,' *Canadian Journal of Political Science* 20 (December 1987):851–63; Kathy Megyery, ed., *Women in Canadian Politics: Towards Equity in Representation* (Toronto: Dundurn Press, 1991); Janine Brodie and Lise Gotell, 'Women and Parties: More than an Issue of Numbers,' in *Party Politics in Canada*, 6th edition, ed. Hugh G. Thorburn (Scarborough: Prentice-Hall, 1991); Sylvia B. Bashevkin, *Toeing the Lines: Women and Party Politics in English Canada*, 2nd edition (Toronto: Oxford University Press, 1993); and Chantal Maillé, 'Women and Political Representation,' in *Canadian Politics*, 2nd edition, ed. James P. Bickerton and Alain G. Gagnon (Peterborough: Broadview Press, 1994).
70 For example, see Lynda Erickson, 'Women and Candidacies for the House of Commons,' in *Women in Canadian Politics*, ed. Megyery.
71 For example, see Yolande Cohen and Michela De Giorgio, Introduction, *Women and Counter Power*, ed. Yolande Cohen (Montreal: Black Rose Books, 1989) and Yolande Cohen, 'Thoughts on Women and Power,' in *Feminism in Canada*, ed. Geraldine Finn and Angela Miles (Montreal: Black Rose Books, 1982). The 'masculinist explanation' tends to emerge in discussions of women politicians and the media. For example, see Gertrude J. Robinson, Armande Saint-Jean, with the assistance of Christine Rioux, 'Women Politicians and Their Media Coverage: A Generational Analysis,' in *Women in Canadian Politics*, ed. Megyery. It also came to the (popular) forefront in the aftermath of Kim Campbell's overwhelming defeat in the last federal election. For example, see 'Woman of the Year: Kim Campbell,' *Chatelaine* 67 (January 1994).
72 For a discussion of how feminist groups in particular have challenged the possibility of integrating women's differences into political life, see Jill McCalla Vickers, 'Feminist Approaches to Women in Politics,' in *Beyond the Vote: Canadian Women and Politics*, ed. Linda Kealey and Joan Sangster (Toronto: University of Toronto Press, 1989).
73 Robert Matas and Miro Cernetig, 'Pro-Choice Doctor Shot at Home,' *Globe and Mail*, 9 November 1994; Joan Breckenridge, 'Abortion Clinics Fear Harassment Will Escalate,' *Globe and Mail*, 14 January 1995.
74 Jane S. Jaquette, 'Power as Theology: A Feminist Analysis,' in *Women's*

Views of the Political World, ed. Judith H. Stiehm (New York: Transnational, 1982).
75 Ibid., 23.
76 A. Paul Pross, *Group Politics and Public Policy*, 2nd edition (Toronto: Oxford University Press, 1992), chapter 6.
77 A. Paul Pross, 'The Pressure Group Conundrum,' in *Canadian Politics*, ed. Bickerton and Gagnon, 177.
78 According to Cott, 'Women's organizations pioneered in, accepted, and published modern methods of pressure-group politics.' Nancy F. Cott, *The Grounding of Modern Feminism* (New Haven: Yale University Press, 1987).
79 Jennifer Nedelsky has pointed out to me that the image that male politicians are dressing up as may nevertheless be a 'male' one.
80 Bashevkin, *Toeing the Lines*, 2nd edition, 86.
81 Janine Brodie with the assistance of Celia Chandler, 'Women and the Electoral Process,' in *Women in Canadian Politics*, ed. Megyery, 34.
82 Brodie notes: 'Three-quarters of the women candidates indicated that women have special financial burdens when seeking election ... First, many identified the costs of child care, the carrying costs of homemaking, and the expense of buying clothes for the campaign.' Ibid., 46.
83 For example, see William Mishler and Harold D. Clarke, 'Political Participation in Canada,' in *Canadian Politics in the 1990s*, 3rd edition, ed. Michael S. Whittington and Glen Williams (Scarborough: Nelson, 1990).
84 Jill Vickers makes the point that women's so-called absence from politics may rest on a methodological problem. Women may become more 'present' when we assume a broader definition of what is 'political.' 'Feminist Approaches to Women in Politics,' in *Beyond the Vote*, ed. Kealey and Sangster, 28–9.
85 Moreover, the solutions offered to the obstacles posed by women's responsibility for the domestic realm often reaffirm that responsibility or suggest structural changes (such as limiting the amount of time members of Parliament need to spend in Ottawa) which are aimed at making it easier to juggle both family life and political office. For example, see Lynda Erickson, 'Women and Candidacies for the House of Commons,' in *Women in Canadian Politics*, ed. Megyery, 120–1.
86 For example, according to Jill Vickers, 'Theories of citizenship and of public service were advanced by suffragists primarily in terms of duties, not of rights.' 'Feminist Approaches to Women in Politics,' in *Beyond the Vote*, ed. Kealey and Sangster, 22.
87 For example, a pilot study on women's attitudes to political involvement found that 'Few of our respondents expressed careerist or "getting ahead"

ambitions in politics. Those who had run for election or were hoping to, tended to express a desire to serve, rather than a desire to "get ahead."' Canadian Research Institute for the Advancement of Women, *Women's Involvement in Political Life: A Pilot Study* (Ottawa: CRIAW/ICREF, 1987), 57.

88 For a discussion of the declining influence of political parties, see John Meisel, 'The Decline of Party in Canada' and 'The Dysfunctions of Canadian Parties: An Exploratory Mapping,' in *Party Politics in Canada*, 6th edition, ed. Hugh G. Thorburn (Scarborough: Prentice-Hall, 1991).

89 Brodie and Gotell suggest that the gains made by the women's movement have even been reduced at the same time as the proportion of women in the House of Commons (approximately 18 per cent after the 1993 election) has risen. 'Women and Parties: More than an Issue of Numbers,' *Party Politics in Canada*, ed. Thorburn, 53–4.

90 'Electing more women to the pinnacle of legislative office, the House of Commons, may thus prove futile in policy terms unless attention is given at the same time to recruitment to senior-level bureaucratic positions, particularly in central agencies of the federal government.' Bashevkin, *Toeing the Lines*, 2nd edition, 172.

91 Ibid., 67–8.

92 *Proceed with Care*, vol. 2, 962–3.

93 Ibid., 56.

CHAPTER 5 Feminist Alternatives

1 For example, Rosalind Delmar, 'What Is Feminism?,' defines feminism simply as 'a desire to change women's position in society,' in *What Is Feminism?*, ed. Juliet Mitchell and Ann Oakley (New York: Pantheon Books, 1986), 13. This definition does not seem to be exclusive enough to disqualify an outlook which, for instance, proposes changing women's position to take away rights they might presently enjoy.

2 bell hooks, 'Feminism: A Movement to End Sexist Oppression,' in *Feminism and Equality*, ed. Anne Phillips (New York: New York University Press, 1987), 68.

3 Alison M. Jaggar, *Feminist Politics and Human Nature* (Totowa: Rowman and Allanheld, 1983).

4 Jaggar briefly mentions Simone de Beauvoir, labelling her as an 'existentialist feminist,' but dismisses her thought as 'implausible.' Ibid., 10.

5 Rosemarie Tong, *Feminist Thought* (Boulder: Westview Press, 1989).

6 Hester Eisenstein, *Contemporary Feminist Thought* (Boston: G.K. Hall, 1983).

7 Josephine Donovan, *Feminist Theory: The Intellectual Traditions of American Feminism* (New York: Frederick Ungar, 1985).
8 According to Nancy F. Cott, *The Grounding of Modern Feminism* (New Haven: Yale University Press, 1987), feminism and the women's movement in the United States have always vacillated between two poles – the desire to eliminate sex-specific limitations and the desire to recognize the unique qualities of women. A similar theme emerges in the Canadian context, according to Nancy Adamson, Linda Briskin, and Margaret McPhail, *Feminist Organizing for Change* (Toronto: Oxford University Press, 1988).
9 Lynne Segal, *Is the Future Female?* (New York: Peter Bedrick, 1987).
10 Karen Offen, 'Defining Feminism: A Comparative Historical Approach,' *Signs* 14 (1988): 119–57.
11 Olive Banks, *Faces of Feminism* (Oxford: Martin Robertson, 1981).
12 Naomi Black, *Social Feminism* (Ithaca: Cornell University Press, 1989).
13 Ibid., 1.
14 By placing Marxist with liberal feminists, Black is perhaps referring to those rare Marxist feminists who simply accept Marx's and Engels' analysis of the 'woman question.' For a discussion of the relationship between Marxism and feminism, see Evelyn Reed, *Problems of Women's Liberation* (New York: Pathfinder Press, 1969); Juliet Mitchell, *Woman's Estate* (New York: Vintage Books, 1973); and Michelle Barrett, *Women's Oppression Today* (London: Verso, 1980). But most feminists who make use of a Marxian framework can more appropriately be labelled as 'feminists of difference' because they base their analysis of women's social and political position on their difference from men, usually on their role in reproduction. They also tend to argue that women's difference from men is their greatest asset and that Marxian principles cannot capture women's unique relations to reproduction. For an example, see Mary O'Brien, *The Politics of Reproduction* (London: Routledge and Kegan Paul, 1981).
15 Judith Grant, *Fundamental Feminism: Contesting the Core Concepts of Feminist Theory* (New York: Routledge, 1993).
16 Ibid., 183.
17 She objects to defining 'post-modernism' or 'post-structuralism' for similar reasons. Judith Butler, 'Contingent Foundations: Feminism and the Question of "Postmodernism,"' in *Feminists Theorize the Political*, ed. Judith Butler and Joan W. Scott (New York: Routledge, 1992), 5.
18 For example, see Nancy Hartsock, *Money, Sex and Power* (Boston: Northeastern University Press, 1985).
19 Examples are Carole Pateman, *The Sexual Contract* (Stanford: Stanford University Press, 1991), and Christine Di Stefano, *Configurations of Masculinity*

(Ithaca: Cornell University Press, 1991), whom I have discussed in the chapters on Locke and Hobbes. See also Genevieve Lloyd, *The Man of Reason: 'Male' and 'Female' in Western Philosophy* (Minneapolis: University of Minnesota Press, 1984), who examines thinkers such as Plato, Descartes, and Rousseau and finds that Western conceptions of Reason are associated with 'maleness' and rest on the exclusion of the 'feminine.' In a similar fashion Wendy Brown, *Manhood and Politics: A Feminist Reading in Political Theory* (Totowa, New Jersey: Rowman and Littlefield, 1988) examines Hannah Arendt, Aristotle, Machiavelli, and Max Weber and finds that their constructions assume a relationship between politics and manhood. Both Lloyd and Brown are leery about offering a 'female reason' or a 'feminine' model of politics as alternatives; nevertheless, their analysis, I suggest, is imbued with assumptions about what 'non-masculine' conceptions would look like.

20 Simone de Beauvoir, *The Second Sex*, ed. and trans. H.M. Parshley (New York: Vintage Books, 1952); also see Margaret Simons, 'The Silencing of Simone de Beauvoir: Guess What's Missing from *The Second Sex*?,' *Women's Studies International Forum* 6 (1983): 559–64.
21 de Beauvoir, *The Second Sex*, 301.
22 Ibid., 694.
23 An interview with Alice Schwartzer, *Simone de Beauvoir Today*, trans. Marianne Howarth (London: Hogarth Press, 1984), 79.
24 Alice Jardine, 'Interview with Simone de Beauvoir,' *Signs* 5 (Winter 1979): 230.
25 de Beauvoir, *The Second Sex*, 73.
26 Schwartzer, *Simone de Beauvoir Today*, 46.
27 de Beauvoir, *The Second Sex*, 798.
28 Ibid., 23.
29 Ibid., 423, 431, 437, 442.
30 Schwartzer, *Simone de Beauvoir Today*, 116. See also Margaret Simons and Jessica Benjamin, 'Simone de Beauvoir: An Interview,' *Feminist Studies* 5 (Summer 1979): 330–45.
31 For example, in her autobiography she writes, 'In the wealth that we [women] take over from them [men] we must very carefully distinguish between those things which are marked by their masculinity.' Simone de Beauvoir, *All Said and Done*, trans. Patrick O'Brien (Middlesex: Penguin Books, 1977), 495.
32 Virginia Held, 'Birth and Death,' in *Feminism and Political Theory*, ed. Cass R. Sunstein (Chicago: University of Chicago Press, 1990), 110.
33 Beauvoir, *The Second Sex*, 774.
34 Simons and Benjamin, 'Simone de Beauvoir: An Interview,' 341. In another

context, she states: 'I think there are some women who really don't stand much of a chance – if they are thirty-five, with four children to cope with, married and lacking any professional qualification – then I don't know what they can do to liberate themselves.' Schwartzer, *Simone de Beauvoir Today*, 43.
35 de Beauvoir, *The Second Sex*, 71.
36 Ibid., 72.
37 Lynda Lange has pointed out to me that mothering might rather be viewed as an engagement in 'transcendence' in the sense that a woman risks her own life in childbirth.
38 According to de Beauvoir, their list of reasons included the following: they had no particular interest in small children; children would not strengthen the bonds between the two of them; they had no need to rediscover themselves in their offspring; they felt indifference and hostility towards their own parents and had little need to experience parenting; they had an aversion to family life; children were incompatible with the freedom and time needed for writing; they would seek 'eternity' through writing rather than through children; they could see no benefits in increasing the world's population; and childbearing seemed a purposeless activity. Simone de Beauvoir, *The Prime of Life*, trans. Peter Green (Middlesex: Penguin Books, 1962), 78.
39 de Beauvoir, *The Second Sex*, 136, 550.
40 Observing a trend that popular guidebooks on pregnancy and early childcare certainly attest to, Olive Banks suggests that greater access to contraception in the twentieth century made it possible for women to have fewer children, but it was coupled with increased social pressure to invest more time and resources in each child. Olive Banks, *Faces of Feminism* (Oxford: Martin Robertson, 1981), 190. In a similar vein, Nancy F. Cott indicates that as the idea that mothering is women's natural destiny diminished in strength in the twentieth century, women felt obliged to engage more time and effort in learning how to mother. Nancy F. Cott, *The Grounding of Modern Feminism*, 168. In my discussion of the new reproductive technologies, a similar theme surfaced – the more rational, the more open to choices mothering becomes, the more it subjects women to social and political pressures.
41 See Susan Moller Okin, *Justice, Gender, and the Family* (New York: Basic Books, 1989), where she examines such modern liberal thinkers as John Rawls, Michael Sandel, and Robert Nozick. In *Women in Western Political Thought* (Princeton: Princeton University Press, 1979) she focuses on traditional thinkers such as Plato, Aristotle, Rousseau, and Mill.
42 Okin, *Justice, Gender, and the Family*, 171.
43 Ibid., 178.
44 Ibid., 175.

45 Ibid., 176.
46 Ibid., 85–6.
47 Ibid., 75.
48 Dorothy Dinnerstein, *The Mermaid and the Minotaur* (New York: Harper and Row, 1976).
49 Ibid., 155.
50 Ibid., 150.
51 Ibid., 78–9.
52 Nancy Chodorow, *The Reproduction of Mothering: Psychoanalysis and the Sociology of Gender* (Berkeley: University of California Press, 1978).
53 Ibid., 19, 218–19.
54 Ibid., 110.
55 Ibid., 176.
56 Ibid., 65.
57 Ibid., 85.
58 Chodorow writes: 'Women come to want and need primary relationships to children. These wants and needs result from wanting intense primary relationships, which men tend not to provide both because of their place in women's oedipal constellations and because of their difficulties with intimacy. Women's desires for intense primary relationship tend not to be with other women, both because of internal and external taboos on homosexuality and because of women's isolation from their primary female kin (especially mothers) and other women.' Ibid., 203–4.
59 Mary O'Brien, *The Politics of Reproduction*, 50.
60 Mary O'Brien, *Reproducing the World: Essays in Feminist Theory* (Boulder: Westview Press, 1989), 22.
61 O'Brien, *The Politics of Reproduction*, 50.
62 'The first priority of feminist politics must be to wrest control of reproductive technology from men, just as, long ago, men partially but effectively wrested the control of sexuality, children, and the social construction of gender from women.' *Reproducing the World*, 16.
63 Ibid., 18–20; a female perspective might offer a 'caring and shared notion of parenthood,' 68.
64 Ibid., 161.
65 Ibid., 73.
66 Ibid., 65.
67 Nancy Hartsock, *Money, Sex, and Power*.
68 Ibid., 241.
69 Ibid., 252.
70 According to Hartsock, 'Women's experience in reproduction represents a

unity with nature that goes beyond the proletarian experience of interchange with nature,' and 'The unity grows from the fact that women's bodies, unlike men's, can be themselves instruments of production: In pregnancy, giving birth, or lactation, arguments about a division of mental from manual labour are fundamentally foreign.' Ibid., 237, 243.
71 Ibid., 257.
72 Ibid., 187, 189, 192.
73 Hartsock finds traces of this way of seeing power in female theorists such as Hannah Arendt, Dorothy Emmett, and Hannah Pitkin. Ibid., 219–23.
74 Heather Jon Maroney, 'Embracing Motherhood: New Feminist Theory,' in *Feminism Now: Theory and Practice*, ed. Marilouise and Arthur Kroker, Pamela McCallum, Mair Verthuy (Montreal: New World Perspectives, 1985), 48. See also Elizabeth Gould Davis, *The First Sex* (Middlesex: Penguin Books, 1971); Joan Bamberger, 'The Myth of Matriarchy: Why Men Rule in Primitive Society,' in *Women, Culture and Society*, ed. Michelle Rosaldo and Louise Lamphere (Stanford: Stanford University Press, 1974).
75 Maroney, 'Embracing Motherhood,' 44.
76 Carol Gilligan, *In a Different Voice: Psychological Theory and Women's Development* (Cambridge: Harvard University Press, 1982).
77 Ibid., 19.
78 Gilligan writes: 'The different voice I describe is characterized not by gender but theme. Its association with women is an empirical observation, and it is primarily through women's voices that I trace its development. But this association is not absolute, and the contrasts between male and female voices are presented here to highlight a distinction between two modes of thought and to focus a problem of interpretation rather than to represent a generalization about either sex.' Ibid., 2.
79 Carol Gilligan, in Linda K. Kerber, Catherine G. Greeno, and Eleanor E. Maccoby, Zella Luria, Carol B. Stack, and Carol Gilligan, 'On *In a Different Voice*: An Interdisciplinary Forum,' *Signs* 11 (Winter 1986): 330.
80 Gilligan describes the confrontation between two characters in a novel as revealing 'two modes of judging, two different constructions of the moral domain – one traditionally associated with masculinity and the public world of social power, the other with femininity and the privacy of domestic interchange. The developmental ordering of these two points of view has been to consider the masculine as more adequate than the feminine and thus as replacing the feminine when the individual moves to maturity. The reconciliation of these two modes, however, is not clear.' *In a Different Voice*, 69.
81 Ibid., 42.
82 Ibid., 67, 70.

83 Ibid., 70.
84 Gilligan, 'On *In a Different Voice*: An Interdisciplinary Forum,' 327.
85 Ibid., 332.
86 Gilligan, *In a Different Voice*, 74.
87 Ibid., 90.
88 Ibid., 94.
89 Ibid., 94.
90 Dorothy Wertz, 'How Parents of Affected Children View Selective Abortion,' in *Issues in Reproductive Technology: An Anthology: I*, ed. Helen Bequaert Holmes (New York: Garland, 1992), 176.
91 Christine Overall, *Human Reproduction: Principles, Practices and Politics* (Toronto: Oxford University Press, 1993), 50.
92 Ibid., 50.
93 Virginia Held, 'Birth and Death,' 89.
94 Virginia Held, 'Non-Contractual Society: A Feminist View,' in *Science, Morality and Feminist Theory*, Supplement to *Canadian Journal of Philosophy* 13, ed. Marsha Hanen and Kai Nielson (Calgary: University of Calgary Press, 1987): 118.
95 Virginia Held, 'Feminism and Moral Theory,' in *Women and Moral Theory*, ed. Eva Feder Kittay and Diana T. Meyers (Totowa: Rowman and Littlefield, 1987), 114.
96 Held, 'Non-Contractual Society,' 115.
97 Ibid., 127.
98 Held, 'Birth and Death,' 107.
99 Ibid., 108.
100 Held, 'Feminism and Moral Theory,' 115.
101 Ibid., 130.
102 Ibid., 123.
103 Virginia Held, 'The Obligations of Mothers and Fathers,' in *Mothering: Essays in Feminist Theory*, ed. Joyce Trebilcot (Totowa: Rowman and Allanheld, 1984), 16.
104 Held, 'Non-Contractual Society,' 131.
105 Ibid., 116.
106 Held, 'Birth and Death,' 113.
107 Ibid., 125.
108 Held, 'Feminism and Moral Theory,' 124.
109 She writes: 'Men (and women) can die out of loyalty, out of duty, out of commitment, and they can die for a better future. Women can give birth, or refuse to give birth from all these motives and others. They can give birth so that a new human being can experience joy, so that humankind can con-

tinue to exist, so that the family of which they are a member can maintain itself, so that the social movement which gives them hope may have another potential adherent, so that the love they share with another may be shared with yet another. They can give birth to express their conceptions for themselves, of humanity, and of life.' Ibid., 91.

110 Ibid., 119.
111 Ibid., 121.
112 Held, 'Birth and Death,' 104.
113 Ibid., 109.
114 Catharine A. MacKinnon, *Towards a Feminist Theory of the State* (Cambridge: Harvard University Press, 1989), 128.
115 Ibid., 170.
116 Ibid., 245–6.
117 Catharine A. MacKinnon, 'Feminism, Marxism, Method, and the State: Toward Feminist Jurisprudence,' *Signs* 8 (Summer 1983): 636.
118 Luce Irigaray, 'When Our Lips Speak Together,' trans. and intro. Carolyn Burke, *Signs* 6 (1980): 66–79; and 'And the One Doesn't Stir without the Other,' trans. and intro. Hélène Vivienne Wenzel, *Signs* 7 (1981): 56–67.
119 Hélène Cixous, 'The Laugh of the Medusa,' trans. Keith and Paula Cohen, in *New French Feminisms*, ed. Elaine Marks and Isabelle de Courtivron (New York: Schocken Books, 1981), 250.
120 Julia Kristeva, 'Woman Can Never Be Defined,' trans. Marilyn A. August, in ibid., 137.
121 Julia Kristeva, 'Oscillation between Power and Desire,' trans. Marilyn A. August, in ibid., 166.
122 Julia Kristeva, ' Women's Time,' trans. Alice Jardine and Harry Blake, *Signs* 7 (1981): 27.
123 Claire Duchen notes that 'the birth metaphor is frequently used to describe intellectual production.' *Feminism in France* (London: Routledge and Kegan Paul, 1986), 63.
124 Julia Kristeva, 'Stabat Mater,' trans. Arthur Goldhammer, in *Contemporary Critical Theory*, ed. Dan Latimer (San Diego: Harcourt, Brace Jovanovich, 1989), 581.
125 Kristeva, 'Women's Time,' 31.
126 Ibid., 33.
127 Luce Irigaray, *This Sex Which Is Not One*, trans. Catherine Porter with Carolyn Burke (Ithaca: Cornell University Press, 1985), 122–3.
128 Kristeva, 'Stabat Mater,' 580.
129 Hélène Cixous refers to the image of the 'hysteric' as the form that resis-

tance to the masculine order might take. 'Castration or Decapitation?' *Signs* 7 (1981): 47–50.

130 For example, see Regenia Gagnier, 'Feminist Postmodernism: The End of Feminism or the Ends of Theory?' and Karen Offen, 'Feminism and Sexual Difference in Historical Perspective,' in *Theoretical Perspectives on Sexual Difference*, ed. Deborah L. Rhode (New Haven: Yale University Press, 1990); Nancy Fraser and Linda J. Nicholson, 'Social Criticism without Philosophy: An Encounter between Feminism and Postmodernism' and Jane Flax, 'Postmodernism and Gender Relations in Feminist Theory,' in *Feminism/Postmodernism*, ed. Linda J. Nicholson (New York: Routledge, 1990); Diana Coole, 'Contemporary Feminism: Towards Postmodernism?,' in *Women in Political Theory: From Ancient Misogyny to Contemporary Feminism*, 2nd edition(Boulder: Lynne Rienner, 1993); Kathleen B. Jones, Introduction to *Compassionate Authority: Democracy and the Representation of Women* (New York: Routledge, 1993); and Judith Butler, 'Contingent Foundations.'
131 Judith Butler, 'Contingent Foundations, 6–7.
132 Judith Butler, *Gender Trouble: Feminism and the Subversion of Identity* (New York: Routledge, 1990).
133 Introduction, *Feminists Theorize the Political*, ed. Butler and Scott, xiv.
134 Ibid., 6.
135 Feminists are working on trying to take important concepts such as autonomy out of their problematic liberal context and to reclaim and redefine them for women. For example, see Jennifer Nedelsky, 'Reconceiving Autonomy: Sources, Thoughts and Possibilities,' *Yale Journal of Law and Feminism* 1 (Spring 1989): 7–36.
136 For example, see Nancy Hartsock, *Money, Sex, and Power*. Christine Di Stefano, *Configurations of Masculinity*, chapter 2, also criticizes Hobbes as being 'masculinist.' The underlying tone of her analysis is similar, although she does not want to assume a 'female' nature.
137 The latter theme is expressed in Dinnerstein, *The Mermaid and the Minotaur*, 112 and in Di Stefano, *Configurations of Masculinity*, chapter 2.

Bibliography

Achilles, Rona. 'Artificial Reproduction: Hope Chest or Pandora's Box?' *Changing Patterns: Women in Canada*. Ed. Sandra Burt, Lorraine Code, and Lindsay Dorney. Toronto: McClelland and Stewart, 1988.
– 'Desperately Seeking Babies: New Technologies of Hope and Despair.' *Delivering Motherhood: Maternal Ideologies and Practices in the Nineteenth and Twentieth Centuries*. Ed. Katherine Arnup, Andrée Lévesque, and Ruth Roach Pierson, with the assistance of Margaret Brennan. New York: Routledge, 1990.
– 'Assisted Reproduction: The Social Issues.' *Changing Patterns: Women in Canada*. 2nd edition. Ed. Sandra Burt, Lorraine Code, and Lindsay Dorney. Toronto: McClelland and Stewart, 1993.
Adamson, Nancy, Linda Briskin, and Margaret McPhail. *Feminist Organizing for Change*. Toronto: Oxford University Press, 1988.
Algren, Nelson. 'The Question of Simone de Beauvoir.' *Harper's Magazine* 230 (May 1965): 134, 136.
Alpern, Kenneth D. 'Genetic Puzzles and Stork Stories: On the Meaning and Significance of Having Children.' *The Ethics of Reproductive Technology*. Ed. Kenneth D. Alpern. New York: Oxford University Press, 1992.
Anderson, Bonnie, and Judith P. Zinsser. *A History of Their Own*. Vol 2. New York: Harper and Row, 1988.
Andrew, Edward. *Shylock's Rights: A Grammar of Lockian Claims*. Toronto: University of Toronto Press, 1988.
Annas, Julia. 'Mill and the Subjection of Women.' *Philosophy* 52 (April 1977): 179–94.
Aries, Phillipe. *Centuries of Childhood*. Trans. Robert Baldick. New York: Random House, 1962.
Ascher, Carol. *Simone de Beauvoir: A Life of Freedom*. Boston: Beacon Press, 1981.

Ashcraft, Richard. *Revolutionary Politics and Locke's Two Treatises of Government.* Princeton: Princeton University Press, 1986.
Atwood, Margaret. *The Handmaid's Tale.* Toronto: McClelland and Stewart, 1985.
Bair, Deidre. *Simone de Beauvoir: A Biography.* New York: Summit Books, 1990.
Bamberger, Joan. 'The Myth of Matriarchy: Why Men Rule in Primitive Society.' *Women, Culture and Society.* Ed. Michelle Rosaldo and Louise Lamphere. Stanford: Stanford University Press, 1974.
Banks, Olive. *Faces of Feminism.* Oxford: Martin Robertson, 1981.
Barrett, Michelle. *Women's Oppression Today.* London: Verso, 1980.
Bashevkin, Sylvia B. *Toeing the Lines: Women and Party Politics in English Canada.* Toronto: University of Toronto Press, 1985.
– *Toeing the Lines: Women and Party Politics in English Canada.* 2nd edition. Toronto: Oxford University Press, 1993.
– 'Women's Participation in Political Parties.' *Women in Canadian Politics: Towards Equity in Representation.* Ed. Kathy Megyery. Toronto: Dundurn Press, 1991.
Bayles, Michael D. 'Limits to a Right to Procreate.' *Having Children.* Ed. Onora O'Neill and William Ruddick. New York: Oxford University Press, 1979.
Bell, Susan Groag, ed., *Women: From the Greeks to the French Revolution.* Belmont: Wadsworth, 1973.
Benhabib, Seyla. 'The Generalized and the Concrete Other: The Kohlberg-Gilligan Controversy and Moral Theory.' *Women and Moral Theory.* Ed. Eva Feder Kittay and Diana T. Meyers. Totowa: Rowman and Littlefield, 1987.
Berns, Laurence. 'Thomas Hobbes.' *History of Political Philosophy.* Ed. Leo Strauss and Joseph Cropsey. Chicago: Rand McNally, 1963, 354–78.
Black, Jerome H., and Nancy E. McGlen. 'Male-Female Political Involvement Differentials in Canada, 1965–1974.' *Canadian Journal of Political Science* 12 (September 1979): 471–97.
Black, Naomi. *Social Feminism.* Ithaca: Cornell University Press, 1989.
Blustein, Jeffrey. *Parents and Children.* New York: Oxford University Press, 1982.
Bolton, Martha Brandt. 'Responsible Women and Abortion Decisions.' *Having Children.* Ed. Onora O'Neill and William Ruddick. New York: Oxford University Press, 1979.
Boraleui, Lea Campos. 'Utilitarianism and Feminism.' *Women in Western Philosophy.* Ed. Ellen Kennedy and Susan Mendus. London: Wheatsheaf Books, 1987.
Braidotti, Rosi. 'Ethics Revisited: Women and/in Philosophy.' *Feminist Challenges.* Ed. Carole Pateman and Elizabeth Gross. Boston: Northeastern University Press, 1986.
Breckenridge, Joan. 'Abortion Clinics Fear Harassment Will Escalate.' Toronto *Globe and Mail.* 14 January 1995.

Brennan, Teresa, and Carole Pateman. ' "Mere Auxiliaries to the Commonwealth": Women and the Origin of Liberalism.' *Political Studies* 22 (June 1979): 183–200.

Brent, Rosalind. '"An Immense Verbosity": Permissive Sexual Advice in the 1970's.' *Feminism, Culture and Politics*. Ed. Rosalind Brent and Caroline Rowan. London: Lawrence and Wishart, 1982.

Brodie, Janine. *Women and Politics in Canada*. Toronto: McGraw-Hill Ryerson, 1985.

Brodie, Janine, and Lise Gotell. 'Women and Parties: More than an Issue of Numbers.' *Party Politics in Canada*. 6th edition Ed. Hugh G. Thorburn. Scarborough: Prentice-Hall, 1991.

Brodie, Janine, with the assistance of Celia Chandler. 'Women and the Electoral Process in Canada.' *Women in Canadian Politics: Towards Equity in Representation*. Ed. Kathy Megyery. Toronto: Dundurn Press, 1991.

Brodie, Janine, Shelley A.M. Gavigan, and Jane Jenson. *The Politics of Abortion*. Toronto: Oxford University Press, 1992.

Brown, Wendy. *Manhood and Politics: A Feminist Reading in Political Theory*. Totowa: Rowman and Littlefield, 1988.

Burt, Sandra. 'Women's Issues and the Women's Movement in Canada since 1970.' *The Politics of Gender, Ethnicity and Language in Canada*. Research Coordinators Alan Cairns and Cynthia Williams. Toronto: University of Toronto Press, 1986.

– 'Legislators, Women, and Public Policy.' *Changing Patterns: Women in Canada*. Ed. Sandra Burt, Lorraine Code, and Lindsay Dorney. Toronto: McClelland and Stewart, 1988.

Butler, Judith. *Gender Trouble: Feminism and the Subversion of Identity*. New York: Routledge, 1990.

– 'Contingent Foundations: Feminism and the Question of "Postmodernism."' *Feminists Theorize the Political*. Ed. Judith Butler and Joan W. Scott. New York: Routledge, 1992.

Butler, Melissa A. 'Early Liberal Roots of Feminism: John Locke and the Attack on Patriarchy.' *American Political Science Review* 72 (March 1978): 135–50.

Campbell, Robert M., and Leslie A. Pal. *The Real Worlds of Canadian Politics*. 2nd edition. Peterborough: Broadview Press, 1991.

Cameron, Barbara. 'Mill's Treatment of Women Workers and Private Property.' *Canadian Journal of Political Science* 13 (December 1980): 775–83.

Canadian Research Institute for the Advancement of Women. *Women's Involvement in Political Life: A Pilot Study*. Ottawa: CRIAF/ICREF, 1987.

Canadian Research Institute for the Advancement of Women. *Submission to the Canadian Royal Commission on New Reproductive Technologies*. Prepared by Jacqueline Best. 1990.

Charvet, John. *Feminism*. London: J.M. Dent and Sons, 1982.
Chodorow, Nancy. *The Reproduction of Mothering: Psychoanalysis and the Sociology of Gender*. Berkeley: University of California Press, 1978.
- 'What Is the Relation between Psychoanalytic Feminism and the Psychoanalytic Psychology of Women?' *Theoretical Perspectives on Sexual Difference*. Ed. Deborah L. Rhode. New Haven: Yale University Press, 1990.
Cixous, Hélène. 'Sorties' (trans. Ann Liddle) and 'The Laugh of the Medusa' (trans. Keith and Paula Cohen). *New French Feminisms*. Ed. Elaine Marks and Isabelle de Courtivron. New York: Schocken Books, 1981.
- 'Castration or Decapitation?' Trans. and intro. Annette Kuhn. *Signs* 7 (1981): 36–55.
- 'Sorties: Out and Out: Attacks/Ways Out/Forays.' Trans. Betsy Wing. *Contemporary Critical Theory*. Ed. Dan Latimer. San Diego: Harcourt, Brace Jovanovich, 1989.
Clark, Lorenne M.G., and Lynda Lange, eds. *The Sexism of Social and Political Theory*. Toronto: University of Toronto Press, 1979.
Clayton, Ellen Wright. 'Women and Advances in Medical Technologies: The Legal Issues.' *Women and New Reproductive Technologies: Medical, Psychosocial, Legal, and Ethical Dilemmas*. Ed. Judith Rodin and Aila Collins. Hillsdale: Lawrence Erlbaum, 1991.
Code, Lorraine, Sheila Mullett, and Christine Overall, eds. *Feminist Perspectives*. Toronto: University of Toronto Press, 1988.
Cohen, Marjorie. 'The Problem of Studying Economic Man.' *Feminism in Canada*. Ed. Geraldine Finn and Angela Miles. Montreal: Black Rose Books, 1982.
Cohen, Yolande. 'Thoughts on Women and Power.' *Feminism in Canada*. Ed. Geraldine Finn and Angela Miles. Montreal: Black Rose Books, 1982.
Cohen, Yolande, and Michela De Giorgio. 'Introduction.' *Women and Counter Power*. Ed. Yolande Cohen. Montreal: Black Rose Books, 1989.
Coltheart, Lenore. 'Desire, Consent and Liberal Theory.' *Feminist Challenges*. Ed. Carole Pateman and Elizabeth Gross. Boston: Northeastern University Press, 1986.
Connolly, William E. *Political Theory and Modernity*. New York: Basil Blackwell, 1988.
Conway, Jill. 'Stereotypes of Femininity in a Theory of Sexual Evolution.' *Suffer and Be Still: Women in the Victorian Age*. Ed. Martha Vicinus. Bloomington: Indiana University Press, 1972.
Coole, Diana. *Women in Political Theory: From Ancient Misogyny to Contemporary Feminism*. 2nd edition. Boulder: Lynne Rienner, 1993.
Copps, Sheila. *Nobody's Baby*. Toronto: Deneau, 1986.
Corea, Gena. *The Mother Machine*. New York: Harper and Row, 1985.
Cott, Nancy F. 'Feminist Theory and Feminist Movements: The Past before Us.'

What Is Feminism? Ed. Juliet Mitchell and Ann Oakley. New York: Pantheon Books, 1986.
- *The Grounding of Modern Feminism*. New Haven: Yale University Press, 1987.
Cox, Kevin. 'Parents Guilty in Starvation Death.' *Toronto Globe and Mail*. 15 June 1995.
Daly, Mary. *Beyond God the Father*. Boston: Beacon Press, 1973.
Davis, Elizabeth Gould. *The First Sex*. Middlesex: Penguin Books, 1971.
de Beauvoir, Simone. *The Second Sex*. Ed. and trans. H.M. Parshley. New York: Vintage Books, 1952.
- *The Prime of Life*. Trans. Peter Green. Middlesex: Penguin Books, 1962.
- *Memoirs of a Dutiful Daughter*. Trans. James Kirkup. Middlesex: Penguin Books, 1963.
- *Force of Circumstance*. Trans. Richard Howard. Middlesex: Penguin Books, 1968.
- *A Very Easy Death*. Trans. Patrick O'Brien. Middlesex: Penguin Books, 1969.
- *All Said and Done*. Trans. Patrick O'Brien. Middlesex: Penguin Books, 1977.
- *Adieux: A Farewell to Sartre*. Trans. Patrick O'Brien. London: Deutsch, Weidenfeld and Nicolson, 1984.
Decter, Midge. *The New Chastity and Other Arguments against Women's Liberation*. New York: Capricorn Books, 1974.
Degler, Carl N. 'Darwinians Confront Gender; or, There Is More to It than History.' *Theoretical Perspectives on Sexual Difference*. Ed. Deborah L. Rhode. New Haven: Yale University Press, 1990.
Delmar, Rosalind. 'What Is Feminism?' *What Is Feminism?* Ed. Juliet Mitchell and Ann Oakley. New York: Pantheon Books, 1986.
Diamond, Irene, ed. *Families, Politics, and Public Policy*. New York: Longman, 1983.
Dijkstra, Sandra. 'Simone de Beauvoir and Betty Friedan: The Politics of Omission.' *Feminist Studies* 6 (Summer 1980): 290–303.
Dinnerstein, Dorothy. *The Mermaid and the Minotaur*. New York: Harper and Row, 1976.
Di Stefano, Christine. 'Masculinity as Ideology in Political Theory: Hobbesian Man Considered.' *Women's Studies International Forum* 6 (1983): 633–44.
- *Configurations of Masculinity*. Ithaca: Cornell University Press, 1991.
Doeuff, Michele. 'Simone de Beauvoir and Existentialism.' *Feminist Studies* 6 (Summer 1980): 278–89.
Donchin, Anne. 'The Future of Mothering: Reproductive Technology and Feminist Theory.' *Hypatia* 1 (Fall 1986): 121–37.
Donovan, Josephine. *Feminist Theory: The Intellectual Traditions of American Feminism*. New York: Frederick Ungar, 1985.

Dubois, Ellen. 'The Radicalism of the Woman Suffrage Movement: Notes toward the Reconstruction of Nineteenth-Century Feminism.' *Feminism and Equality.* Ed. Anne Phillips. New York: New York University Press, 1987.
Duchen, Claire. *Feminism in France.* London: Routledge and Kegan Paul, 1986.
Eichler, Margrit. 'Sexism in Research and Its Policy Implications.' *Taking Sex into Account: The Policy Consequences of Sexist Research.* Ed. Jill McCalla Vickers. Ottawa: Carleton University Press, 1984.
Eisenstein, Hester. *Contemporary Feminist Thought.* Boston: G.K. Hall, 1983.
Eisenstein, Zillah R. *The Radical Future of Liberal Feminism.* New York: Longman, 1981.
– *Feminism and Sexual Equality.* New York: Monthly Review Press, 1984.
Elshtain, Jean Bethke. 'Moral Woman and Immoral Man: A Consideration of the Public-Private Split and Its Political Ramifications.' *Politics and Society* 4 (1974): 453–73.
– *Public Man, Private Woman.* Princeton: Princeton University Press, 1981.
– '"Thank Heaven for Little Girls": The Dialectics of Development' and 'Aristotle, the Public-Private Split, and the Case of the Suffragists.' *The Family in Political Thought.* Ed. Jean Bethke Elshtain. Amherst: University of Massachusetts Press, 1982.
– 'Against Androgyny.' *Feminism and Equality.* Ed. Anne Phillips. New York: New York University Press, 1987.
– *Power Trips and Other Journeys.* Madison: University of Wisconsin Press, 1990.
Erickson, Lynda. 'Women and Candidacies for the House of Commons.' *Women in Canadian Politics: Towards Equity in Representation.* Ed. Kathy Megyery. Toronto: Dundurn Press, 1991.
Evans, Judith. 'Feminism and Political Theory' and 'Feminist Theory and Political Analysis.' *Feminism and Political Theory.* London: Sage Publications, 1986.
Evans, Mary. *Simone de Beauvoir: A Feminist Mandarin.* London: Tavistock, 1985.
Faden, Ruth. 'Autonomy, Choice, and the New Reproductive Technologies: The Role of Informed Consent in Prenatal Genetic Diagnosis.' *Women and New Reproductive Technologies: Medical, Psychosocial, Legal, and Ethical Dilemmas.* Ed. Judith Rodin and Aila Collins. Hillsdale, New Jersey: Lawrence Erlbaum, 1991.
Felstiner, Mary Lowenthal. 'Seeing the Second Sex through the Second Wave.' *Feminist Studies* 6 (Summer 1980): 247–75.
Figes, Eva. *Patriarchal Attitudes.* London: Virago, 1978.
Firestone, Shulamith. *The Dialectic of Sex.* London: Jonathan Cape, 1971.
Flax, Jane. 'Mother-Daughter Relationships: Psychodynamics, Politics and Philosophy.' *The Future of Difference.* Ed. Hester Eisenstein and Alice Jardine. Boston: G.K. Hall, 1980.

- 'The Family in Contemporary Feminist Thought: A Critical Review.' *The Family in Political Thought*. Ed. Jean Bethke Elshtain. Amherst: University of Massachusetts Press, 1982.
- 'Postmodernism and Gender Relations in Feminist Theory.' *Feminism/Postmodernism*. Ed. Linda J. Nicholson. New York: Routledge, 1990.
Fraser, Antonia. *The Weaker Vessel: Woman's Lot in Seventeenth-Century England*. London: Methuen, 1985.
Fraser, Nancy, and Linda J. Nicholson. 'Social Criticism without Philosophy: An Encounter between Feminism and Postmodernism.' *Feminism/Postmodernism*. Ed. Linda J. Nicholson, New York: Routledge, 1990.
Freeman, Jo. 'The Woman's Liberation Movement: Its Origin, Structures, Impact and Ideas.' *Women: A Feminist Perspective*. Ed. Jo Freeman. Palo Alto: Mayfield, 1975.
Friedan, Betty. *The Feminine Mystique*. New York: Dell Publishing, 1963.
- *The Second Stage*. New York: Summit Books, 1981.
Friedman, Marilyn. 'Beyond Caring: The De-Moralization of Gender.' *Science, Morality and Feminist Theory*. Ed. Marsha Hanen and Kai Nielson. Calgary: University of Calgary Press, 1987. Supplement to *Canadian Journal of Philosophy* 13.
Fuchs, Jo-Ann P. 'Female Eroticism in the Second Sex.' *Feminist Studies* 6 (Summer 1980): 304–13.
Funderburk, Charles, and Robert G. Thobaber. *Political Ideologies: Left, Center, Right*. New York: Harper and Row, 1989.
Gagnier, Regenia. 'Feminist Postmodernism: The End of Feminism or the Ends of Theory?' *Theoretical Perspectives on Sexual Difference*. Ed. Deborah L. Rhode. New Haven: Yale University Press, 1990.
Gatens, Moira. 'Feminism, Philosophy and Riddles without Answers.' *Feminist Challenges*. Ed. Carole Pateman and Elizabeth Gross. Boston: Northeastern University Press, 1986.
- *Feminism and Philosophy*. Bloomington: Indiana University Press, 1991.
Gelb, Joyce. *Feminism and Politics: A Comparative Perspective*. Berkeley: University of California Press, 1989.
Gerassi, John. 'Simone de Beauvoir: The Second Sex Twenty-five Years Later.' *Society* 13 (January/February 1976): 79–85.
Gettell, Raymond G., and Lawrence C. Wanlass, eds. *History of Political Thought*. 2nd edition. New York: Appleton-Century-Crofts, 1953.
Gillespie, Michael, and Michael Lienesch. 'Religion and the Resurgence of Conservatism.' *The Resurgence of Conservatism in Anglo-American Democracies*. Ed. Barry Cooper, Allan Kornberg, and William Mishler. Durham: Duke University Press, 1988.

Gilligan, Carol. *In a Different Voice: Psychological Theory and Women's Development.* Cambridge, Massachusetts: Harvard University Press, 1982.
- 'Moral Orientation and Moral Development.' *Women and Moral Theory.* Ed. Eva Feder Kittay and Diana T. Meyers. Totowa: Rowman and Littlefield, 1987.

Goldwin, Robert A. 'John Locke.' *History of Political Philosophy.* Ed. Leo Strauss and Joseph Cropsey. Chicago: Rand McNally, 1963.

Gordon, Linda. 'Feminism and Social Control: The Case of Child Abuse and Neglect.' *What Is Feminism?* Ed. Juliet Mitchell and Ann Oakley. New York: Pantheon Books, 1986.

Gough, Kathleen. 'The Origin of the Family.' *Women: A Feminist Perspective.* Ed. Jo Freeman. Palo Alto: Mayfield, 1975.

Grant, Judith. *Fundamental Feminism: Contesting the Core Concepts of Feminist Theory.* New York: Routledge, 1993.

Greer, Germaine. *The Female Eunuch.* London: Paladin, 1971.
- *Sex and Destiny.* Toronto: Stoddart, 1984.

Grimshaw, Jean. *Philosophy and Feminist Thinking.* Minneapolis: University of Minnesota Press, 1986.

Gross, Elizabeth. 'Philosophy, Subjectivity and the Body: Kristeva and Irigaray.' *Feminist Challenges.* Ed. Carole Pateman and Elizabeth Gross. Boston: Northeastern University Press, 1986.

Hagopian, Mark N. *The Phenomenon of Revolution.* New York: Harper and Row, 1974.

Hartsock, Nancy C.M. *Money, Sex, and Power.* Boston: Northeastern University Press, 1985.

Hekman, Susan J. 'John Stuart Mill's *The Subjection of Women*: The Foundations of Liberal Feminism,' *History of European Ideas* 15 (1992): 681–6.

Held, Virginia. 'The Obligations of Mothers and Fathers.' *Mothering: Essays in Feminist Theory.* Ed. Joyce Trebilcot. Totowa: Rowman and Allenheld, 1984.
- 'Feminism and Moral Theory.' *Women and Moral Theory.* Ed. Eva Feder Kittay and Diana T. Meyers. Totowa: Rowman and Littlefield, 1987.
- 'Non-Contractual Society: A Feminist View.' *Science, Morality and Feminist Theory.* Ed. Marsha Hanen and Kai Nielson. Calgary: University of Calgary Press, 1987. Supplement to *Canadian Journal of Philosophy* 13.
- 'Birth and Death.' *Feminism and Political Theory.* Ed. Cass R. Sunstein. Chicago: University of Chicago Press, 1990.

Hewlett, Sylvia Ann. *A Lesser Life.* New York: William Morrow, 1986.

Himmelfarb, Gertrude. *On Liberty and Liberalism.* New York: Alfred A. Knopf, 1974.

Hill, Thomas E., Jr. 'Autonomy: Self and Other.' *Women and Moral Theory.* Ed.

Eva Fedor Kittay and Diana T. Meyers. Totowa: Rowman and Littlefield, 1987.
Hobbes, Thomas. *De Cive or The Citizen*. Ed. and intro. Sterling P. Lamprecht. New York: Appleton-Century-Crofts, 1949.
– 'De Corpore Politico, or the Elements of Law.' *The English Works of Thomas Hobbes*. vol. 4. Ed. Sir William Molesworth. London: Scientia Aalen, 1962.
– *Leviathan*. Ed. and intro. C.B. Macpherson. Middlesex: Penguin Books, 1968.
Hole, Judith, and Ellen Levine. 'The First Feminists.' *Women: A Feminist Perspective*. Ed. Jo Freeman. Palo Alto: Mayfield, 1975.
hooks, bell. 'Feminism: A Movement to End Sexist Oppression.' *Feminism and Equality*. Ed. Anne Phillips. New York: New York University Press, 1987.
– 'Feminism: A Transformational Politics.' *Theoretical Perspectives on Sexual Difference*. Ed. Deborah L.Rhode. New Haven: Yale University Press, 1990.
Houston, Barbara. 'Gilligan and the Politics of a Distinctive Women's Morality.' *Feminist Perspectives*. Ed. Lorraine Code, Sheila Mullet, and Christine Overall. Toronto: University of Toronto Press, 1988.
– 'Rescuing Womanly Virtues: Some Dangers of Moral Reclamation.' *Science, Morality and Feminist Theory*. Ed. Marsha Hanen and Kai Nielson. Calgary: University of Calgary Press, 1987. Supplement to *Canadian Journal of Philosophy* 13.
Hughes, Patricia. 'Fighting the Good Fight: Separation or Integration?.' *Feminism in Canada*. Ed. Geraldine Finn and Angela Miles. Montreal: Black Rose Books, 1982.
Hunt, Karen. 'Crossing the River of Fire: The Socialist Construction of Women's Politicization.' *Feminism and Political Theory*. London: Sage Publications, 1986.
Irigaray, Luce. 'When Our Lips Speak Together.' Trans. and intro. Carolyn Burke. *Signs* 6 (1980): 66–79.
– 'And the One Doesn't Stir without the Other.' Trans. and intro. Hélène Vivienne Wenzel. *Signs* 7 (1981): 56–67.
– 'This Sex Which Is Not One' and 'When the Goods Get Together.' Trans. Claudia Reeder. *New French Feminisms*. Ed. Elaine Marks and Isabelle de Courtivron. New York: Schocken Books, 1981.
– *This Sex Which Is Not One*. Trans. Catherine Porter with Carolyn Burke. Ithaca: Cornell University Press, 1985.
Jaggar, Alison M. *Feminist Politics and Human Nature*. Totowa: Rowman and Allanheld, 1983.
Jaquette, Jane S. 'Power as Theology: A Feminist Analysis.' *Women's Views of the Political World*. Ed. Judith H. Stiehm. New York: Transnational, 1982.
Jardine, Alice. 'Interview with Simone de Beauvoir.' *Signs* 5 (Winter 1979): 224–36.

Jenson, Jane. 'Struggling for Identity: The Women's Movement and the State in Western Europe.' *West European Politics* 8 (October 1985): 5–18.

Johnson, Miriam M. *Strong Mothers, Weak Wives*. Berkeley: University of California Press, 1988.

Jones, Kathleen B. *Compassionate Authority: Democracy and the Representation of Women*. New York: Routledge, 1993.

Katzenstein, Mary Fainsod, and David D. Laitin. 'Politics, Feminism, and the Ethics of Caring.' *Women and Moral Theory*. Ed. Eva Feder Kittay and Diana T. Meyers. Totowa: Rowman and Littlefield, 1987.

Kay, Herma Hill. 'Perspectives on Sociobiology, Feminism, and the Law.' *Theoretical Perspectives on Sexual Difference*. Ed. Deborah L. Rhode. New Haven: Yale University Press, 1990.

Kay, Barry J., Ronald D. Lambert, Steven D. Brown, and James E. Curtis. 'Gender and Political Activity in Canada, 1965–1984.' *Canadian Journal of Political Science* 20 (December 1987): 851–63.

Kennedy, Ellen, and Susan Mendus, eds. *Women in Western Political Philosophy*. London: Wheatsheaf Books, 1987.

Kerber, Linda K., Catherine G. Greeno and Eleanor E. Maccoby, Zella Luria, Carol B. Stack, and Carol Gilligan. 'On *In a Different Voice*: An Interdisciplinary Forum.' *Signs* 11 (1986): 304–33.

Kome, Penny. *The Taking of Twenty-Eight: Women Challenge the Constitution*. Toronto: Women's Press, 1983.

Kristeva, Julia. *Desire in Language*. Ed. Leon Roudiez. New York: Columbia University Press, 1980.

– 'Woman Can Never Be Defined' and 'Oscillation between Power and Desire.' Trans. Marilyn A. August. *New French Feminisms*. Ed. Elaine Marks and Isabelle de Courtivron. New York: Schocken Books, 1981.

– 'Women's Time.' Trans. Alice Jardine and Harry Blake, intro. Alice Jardine. *Signs* 7 (1981): 5–35.

– 'Stabat Mater.' Trans. Arthur Goldhammer. *Contemporary Critical Theory*. Ed. Dan Latimer. San Diego: Harcourt, Brace Jovanovich, 1989.

Krouse, Richard W. 'Patriarchal Liberalism and Beyond: From John Stuart Mill and Harriet Taylor.' *The Family in Political Thought*. Ed. Jean Bethke Elshtain. Amherst: University of Massachussetts Press, 1982.

Kuykendall, Eleanor H. 'Toward an Ethic of Nurturance: Luce Irigaray on Mothering and Power.' *Mothering: Essays in Feminist Theory*. Ed. Joyce Trebilcot. Totowa: Rowman and Allanheld, 1984.

Lasch, Christopher. *Haven in a Heartless World*. New York: Basic Books, 1977.

Levin, David S. 'Thomson and the Current State of the Abortion Controversy.' *Journal of Applied Ethics* 2, 1(1985):125.

Levin, Michael. *Feminism and Freedom*. New Jersey: Transaction Books, 1987.

Lewis, Jane. 'Feminism and Welfare.' *What Is Feminism?* Ed. Juliet Mitchell and Ann Oakley. New York: Pantheon Books, 1986.

Lloyd, Genevieve. *The Man of Reason: 'Male' and 'Female' in Western Philosophy.* Minneapolis: University of Minnesota Press, 1984.

– 'Selfhood, War and Masculinity.' *Feminist Challenges.* Ed. Carole Pateman and Elizabeth Gross. Boston: Northeastern University Press, 1986.

Locke, John. *An Essay Concerning Human Understanding.* vol. 1 and 2. Ed. John W. Yolton. London: J.M. Dent and Sons, 1961.

– *A Letter on Toleration.* Ed. Raymond Klibansky and J.W. Gough. Oxford: Clarendon Press, 1968.

– 'Locke's Letter to Edward Clarke on Education, 1684–91' and 'Some Thoughts Concerning Education.' *The Educational Writings of John Locke.* Ed. James L. Axtell. New York: Cambridge University Press, 1968.

– *The Reasonableness of Christianity.* Ed. I.T. Ramsey. Stanford: Stanford University Press, 1958.

– *Two Treatises of Government.* Rev. edition. Ed. Peter Laslett. New York: Cambridge University Press, 1963.

Mackenzie, Catriona. 'Simone de Beauvoir: Philosophy and/or the Female Body.' *Feminist Challenges.* Ed. Carole Pateman and Elizabeth Gross. Boston: Northeastern University Press, 1986.

MacKinnon, Catharine A. 'Feminism, Marxism, Method, and the State: An Agenda for Theory.' *Signs* l7 (1982): 515–44.

– 'Feminism, Marxism, Method, and the State: Toward Feminist Jurisprudence.' *Signs* 8 (1983): 635–57.

– *Towards a Feminist Theory of the State.* Cambridge: Harvard University Press, 1989.

– 'Legal Perspectives on Sexual Difference.' *Theoretical Perspectives on Sexual Difference.* Ed. Deborah L. Rhode. New Haven: Yale University Press, 1990.

Macpherson, C.B. *The Political Theory of Possessive Individualism.* London: Oxford University Press, 1962.

Maillé, Chantal. 'Women and Political Representation.' *Canadian Politics.* 2nd edition. Ed. James P. Bickerton and Alain G. Gagnon. Peterborough: Broadview Press, 1994.

Manzer, Ronald. *Public Policies and Political Development in Canada.* Toronto: University of Toronto Press, 1985.

Marchak, Patricia. 'Rational Capitalism and Women as Labour.' *Feminism and Political Economy.* Ed. Heather Jon Maroney and Meg Luxton. Toronto: Methuen, 1987.

Marks, Elaine, and Isabelle de Courtivron, eds. *New French Feminisms.* New York: Schocken Books, 1981.

Maroney, Heather Jon. 'Embracing Motherhood: New Feminist Theory.' *Feminism Now: Theory and Practice*. Ed. Marilouise and Arthur Kroker, Pamela McCallum, Mair Verthuy. Montreal: New World Perspectives, 1985.

Matas, Robert, and Miro Cernetig. 'Pro-Choice Doctor Shot at Home.' *Toronto Globe and Mail*. 9 November 1994.

McCormack, Thelma. *Politics and the Hidden Injuries of Gender*. Ottawa: CRIAW/ICREF, 1991.

– 'Reproductive Technologies: Rights, Choice, and Coercion.' *Women and Canadian Public Policy*. Ed. Janine Brodie. Toronto: Harcourt Brace, 1996.

McDaniel, Susan A. 'The Changing Canadian Family: Women's Roles and the Impact of Feminism.' *Changing Patterns: Women in Canada*. Ed. Sandra Burt, Lorraine Code, and Lindsay Dorney. Toronto: McClelland and Stewart, 1988.

McLaren, Angus, and Arlene Tigar McLaren. *The Bedroom and the State: The Changing Practices and Politics of Contraception and Abortion in Canada 1880–1980*. Toronto: McClelland and Stewart, 1986.

McMillan, Carol. *Women, Reason, and Nature*. Princeton: Princeton University Press, 1982.

Megyery, Kathy, ed. *Women in Canadian Politics: Towards Equity in Representation*. Toronto: Dundurn Press, 1991.

Meisel, John. 'The Decline of Party in Canada' and 'The Dysfunctions of Canadian Parties: An Exploratory Mapping.' *Party Politics in Canada*. 6th edition Ed. Hugh G. Thorburn. Scarborough: Prentice-Hall, 1991.

Meyers, Diana T. 'The Socialized Individual and Individual Autonomy: An Intersection between Philosophy and Psychology.' *Women and Moral Theory*. Ed. Eva Feder Kittay and Diana T. Meyers. Totowa: Rowman and Littlefield, 1987.

Miles, Angela. 'Ideological Hegemony in Political Discourse: Women's Specificity and Equality.' *Feminism in Canada*. Ed. Geraldine Finn and Angela Miles. Montreal: Black Rose Books, 1982.

– *Culture Texts: Feminist Radicalism in the 1980's*. Montreal: New World Perspectives, 1985.

Mill, Harriet Taylor, and John Stuart. 'Early Essays on Marriage and Divorce (1832).' *Essays on Sex Equality*. Ed. Alice S. Rossi. Chicago: University of Chicago Press, 1970.

Mill, John Stuart. *The Collected Works of John Stuart Mill*. Ed. John M. Robson. Toronto: University of Toronto Press, 1963–84.

Mishler, William, and Harold D. Clarke. 'Political Participation in Canada.' *Canadian Politics in the 1990s*. 3rd edition. Ed. Michael S. Whittington and Glen Williams. Scarborough: Nelson, 1990.

Mitchell, Alanna. 'Abortion Numbers Continue to Climb.' Toronto *Globe and Mail*. 13 July 1995.
- 'Abortion Rate Increase Linked to Recession.' Toronto *Globe and Mail*. 4 October 1994.

Mitchell, Juliet. *Woman's Estate*. New York: Vintage Books, 1973.
- 'Reflections on Twenty Years of Feminism.' *What Is Feminism?* Ed. Juliet Mitchell and Ann Oakley. New York: Pantheon Books, 1986.
- 'Women and Equality.' *Feminism and Equality*. Ed. Anne Phillips. New York: New York University Press, 1987.

Morgan, Kathryn Pauly. 'Women and Moral Madness.' *Feminist Perspectives*. Ed. Lorraine Code, Sheila Mullett, and Christine Overall. Toronto: University of Toronto Press, 1988.

Morton, F.L. *Morgentaler v. Borowski: Abortion, the Charter, and the Courts*. Toronto: McClelland and Stewart, 1992.

Mullett, Sheila. 'Shifting Perspectives: A New Approach to Ethics.' *Feminist Perspectives*. Ed. Lorraine Code, Sheila Mullett, and Christine Overall. Toronto: University of Toronto Press, 1988.

Nedelsky, Jennifer. 'Reconceiving Autonomy: Sources, Thoughts and Possibilities.' *Yale Journal of Law and Feminism* 1 (Spring 1989): 7–36.
- 'Choosing a Legal Framework for Potential Life.' Unpublished paper.
- 'Reconceiving Rights as Relationship.' Unpublished paper.

Nicholson, Linda J., ed. *Feminism/Postmodernism*. New York: Routledge, 1990.

Noddings, Nel. 'Ethics from the Standpoint of Women.' *Theoretical Perspectives on Sexual Difference*. Ed. Deborah L. Rhode. New Haven: Yale University Press, 1990.

Oakley, Ann. *Taking It Like a Woman*. London: Jonathan Cape, 1984.
- 'Feminism, Motherhood and Medicine – Who Cares?' *What Is Feminism?* Ed. Juliet Mitchell and Ann Oakley. New York: Pantheon Books, 1986.

O'Brien, Mary. 'Reproducing Marxist Man.' *The Sexism of Social and Political Theory*. Ed. Lorenne M.G. Clark and Lynda Lange. Toronto: University of Toronto Press, 1979.
- *The Politics of Reproduction*. London: Routledge and Kegan Paul, 1981.
- *Reproducing the World: Essays in Feminist Theory*. Boulder: Westview Press, 1989.
- 'Feminism and Sexual Difference in Historical Perspective.' *Theoretical Perspectives on Sexual Difference*. Ed. Deborah L. Rhode. New Haven: Yale University Press, 1990.

Offen, Karen. 'Defining Feminism: A Comparative Historical Approach.' *Signs* 14 (1988): 119–57.
- 'Feminism and Sexual Difference in Historical Perspective.' *Theoretical Per-

spectives on Sexual Difference. Ed. Deborah L. Rhode. New Haven: Yale University Press, 1990.

Okely, Judith. *Simone de Beauvoir: A Re-Reading.* London: Virago Press, 1986.

Okin, Susan Moller. *Women in Western Political Thought.* Princeton: Princeton University Press, 1979.

– *Justice, Gender, and the Family.* New York: Basic Books, 1989.

– 'Afterward to the 1992 Edition.' *Women in Western Political Thought.* Princeton: Princeton University Press, 1992.

O'Neill, Onora. 'Begetting, Bearing, and Rearing.' *Having Children.* Ed. Onora O'Neill and William Ruddick. New York: Oxford University Press, 1979.

Ortner, Sherry B. 'Is Female to Male as Nature is to Culture?' *Woman, Culture and Society.* Ed. Michelle Rosaldo and Louise Lamphere. Stanford: Stanford University Press, 1974.

Overall, Christine. 'Surrogate Motherhood.' *Science, Morality and Feminist Theory.* Ed. Marsha Hanen and Kai Nielson. Calgary: University of Calgary Press, 1987. Supplement to *Canadian Journal of Philosophy* 13.

– 'Selective Termination in Pregnancy and Women's Reproductive Autonomy.' *Issues in Reproductive Technology I: An Anthology.* Ed. Helen Bequaert Holmes. New York: Garland, 1992.

– *Human Reproduction: Principles, Practices and Policies.* Toronto: Oxford University Press, 1993.

Packe, Michael St. John. *The Life of John Stuart Mill.* New York: Macmillan, 1954.

Parry, Geraint. 'The Idea of Political Participation.' *Participation in Politics.* Ed. Geraint Parry. Manchester: Manchester University Press, 1972.

Pateman, Carole. *Participation and Democratic Theory.* New York: Cambridge University Press, 1970.

– 'The Shame of the Marriage Contract.' *Women's Views of the Political World of Men.* Ed. Judith H. Stiehm. New York: Transnational, 1982.

– 'Feminist Critique of the Public/Private Dichotomy.' *Public and Private in Social Life.* Ed. S.I. Benn and G.F. Gaus. Canberra: Croom Helm, 1983.

– *The Problem of Political Obligation.* Berkeley: University of California Press, 1985.

– *The Sexual Contract.* Stanford: Stanford University Press, 1988.

– *The Disorder of Women.* Cambridge: Polity Press, 1989.

– '"God Hath Ordained to Man a Helper": Hobbes, Patriarchy and Conjugal Right.' *Feminist Interpretations and Political Theory.* Ed. Mary Lyndon Shanley and Carole Pateman. Pennsylvania: Pennsylvania State University Press, 1991.

Pitkin, Hanna. *Fortune Is a Woman.* Berkeley: University of California Press, 1984.

Plamenatz, John. *Man and Society.* Vol 1. New York: McGraw-Hill, 1963.

Polatnick, M. Riva. 'Why Men Don't Rear Children: A Power Analysis.' *Mothering: Essays in Feminist Theory.* Ed. Joyce Trebilcot. Totowa: Rowman and Allanheld, 1984.

Proceed with Care: Final Report of the Royal Commission on New Reproductive Technologies. Vols. 1 and 2. Ottawa: Minister of Supply and Services Canada, 1993.

Pross, A. Paul. *Group Politics and Public Policy.* 2nd edition. Toronto: Oxford University Press, 1992.

– 'The Pressure Group Conundrum.' *Canadian Politics.* 2nd edition. Ed. James P. Bickerton and Alain G. Gagnon. Peterborough: Broadview Press, 1994.

Rebick, Judy. 'Is the Issue Choice?' *Misconceptions: The Social Construction of Choice and the new Reproductive and Genetic Technologies.* Vol. 1. Ed. Gwynne Basen, Margrit Eichler, and Abby Lippman. Hull: Voyageur, 1993.

Reed, Evelyn. *Problems of Women's Liberation.* New York: Pathfinder Press, 1969.

The Research Studies of the Royal Commission on Reproductive Technologies. Ottawa: Minister of Supply and Services, 1993.

Rich, Adrienne. *Of Woman Born.* New York: W.W. Norton, 1986.

Richards, Janet Radcliffe. *The Sceptical Feminist.* Middlesex: Penguin Books, 1980.

Ring, Jennifer. *Modern Political Theory and Contemporary Feminism.* Albany: State University of New York Press, 1991.

Robinson, Gertrude J., and Armande Saint-Jean, with the assistance of Christine Rioux. 'Women Politicians and Their Media Coverage: A Generational Analysis.' *Women in Canadian Politics: Towards Equity in Representation.* Ed. Kathy Megyery. Toronto: Dundurn Press, 1991.

Robson, Ann P. and John M. *Sexual Equality: Writings by John Stuart Mill, Harriet Taylor Mill, and Helen Taylor.* Toronto: University of Toronto Press, 1994.

Rosenberg, Harriet. 'Motherwork, Stress and Depression: The Costs of Privatized Social Reproduction.' *Feminism and Political Economy.* Ed. Heather Jon Maroney and Meg Luxton. Toronto: Methuen, 1987.

Rosenblum, Nancy L. *Another Liberalism: Romanticism and the Reconstruction of Liberal Thought.* Cambridge: Harvard University Press, 1987.

Rossi, Alice S. 'Sentiment and Intellect: The Story of John Stuart Mill and Harriet Taylor Mill.' *Essays on Sex Equality.* Ed. Alice S. Rossi. Chicago: University of Chicago Press, 1970.

Rowbotham, Sheila. *Women, Resistance and Revolution.* Middlesex: Penguin Books, 1972.

Ruddick, Sara. 'Maternal Thinking.' *Mothering: Essays in Feminist Theory.* Ed. Joyce Trebilcot. Totowa: Rowman and Allanheld, 1984.

– 'Remarks on the Sexual Politics of Reason.' *Women and Moral Theory.* Ed. Eva Feder Kittay and Diana T. Meyers. Totowa: Rowman and Littlefield, 1987.

Sabine, George H. *A History of Political Theory.* 3rd edition. New York: Holt, Rinehart and Winston, 1961.

Sabrosky, Judith A. *From Rationality to Liberation: The Evolution of Feminist Ideology.* Westport: Greenwood Press, 1979.

Sargent, Lyman Tower. *Contemporary Political Ideologies.* 7th edition. Chicago: Dorsey Press, 1987.

Saxonhouse, Arlene W. 'Classical Greek Conceptions of Public and Private.' *Public and Private in Social Life.* Ed. S.I. Benn and G.F. Gaus. Canberra: Croom Helm, 1983.

– *Women in the History of Political Thought.* New York: Praeger, 1985.

Schlafly, Phyllis. *The Power of the Positive Woman.* New York: Arlington House, 1977.

Schochet, Gordon J. *Patriarchalism in Political Thought.* Oxford: Basil Blackwell, 1975.

Schwarzer, Alice. *Simone de Beauvoir Today.* Trans. Marianne Howarth. London: Hogarth Press, 1984.

Scruton, Roger. *A Dictionary of Political Thought.* London: Pan Books, 1983.

Segal, Lynne. *Is the Future Female?* New York: Peter Bedrick, 1987.

Shanley, Mary Lyndon. 'Marital Slavery and Friendship: John Stuart Mill's "The Subjection of Women."' *Political Theory* 9 (May 1981): 229–47.

– 'Marriage Contract and Social Contract in Seventeenth Century English Political Thought.' *The Family and Political Thought.* Ed. Jean Bethke Elshtain. Amherst: University of Massachussetts Press, 1982.

– 'Afterward: Feminism and Families in a Liberal Polity.' *Families, Politics and Public Policy.* Ed. Irene Diamond. New York: Longman, 1983.

– 'Surrogate Mothering and Women's Freedom: A Critique of Contracts for Human Reproduction.' *Signs* 18 (1993): 618–39.

Sherwin, Susan. 'Feminist Ethics and In Vitro Fertilization.' *Science, Morality and Feminist Theory.* Ed. Marsha Hanen and Kai Nielson. Calgary: University of Calgary Press, 1987. Supplement to *Canadian Journal of Philosophy* 13.

Shevory, Thomas C. 'Through a Glass Darkly: Law, Politics, and Frozen Human Embryos.' *Issues in Reproductive Technology I: An Anthology.* Ed. Helen Bequaert Holmes. New York: Garland, 1992.

Shrage, Laurie. 'Fetal Ideologies and Maternal Desires: A Post-Enlightenment Account of Abortion.' *Moral Dilemmas of Feminism.* New York: Routledge, 1994.

Siltaness, Janet, and Michelle Stanworth. 'The Problem of Private Woman and Public Man.' *Women and the Public Sphere.* Ed. Janet Siltaness and Michelle Stanworth. London: Hutchinson, 1984.

Simons, Margaret. 'The Silencing of Simone de Beauvoir: Guess What's Missing from *The Second Sex?*' *Women's Studies International Forum* 6 (1983): 559–64.

Simons, Margaret, and Jessica Benjamin. 'Simone de Beauvoir: An Interview.' *Feminist Studies* 5 (Summer 1979): 330–45.
Smith, Janet Farrell. 'Parenting and Property.' *Mothering: Essays in Feminist Theory.* Ed. Joyce Trebilcot. Totowa: Rowman and Allanheld, 1984.
Spallone, Patricia. *Beyond Conception: The New Politics of Reproduction.* Massachusetts: Bergin and Garvey, 1989.
Stacey, Judith. 'Are Feminists Afraid to Leave Home? The Challenge of Conservative Pro-Family Feminism.' *What Is Feminism?* Ed. Juliet Mitchell and Ann Oakley. New York: Pantheon Books, 1986.
Stearns, Peter N. 'Working-Class Women in Britain, 1890–1914.' *Suffer and Be Still.* Ed. Martha Vicinus. Bloomington: Indiana University Press, 1972.
Taylor, Fabrice. 'More Choosing to Be Childless.' Toronto *Globe and Mail.* 8 July 1995.
Teichrob, Ruth. 'Spanking Statute Flayed.' *Winnipeg Free Press.* 7 November 1993.
Thiele, Beverly. 'Vanishing Acts in Social and Political Thought: Tricks of the Trade.' *Feminist Challenges.* Ed. Carole Pateman and Elizabeth Gross. Boston: Northeastern University Press, 1986.
Thompson, Janna. 'Women and Political Rationality.' *Feminist Challenges.* Ed. Carole Pateman and Elizabeth Gross. Boston: Northeastern University Press, 1986.
Tong, Rosemarie. *Feminist Thought.* Boulder: Westview Press, 1989.
Tronto, Joan C. 'Beyond Gender Difference to a Theory of Care.' *Signs* 12 (1987): 644–63.
Urbinati, Nadia. 'John Stuart Mill on Androgyny and Ideal Marriage.' *Political Theory* 19 (November 1991): 626–48.
Valeska, Lucia. 'If All Else Fails, I'm Still a Mother.' *Mothering: Essays in Feminist Theory.* Ed. Joyce Trebilcot. Totowa: Rowman and Allanheld, 1984.
Vickers, Jill McCalla. 'Memoirs of an Ontological Exile: The Methodological Rebellions of Feminist Research.' *Feminism in Canada.* Ed. Geraldine Finn and Angela Miles. Montreal: Black Rose Books, 1982.
– 'Feminist Approaches to Women in Politics.' *Beyond the Vote: Canadian Women and Politics.* Ed. Linda Kealey and Joan Sangster. Toronto: University of Toronto Press, 1989.
Vogel, Ursula. 'Rationalism and Romanticism: Two Strategies for Women's Liberation.' *Feminism and Political Theory.* London: Sage Publications, 1986.
Walters, Margaret. 'The Rights and Wrongs of Women: Mary Wollstonecraft, Harriet Martineau, Simone de Beauvoir.' *The Rights and Wrongs of Women.* Ed. Juliet Mitchell and Ann Oakley. Middlesex: Penguin Books, 1976.
Warren, Mary Anne. 'Abortion: New Complexities.' *Issues in Reproductive Technology I: An Anthology.* Ed. Helen Bequaert Holmes. New York: Garland, 1992.

Wearing, Joseph. *The Ballot and Its Message.* Toronto: Copp Clark Pitman, 1991.
Wertz, Dorothy. 'How Parents of Affected Children View Selective Abortion.' *Issues in Reproductive Technology I: An Anthology.* Ed. Helen Bequaert Holmes. New York: Garland, 1992.
Whitbeck, Caroline. 'The Maternal Instinct (1972).' *Mothering: Essays in Feminist Theory.* Ed. Joyce Trebilcot. Totowa: Rowman and Allanheld, 1984.
Williams, Linda S. 'Biology or Society? Parenthood Motivation in a Sample of Canadian Women Seeking In Vitro Fertilization.' *Issues in Reproductive Technology I: An Anthology.* Ed. Helen Bequaert Holmes. New York: Garland, 1992.
Wolin, Sheldon. *Politics and Vision.* Boston: Little, Brown and Co., 1960.
Wollstonecraft, Mary. *The Rights of Woman.* New York: J.Dent and Sons, 1955.
Young, Iris Marion. 'The Ideal of Community and the Politics of Difference.' *Feminism/Postmodernism.* Ed. Linda J. Nicholson. New York: Routledge, 1990.
– *Justice and the Politics of Difference.* Princeton: Princeton University Press, 1990.
Young, Lisa. 'Legislative Turnover and the Election of Women to the Canadian House of Commons.' *Women in Canadian Politics: Towards Equity in Representation.* Ed. Kathy Megyery. Toronto: Dundurn Press, 1991.
Zvesper, John. 'Hobbes' Individualistic Analysis of the Family.' *Politics* 5 (October 1985): 28–33.

Index

Abortion, 86, 127, 131, 134–8, 141–5, 147–9, 167–9, 179–81, 196, 231, 235, 244
Achilles, Rona, 138, 232, 233
Adam/Eve, 62–3, 84
Adoption, 130, 138
Adultery, 67, 82
Alpern, Kenneth, 138–9, 232
American women's suffrage movement, 159
Andrew, Edward, 52, 208, 212, 213, 216
Androgyny, 94
Annas, Julia, 93, 222
Arendt, Hannah, 240, 243
Aristotle, 64, 240, 241
Ashcraft, Richard, 221

Baird, Patricia, 233
Bamberger, Joan, 243
Banks, Olive, 159–60, 239, 241
Barrett, Michelle, 239
Bashevkin, Sylvia, 154–5, 236–8
Berns, Laurence, 42, 201, 209, 210
Birth, as 'natural,' 9; philosophy of, 174
Black, Naomi, 160, 239

Blustein, Jeffrey, 205
Bolton, Martha, 135, 231
Borowski, Joe, 234
Breckenridge, Joan, 236
Brennan, Teresa, 201, 206
Brodie, Janine, 134, 136–7, 154, 199, 200, 231, 232, 235, 236, 237, 238
Brown, Stephen, 236, 240
Butler, Judith, 161, 239, 246
Butler, Melissa, 55, 57, 212

Cameron, Barbara, 94, 223
Campbell, Kim, 236
Campbell, Robert, 135, 231
Canada, 6, 154, 199, 231, 235; and abortion, 134, 137, 142; absence of women in elected office, 151; population issues, 129–30
Cernetig, Miro, 236
Chandler, Celia, 200
Charlottetown Accord, 130
Child abuse, 110, 129–30, 226
Childbearing, 93, 138
Child-care, 68–9, 76–7, 120, 128–30, 135, 137, 141, 156, 168–9, 171–2, 181, 196–7
Children, 14; as irrational, 14, 22;

expense of, 140; and 'natural' desires of, 57-8; and political community, 39; and political necessity of, 53, 149; and rights, 29; as weak, 133
Chodorow, Nancy, 158, 159, 169-73, 176, 178, 242
Cixous, Helene, 190-2, 245
Clayton, Ellen Wright, 234
Clark, Lorenne, 57, 82, 199, 212, 219
Clarke, Harold D., 237
Cohen, Yolande, 236
Conjugal relations, 55, 57, 62, 64-7, 70-1, 77, 81-4, 88, 90, 92, 110
Connolly, William, 201, 209
Consent, 72-3, 89-90
Contract theory, 184-6
Coole, Diana, 94, 199, 222, 223, 246
Corporal punishment, 58, 60, 131
Cott, Nancy F., 153, 237, 239, 241
Cowardice, 48
Curtis, James, 236

Daly, Mary, 158
Davis, Elizabeth Gould, 243
de Beauvoir, Simone, 18-19, 158, 162-9, 185, 188, 203, 238, 240, 241
De Giorgio, Michela, 236
Delmar, Rosalind, 238
Descartes, René, 240
Dickson, Brian, 134
Di Stefano, Christine, 4, 11-14, 15, 93-4, 199, 201, 202, 222, 239, 246
Division of labour, 178, 195
Domestic duty, 99-100, 102-3, 114, 116, 118, 120, 123, 151, 189, 237
Donchin, Anne, 233
Donovan, Josephine, 159, 239
Dualism, 12, 174, 176

Duchen, Claire, 245

Economics, 27, 107, 184
Education, 24, 34, 38, 40, 54, 57-61, 73-6, 97, 102, 105-6, 108, 111, 120, 125
Eisenstein, Zillah R., 4, 54-5, 57, 83, 94, 158-9, 199, 212, 220, 222, 223, 238
Elshtain, Jean Bethke, 4, 199, 233
Emmett, Dorothy, 243
Equal Rights Amendment, 159
Equality, 45, 48-9, 87, 229; of opportunity, 6, 95-6, 108, 112-13, 117, 151; of outcome, 95, 117, 122, 151; of reason, 150; of rights, 107, 126
Erickson, Lynda, 236, 237
'Ethic of care,' 131, 143-5, 150, 155-6, 179-83, 187

Faden, Ruth, 232
Fear, 15, 36-7, 43, 44, 47
Female sexuality, 189, 191
Female values, 164
Feminism: and Hobbes, 196; and liberalism, 193-4; and reproductive technology, 142; as adversarial, 7; cultural, 159; defining, 157-62, 200; equity, 160; experiential, 178, 196; Freudian, 159; liberal, 157-60, 162, 239; maternal, 158, 165, 169, 178, 196; Marxist, 159, 160, 239; of difference, 169, 178, 189; of sameness, 163, 167, 169; sexual, 189-90, 192; social, 160; socialist, 157, 160; post-modern, 161, 192, 239, 246; post-structural, 161, 192-3, 197, 239, 246; psychoanalytical, 159, 172; radical, 157-9; reactionary, 158-9; welfare, 159

'Feminization of Politics,' 151–3
Fetus, 136, 142–3, 145–6, 232, 234, 235
Flax, Jane, 11, 14, 201, 202, 246
Fraser, Antonia, 221
Fraser, Nancy, 246
Friedan, Betty, 158

Gagnier, Regenia, 246
Gatens, Moira, 93, 222
Gavigan, Shelley, 146–7, 231, 232, 235
Generation, 15, 20–1, 30, 34–5, 37, 53, 127
Genetic testing, 138, 148–9
Genetics and natality, 232–3
Gillespie, Michael, 231
Gilligan, Carol, 143–4, 179–82, 234, 243, 244
God, 37, 53, 67–9, 74, 78–9, 81, 85–6, 128, 131, 209, 232
Gotell, Lise, 236, 238
Grant, Judith, 160, 239
Greer, Germaine, 137, 232
Griffin, Susan, 158

Hartsock, Nancy, 169, 176–8, 210, 239, 242, 243, 246
Hekman, Susan J., 95, 223
Held, Virginia, 9, 165–6, 183–9, 201, 240, 244, 245
Hewlett, Sylvia, 235
Hobbes, Thomas, 54, 93, 111, 126, 127, 130, 185, 194, 199, 202–7, 240
– abortion, 136; pro-choice, 135, 137
– Amazon women, 29
– biological bonds, 16, 20
– child-care, 26, 128, 135, 141
– children: law, 23; civil society, 23; political necessity of, 53; rights of, 29; state of nature, 23; property, 27, 139; weakness of, 133
– civil law, 31, 34, 49, 51, 206, 208, 211
– civil society, 15, 23–7, 32, 33, 35, 37, 39, 40, 42, 45, 51, 206
– consent, 14, 42, 210
– contracts, 26–7, 33, 44; parent/child, 22, 33
– cowardice, 48
– dominion, 27
– economics, 27
– education 24, 34, 38–40
– equality, 45, 48–9, 50, 210, 211
– family, 34
– fear, 15, 36–7, 43, 44, 47
– generation, 15, 20–1, 30, 34–5, 37, 53
– God, 37, 53
– good and evil, 31, 32
– honour, 25
– infanticide, 17
– law of gratitude, 22, 24–5, 36, 40, 205, 210
– laws of nature, 22, 24, 25, 30, 33, 36, 39, 43, 48, 50, 52, 204, 211
– image of Leviathan, 44, 46, 47, 49
– liberty, 30, 44, 208
– Locke, 10
– love (child for parent), 21
– view of the male, 45; male superiority, 33
– marriage, 24, 26–8, 40, 51, 53
– 'masculine canon,' 12
– masculine concept of self, 12–14
– as 'masculinist,' 246
– maternal dominion, 15–17, 19, 29, 33, 34, 43, 47, 50–3, 128, 141, 177, 186, 203
– maternal instinct, 13–14, 19, 44
– maternal rationality, 184, 195

- maternal rights, 26, 27, 136
- monarchy, 35
- moral theory, 184
- mother/child relations, 18, 40
- parental dominion, 22–3, 28
- parent/child relations, 8, 13, 15, 16–17, 20–5, 31–4, 42, 53, 127, 131, 166
- passions, 43, 45
- paternal dominion, 15, 16, 30–1, 33, 34, 53; artificiality of, 128
- paternal rights, 26, 40
- patricide/matricide, 32
- peace, 30
- physical differences between men and women, 152
- political action, 52
- political citizenship, 47, 52, 200
- political maintenance, 34, 42, 52
- political participation, 6, 42, 44, 200
- political rights, 47, 49
- power, 20–2, 25, 35, 44–7
- private/public duality, 30, 31–2, 131
- punishment, 209
- rationality of children, 22
- rationality/mothering, 9, 18–19, 22, 136, 166, 184
- reasons for having children, 22
- religion, 37
- reproduction, 7, 12, 50, 147, 150, 195
- reproductive labour, 51, 129
- reproductive rights, 53, 132–3, 163, 194–5
- right reason, 36–8
- self-interest, 18, 21, 26, 36, 38–40, 42, 43, 48, 52, 53, 111, 127, 132–3, 137
- self-preservation, 48
- sexual contract, 4, 10
- siblings, 21
- sovereign authority, 15, 27, 30–1, 36, 37, 41, 44, 46, 48, 49, 207, 208, 211
- speech/reason, 22
- state of nature, 10, 12, 15, 16, 18–20, 22, 23–4, 28–35, 37, 39, 44–5, 47–9, 51, 128, 130, 132, 167, 204, 206, 207
- warrior hero, 47–8, 50, 151
- view of women, 6, 10–11, 29, 42, 43, 44, 46, 48, 51
- women and liberal state, 5

hooks, bell, 238
Human nature, 12, 38

Incest, 67
Infanticide, 17, 69
In vitro fertilization, 127, 138, 140, 147, 182, 236
Irigaray, Luce, 190, 192, 245

Jaggar, Alison, 157–8, 238
Jaquette, Jane S., 153, 236
Jardine, Alice, 240
Jensen, Jane, 231, 232, 235
Jones, Kathleen, B., 246

Kay, Barry, 236
Kristeva, Julia, 190–2, 245

Lambert, Ronald, 236
Lange, Lynda, 199, 203, 241
Levin, David S., 231
Liberty, 30, 44, 55, 57, 73, 87, 108
Lienesch, Michael, 231
Literature, 118
Lloyd, Genevieve, 240
Locke, John, 53, 93, 111, 126, 127, 130, 194, 201, 206, 222, 240
- abortion, 86; and pro-life, 135, 137
- Adam/Eve, 62–3, 84, 215
- adultery, 67, 82

- breeding, 214
- child abuse, 216
- child-care, 68, 69, 76–7, 84, 128, 135, 141
- children, 139; benefits of, 219; labour power, 79; natural desires of, 57–8; obligation to parents, 74, 83; property, 79–80, 216–18, 220
- civil laws, 213
- civil rights, 92
- civil society, 72, 76, 87, 89, 221
- conjugal relations, 55, 57, 62, 64–7, 70, 77, 81–4, 88, 90, 92
- consent, 72–3, 89–90, 217, 221
- contracts, 83
- corporal punishment, 58, 60
- divine laws, 213
- domestic duty of women, 137, 188
- education, 54, 57–61, 73, 74, 75, 76, 77, 92, 213, 214, 217
- equality, 87, 221
- federative power, 89, 91
- fetus, 220
- Filmer, 54, 56, 62, 68, 70, 83
- geography, 61
- God, 67–9, 74, 78–9, 80, 81, 85–6, 128, 131, 214, 217, 218, 232
- government, 70
- Hobbes, 10
- humans/animals, 70
- incest, 67
- industry, 218
- infanticide, 69
- inheritance, 78–81
- labour power, 68, 79, 83, 86, 92, 219
- laws of nature, 58, 69, 74, 88–9
- laziness, 58
- liberty, 57, 73, 87, 217, 218
- majoritarianism, 73
- male/female relations, 54

- marriage, 62, 215
- maternal duty, 74
- maternal power, 54, 85
- maternal relationship to reproduction, 147
- maternal rights, 56
- money, 77
- 'natural' freedom, 55
- neo-conservatism, 131
- parental dominion, 75, 76, 79, 82–3, 218
- paternal uncertainty, 82, 133, 219
- patriarchy, 54, 56
- philosophical thinking, 59
- physical differences between male/female, 59–60, 66, 89–92, 152
- political allegiance, 71
- political citizenship, 72, 88, 91, 200
- political importance of family, 76–7, 150
- political participation, 6, 55, 92, 200
- political power, 75
- population issues, 68, 70, 85, 129, 216
- procreation, 67
- property, 54, 55, 57, 64–6, 70, 72, 77–80, 82, 83–4, 86, 90, 92, 128, 215, 216, 221
- private/public duality, 55, 61
- quality of species, 71
- religious tolerance, 230
- reproduction and sexual desire, 133
- reproductive rights, 7, 87–8, 92, 132–3, 163
- reproductive labour, 85–8, 128–9, 132
- right to rebellion, 58, 90–1, 213
- self-interest, 88, 111, 132–3
- self-preservation, 77
- sex, 67, 133

270 Index

- sexual contract, 4, 56
- social contract, 56
- socialization, 59
- sodomy, 67
- spoilage principle, 218
- state of nature, 85, 89
- strictness of parents, 76
- suffrage, 90, 221
- taxation, 221
- view of women, 4, 6, 11, 54, 55; 'common sense' of, 61–2, 64; independence of will, 65; 'natural' inferiority, 57, 63; punishment of, 63; status in political realm, 54; property, 54, 215; rationality of, 54, 55, 57, 82, 86–9, 92, 136, 166, 184; war, 91; wisdom, 214; women and liberal state, 5

Machiavelli, Niccolò, 240
MacKinnon, Catharine, 189–90, 245
Macpherson, C.B., 213, 218, 220
Maille, Chantal, 236
Male language, 191–2
Male sexuality, 189
Market relations, 184
Maroney, Heather, 178, 243
Marriage, 24, 26–8, 40, 51, 53, 62, 94–5, 97, 107, 109, 111–12, 118, 206, 215
Masculinity, as rejection of feminine, 176
Matas, Robert, 236
Maternal instinct, 19, 140, 170, 175, 194
Maternal dominion, 13, 15, 16, 19, 29, 33, 34, 35, 43, 47, 50–2, 54, 85, 132, 136, 141, 177, 186, 196, 203
Maternal rights, 26, 27, 41, 56, 110, 128, 136, 143
Matriarchy, 178, 186–7, 192

Matricide/patricide, 32
McDaniel, Susan A., 137, 231
McClaren, Angus, 230
McClaren, Arlene, 230
Meisel, John, 238
Men, and absence of women in elected office, 152; male perspective in Western political thought, 3; masculinist perspective, 4; and view of mother, 169–70, 176; nature of, 45; view of reproduction, 143; and reproductive technology, 149
Mill, Harriet Taylor, 93, 122, 222, 224, 225, 229
Mill, John Stuart, 92, 93, 127, 130, 137, 157, 159, 194, 222, 223, 241
- animal instinct, 226
- child abuse, 110, 129
- child care, 120, 155
- competition in marketplace, 96–7
- conjugal rights, 110
- creativity of women, 224, 228
- domestic life/duties of women, 98–100, 102–3, 114, 116, 118, 120, 123, 140, 151, 154, 181, 227
- domestic labour, 139
- economic benefits of women in work force, 227
- economics of families, 107
- education, 97, 102, 105–6, 108, 111, 120, 125
- 'elitism,' 94
- employment, 228–9
- equality of opportunity, 6, 95–6, 108, 112–13, 117, 151
- equality of outcome, 95, 97, 117, 122, 151
- equality of rights, 107
- equality of political status, 151, 229

- 'ethic of care,' 131, 138, 150, 155–6, 183, 188, 195
- family relations, 105–7
- freedom of choice, 96
- good government, 227
- individualism, 94, 117
- individual rights, 228
- justice, 108
- labour power, 111
- liberty, 105, 108
- literature, 118, 228
- male/female differences, 111, 113, 163, 225
- marriage, 94–5, 97, 107, 109, 111–12, 118, 225
- masculine bias of, 93–4
- maternal instinct, 140, 166
- maternal rights, 110
- moral virtue, 110
- motherhood, 94
- parental dominion, 109, 121
- parent/child relations, 8, 109, 127
- parental rights, 226
- political citizenship, 200
- political participation, 97, 99, 200
- political power, 6, 105, 117, 224
- political realm, 118
- political representation, 115–17, 122
- political rights, 112–13
- political status of women, 93, 115–16, 151
- population issues, 105–7, 112, 121, 129
- private/public duality, 94–5, 102, 107
- property rights, 111–12, 124
- public interest, 123–4
- regulation of reproduction, 105–7, 121, 129, 134
- reproductive duty, 134, 150
- reproductive labour, 139
- restraints placed on women, 96–7
- self-interest, 102–3, 112, 125
- selfishness of women, 224
- sexual contract, 94
- social constructions, 95
- socialization, 105, 108–9, 124–5
- spousal abuse, 110, 119, 121–2, 229
- suffrage, 93, 115, 117, 123, 215, 230
- training, 105
- view of women, 4, 93–6, 102, 104; and caring nature, 103–4, 123–6, 129, 138; as inhibited, 98; as morally sensible, 100–1, 103, 110; and physical stature, 100, 123, 152; political suitability of, 114, 118, 122, 123; practical intelligence of, 97–8, 101–2, 114, 227; and relationship to family, 93, 95; and rights of body, 110; and self-sacrifice, 103; and war, 122–3
- virtue, 224
- wealthy women, 119–21
- women and liberal state, 5
- working-class women, 118–22

Mishler, William, 237
Mitchell, Alanna, 231
Mitchell, Juliet, 239
Monarchy, 207
Moral majority, 131
Morgan, Kathryn, 4, 199
Morton, F.L., 231
Mother/child relations, 11, 18, 168, 171–2
Mother/fetus relations, 143, 147
Motherhood, 4, 6, 8, 9, 94; and maternal certainty, 16–17; as rational/irrational, 9, 18–19, 86, 137, 172, 187–9 (*see also* Maternal dominion)

272 Index

Nedelsky, Jennifer, 237, 246
Neo-conservatism, 131, 156
Nicholson, Linda J., 246
Nozick, Robert, 168, 241
Nursing, women's suitability for, 104

Object relations theory, 11–12, 14, 170
O'Brien, Mary, 8, 43, 169, 173–6, 178, 200, 210, 242
Offen, Karen, 159, 239, 246
Okin, Susan Moller, 94, 162, 167–9, 199, 223, 241
Overall, Christine, 134–5, 145–6, 182, 231, 234, 244

Packe, Michael St. John, 230
Pal, Leslie, 135, 231
Parental dominion, 22–3, 75, 76, 79, 82–3, 109
Parent/child relations, 7–9, 13–14, 16–17, 20–5, 31, 32, 33, 34, 53, 56–7, 59, 66, 73–4, 83, 105–6, 109, 131, 138–9, 169, 183–5, 189–90, 194, 196, 241
Parental rights, 56, 121
Parry, Geraint, 200
Pateman, Carole, 4, 10, 15, 26, 28, 29, 30, 43, 52, 55–7, 62, 83–4, 88, 94, 199, 200, 201, 202, 205–7, 210, 214–15, 219–21, 223, 235, 239
Paternal dominion, 15, 16, 30–1, 33, 34, 35, 41, 54, 128, 204, 207
Paternal rights, 26, 40, 41, 136, 146; over fetus, 188
Paternity, and uncertainty, 8, 133
Patriarchy, 10, 15, 25, 28, 35, 36, 41, 54, 56, 149, 157, 178, 186, 189–92, 195
Pitkin, Hannah, 243
Plamenatz, John, 210, 218
Plato, 240, 241
Political action, 52

Political allegiance, 71
Political citizenship, 5, 47, 52, 72, 89–91, 154, 237
Political interests, women and, 6, 114
Political office, women and, 115–16
Political participation, 44; women and, 5, 92, 97, 99
Political representation, of women, 115–17, 122
Politics, and practical reason, 114
Population issues, 68, 70, 85, 105–7, 112, 129, 216
Post-modernism, and feminism, 161, 192, 239, 246
Post-structuralism, and feminism, 161–2, 192–3, 197, 239, 246
Power, 5, 20–2, 30, 35, 44–7, 75, 105, 117, 153, 176, 186, 205
Pregnancy, 168, 192, 241
Pro-choice movement, 142
Procreation, 67, 137
Pross, A. Paul, 237
Prostitution, 212
Private/public duality, 3, 4, 8, 30, 31, 32, 43, 55, 61, 94–5, 102, 107, 147–8, 179

Quebec, 129

Rape, 190
Rawls, John, 241
Rebick, Judy, 142, 234
Reed, Evelyn, 239
Religion, 37
Reproduction, 50, 121, 127, 165, 167, 169; and nature, 173, 175; and oppression, 169; and the private realm, 6; and state regulation of, 105–6, 121, 129; as rational, 7, 9, 132–3, 175–6, 196

Reproductive consciousness, 173, 175–6
Reproductive duty, 134
Reproductive labour, 51, 68, 83, 85–7, 111, 128–9, 132–3, 135, 139, 187
Reproductive rights, 5, 7, 9, 53, 87, 92, 127, 132–3, 144, 146, 147–8, 169, 177, 182, 189–90, 194; and liberalism, 127; rationality and reproduction, 7, 9, 132–3, 175–6, 196
Reproductive technology, 131, 138–9, 141–2, 149, 233, 234, 242
Rich, Adrienne, 159
Ring, Jennifer, 96, 126, 223
Rights/duties, tension between, 181
Rioux, Christine, 236
Robinson, Gertrude, 236
Robson, Ann, 222, 223, 226
Robson, John, 222, 223, 226
Roe v. Wade, 231
Rossi, Alice, 222
Rousseau, Jean-Jacques, 240, 241
Royal Commission on New Reproductive Technologies, 140, 144, 233, 234

Sabine, George H., 201
Saint-Jean, Armande, 236
Sameness/difference, 6, 159, 161–3, 165, 196
Sandel, Michael, 241
Sartre, Jean-Paul, 166
Schochet, Gordon, 25, 35, 36, 204, 205, 206, 208
Schwartzer, Alice, 240, 241
Scruton, Roger, 200
Segal, Lynne, 159, 239
Sex, 67, 165, 190; and sexual contract, 4, 10, 14, 56, 83, 94; male access to women, 3, 83

Shanley, Mary, 95, 206, 223, 234
Sherwin, Susan, 233, 234
Shevory, Thomas C., 233
Shrage, Laurie, 137, 232, 235
Simons, Margaret, 240
Social construction, 95, 195
Socialization, 41, 59, 108–9, 124–5, 140
Sodomy, 67
Spallone, Patricia, 143, 148, 234, 235
Spousal abuse, 110, 119, 121–2, 226, 229
Suffrage, 90, 93, 115, 117, 123, 225, 230
Supreme Court of Canada, 134
Surrogacy, 138–40, 147, 234

Taylor, Fabrice, 231
Taylor, Helen, 93, 104, 125, 222, 224, 225, 227, 230
Teaching, women's suitability for, 111
Teichrob, Ruth, 230
Tong, Rosemarie, 158, 238

Urbinati, Nadia, 94, 125–6, 223, 230

Vickers, Jill McCalla, 236, 237

Warren, Mary Anne, 148, 235
Warrior hero, 47–8, 50, 151, 177
Weber, Max, 240
Wertz, Dorothy, 182, 244
Williams, Linda, 140, 233
Wolin, Sheldon, 201, 206, 208
Wollstonecroft, Mary, 157, 159
Women
– biological relationship to reproduction, 163
– caring nature, 103–4, 123–6, 129, 131, 140, 155, 160, 186, 188
– difference of, 162
– family, 93, 95

- independence of will, 65; women's bodies, 51–2, 110, 134, 142
- liberal state, 5
- moral sensibility, 100–1, 103, 110
- mother/child relations, 11, 18, 242
- mothering, 4, 6, 8, 131, 167–8, 171, 183
- 'natural subordination,' 55, 57, 63, 88, 96
- oppression, 161, 169, 170–1
- as 'other,' 11
- physical strength, 100, 123
- political citizenship, 5, 62
- political participation, 5, 54, 115, 122, 155
- political status, 93, 118
- political theory, 174
- rationality of, 4, 54, 57, 61–2, 64, 87–9, 97–8, 101–2, 136, 150, 191
- selfishness of, 137, 182

Working-class women, 118–21

Zvesper, John, 204